THE POLITICS OF ENVIRONMENTAL MEDIATION

The Politics
of Environmental
Mediation

Douglas J. Amy

New York   **Columbia University Press**   **1987**

Library of Congress Cataloging-in-Publication Data

Amy, Douglas J.
  The politics of environmental mediation.

  Bibliography: p.
  Includes index.
  1. Environmental mediation—United States.
  2. Environmental policy—United States. I. Title.
  KF3775.A949   1987   344.73′046′0269   86-24445
  ISBN 0-231-06424-1   347.304460269

Columbia University Press
New York   Guildford, Surrey
Copyright © 1987 Columbia University Press
All rights reserved

Printed in the United States of America

This book is Smyth-sewn.

Book design by J. S. Roberts

TO HILDE AMY AND GLENN AMY

Contents

Acknowledgments

A book like this cannot come into existence without the help of a number of other people. First, I would like to acknowledge the assistance and patience of all those who allowed themselves to be interviewed for this work: Howard Bellman, James Benson, Gail Bingham, William Dittrich, David Doniger, Dana Duxbury, Ellen Hardabeck, Jonathan Lash, Joan Murphy, and David Phillips. I am particularly grateful to those mediators who strongly disagreed with some of my analysis and yet remained open and communicative. Naturally, all of these people are absolved of any responsibility for the conclusions reached in this book.

I would also like to thank several people who kindly shared their research on environmental mediation with me. David Sachs allowed me to look through an intriguing series of interviews of professional mediators that he completed for his masters thesis at MIT. Kai Lee, Larry Susskind, Timothy Sullivan, Susan Silbey, and Sally Merry were kind enough to send me drafts of books and articles before they were published. Dorothy Lagerroos and Caryl Terrell of the Wisconsin League of Women Voters were consistently supportive and gave me access to survey data they collected in their study of the use of mediation in Wisconsin State politics. I am also indebted to Peter Evans who shared information and ideas generated in his senior thesis at Hampshire College—our conversations were as useful as they were enjoyable.

I also appreciate the help of several individuals who reviewed articles and earlier drafts of this work and provided encouragement and useful suggestions, including Christine Harrington, John Brigham, Richard Hofrichter, Lettie Wenner, Brad Crenshaw, Ben Schiff, and Paul Dawson. Thanks also go to Bob Wagner and Mary Beth Cardin for help in preparing this manuscript.

And finally, I am most grateful to my two constant companions during this long endeavor: Maggie, who provided amusement during the long hours of research and writing; and Susan, who somehow manages to be my best critic and my best fan, and who always reminds me about what is really important and what is not.

Parts of this book originally appeared in an earlier form in *Policy Sciences* and *Ecology Law Quarterly* and are reprinted here with permission.

Introduction

In the Francis Marion National Forest in South Carolina, there lies a marshy area of several thousand acres known as Ion Swamp. The swamp is one of the last known nesting places of the Bachman's Warbler—described in *Peterson's Field Guide* as "the rarest North American songbird." Environmentalists in the area became upset when, in 1976, the U. S. Forest Service announced its intention to permit logging in the area. At first it appeared that the ensuing dispute would go the same route of many such environmental controversies and become entangled in a long and expensive court battle. However, Robert Golten, an attorney for the National Wildlife Federation, investigated the situation and suggested that the parties try to mediate their dispute. A mediation panel was chosen and the parties agreed to a moratorium on both litigation and lumbering during the mediation process. After several months of dialogue, field trips, and research, the panel recommended a compromise: that lumbering be permitted, but not in the bottom land areas that served as nesting places for the warblers. Both the Forest Service and the environmentalists quickly accepted this proposal and the dispute was resolved.[1]

The resolution of the Ion Swamp controversy was one of the earliest examples of environmental mediation—a process that has since developed into a significant trend in environmental politics. Briefly, environmental mediation is an informal process in which a neutral, third-party mediator facilitates the resolution of an environmental dispute. In this approach, representatives of government, business, and environmental groups sit down with the mediator to negotiate a binding settlement to a particular controversy. The process is completely voluntary. Unlike arbitrators, mediators have no power to impose a settlement on the parties; they must rely on their skills at negotiation and facilitation to encourage the parties to agree to a compromise that will settle the issue. The growing interest in this new process has been primarily due to the fact that it can serve as an alternative to litigation, currently the most common way that environmental disputes get resolved. Proponents of mediation argue that in many environmental cases litigation has proved to be a very expensive and time-consuming approach, and one that does not always produce satisfactory decisions for any of the parties involved. Environmental mediation has been billed as an alternative to the frustrations of the courts, a less confrontational and more cooperative process that can resolve disputes in a cheaper, fairer, and more timely fashion.

This kind of cooperative approach to environmental disputes seems to run against the grain of much of environmental politics in the 1980s. For much of this decade, attention has been focused on the intense political conflicts generated by the Reagan administration's dramatic changes in environmental policies and priorities. This was especially true during the first Reagan administration when the arbitrary environmental decisions of appointees like James Watt and Ann Burford helped to foster a climate of polarization and bitterness in environmental politics. But even during this period of intense conflict, there were other more co-operative forces at work behind the scenes, including a growing movement supporting approaches like environmental mediation. And more recent Reagan appointees in the environmental area have begun to publicly endorse and promote the use of environmental mediation as a preferred technique for settling many disputes. During his tenure at the Environmental Protection Agency, William Ruckelshaus became a champion of this nonconfrontational approach, and enthusiastically sponsored several experiments in negotiated rule-making in his agency. In a 1984 speech at the National Conference on Environmental Dispute Resolution, Ruckelshaus underlined the significance of this new approach by arguing that it "has an almost transcendent importance in the future of our country's dealing with problems like the protection of the environment."[2] Secretary of the Interior William Clark has also been an articulate advocate of increased cooperation between environmentalists, developers, and government. In one of his first major speeches after his appointment in 1983, he told the National Wildlife Federation that there was no inherent conflict between the basic goals of industry and environmentalists, and that it was time that we abandon the "us guys" versus "you guys" attitude and learn to work together to ensure both economic prosperity and a clean environment.[3]

Environmental mediation has also received enthusiastic support from some parts of the environmental community. Most notably, Jay Hair, executive vice-president of the National Wildlife Federation, and William Reilly, president of the Conservation Foundation have energetically promoted the use of this cooperative approach.[4] Their organizations have sponsored conferences and workshops on this approach, and have helped to fund or mediate several actual negotiation efforts. On the other side, there has been a significant interest in this process on the part of industry as well. Elements of the coal, oil, and chemical industries have endorsed the process and contributed considerable funds for its study and use. Louis Fernandez, chairman of the Board of Monsanto Company, has been one of the most vocal supporters. In one typical speech, he argued that business and environmentalists must "discard old, combative ways of thinking and acting. . . . Cooperation must become the theme of this country's environmental efforts. The alternatives of continued bickering, continued pulling and tugging at the regulatory agencies, and finally, continued litigation are simply more expensive than any of us can afford and more time-consuming than the public will tolerate."[5] This kind of support from parts of the business, environmental, and government communities certainly suggests that environmental mediation has now become a significant trend in environmental politics—it is an idea whose time seems to have come.

THE BEGINNINGS

It has taken almost a decade for environmental mediation to emerge as an important part of environmental politics. The earliest experiments with mediation began in the mid-1970s. Credit for first bringing the tools of mediation to bear on environmental problems usually goes to Gerald Cormick and Jane McCarthy.[6] While at the Community Crisis Intervention Center in St. Louis in 1973, Cormick and McCarthy had a series of talks with environmentalists, lawyers, industry representatives, and government officials that revealed an increasing frustration with the impasses caused by confrontational approaches to environmental disputes. Many also responded positively to the possibility of extending the dispute resolution techniques that were being used successfully in community disputes into the area of environmental controversies. Buoyed by this response, Cormick and McCarthy sought out resources to fund an exploratory project. After securing grants from the Ford and Rockefeller Foundations to examine the possibility of using mediation in environmental issues, they sought out a suitable test case. Eventually they became involved in mediating a dispute in Washington State between environmentalists, farmers, developers and public officials over the damming of the Snoqualmie River—a case that has since become a classic in the annals of environmental dispute resolution.

The Snoqualmie River controversy was in many ways a typical, frustrating environmental dispute.[7] The river is flood-prone and following a particularly devastating flood, the U.S. Corp of Engineers proposed a flood control dam to deal with this continuing problem. The dam was hardly endorsed by homeowners, businessmen, and farmers in the affected areas. Opposing the dam, however, was a coalition of citizen and environmental groups who maintained that the dam would open the flood plain to urban sprawl, interrupt a free-flowing river, and could not be justified on a benefit-cost basis. Eventually the governor agreed with the environmentalists and said no to the dam proposal. However, as often happens in environmental disputes, the fighting over this issue continued unabated. In desperation, the governor agreed to a suggestion that Cormick and McCarthy be appointed to head a mediation effort to try to resolve this controversy once and for all. Finally, after seven months of difficult negotiations, including several months spent in formalizing the specific language of an agreement, all of the parties in the mediation effort signed a joint agreement which was forwarded to the governor. The agreement illustrated what proponents of mediation claim is its main asset— its ability to generate creative solutions that satisfy the interests of all the various parties involved. In this case, the agreement provided, among other things, for a smaller dam at a different site on the river to control flooding, and a river basin planning council to coordinate planning for the entire area. The agreement was hailed by residents, environmentalists, and state and federal officials alike, and the announcement of the agreement received feature coverage from both the print and electronic media. Environmental mediation was off and running.

After this optimistic beginning, Cormick moved to Seattle and started the Office of Environmental Mediation (now the Mediation Institute) and took on several additional mediation efforts in the Northwest. His successes soon garnered national attention, and interest in mediation began to grow. Slowly, throughout the late 1970s an increasing number of scholars, environmentalists, and developers began to explore the possibilities present in mediation. By the 1980s, environmental mediation had moved out of the experimental stage and had become more institutionalized and professionalized. There are now a number of mediation institutes around the country involved in training mediators and offering mediation services. Besides Cormick's office, there are organizations located in ten states and the District of Columbia. They include, among others, the Institute for Environmental Negotiation at the University of Virginia, Charlottesville, the New England Environmental Mediation Center in Boston, ACCORD Associates in Boulder, and the Public Disputes Program of the Harvard Law School.[8]

Environmental mediation itself has now taken a number of different forms—moving beyond its typical use in local, site-specific disputes.⁹ For example, one kind of negotiations, usually called "policy dialogue," takes place not over a particular site-specific problem, but over basic environmental policy issues on the national level. The National Coal Policy Project was an example of this kind of negotiation. It brought together coal companies, utilities and environmentalists in a yearlong series of meetings, which in this case did not even utilize the services of a formal third-party mediator.¹⁰ "Reg-neg" or regulatory negotiations is another form of mediation; this one involving efforts by regulatory agencies to design environmental regulations by first negotiating with environmentalists and industry. The intention is to avoid the litigation that usually is used to challenge new rules.¹¹ Reg-neg is an example of new and potentially very significant development in the area of environmental mediation—the formal institutionalization of mediation within governmental policymaking processes. Before the 1980s, mediation efforts were largely sporadic and ad-hoc affairs which took place only when the individual disputing parties became interested in this approach. More recently, mediation has begun to make the transition to a more regular and official part of environmental policymaking. For example, several states now have laws which allow or require mediation in disputes over such things as the location of hazardous waste disposal facilities.¹² Some proponents see this as only the beginning of a larger trend toward widespread incorporation of mediation into government. They envision mediation becoming a normal stage of the legislative and the rule-making processes used by governments on the local, state, and federal levels.

In all of its various forms, environmental mediation has accumulated a growing list of successes in a variety of environmental controversies. Successful agreements have been fashioned in such difficult areas as power plant siting, land use, pollution abatement, preservation of park lands, mass transit planning, and others.¹³ Many proponents of environmental mediation now believe that the 1980s will be a time when mediation will increasingly replace litigation as a means of resolving environmental disagreements. Jay Hair of the National Wildlife Federation has suggested that "as (we) move away from 'the environmental position' and 'the business position' to concentrate on underlying interests, the demand for mediators will increase."[14] He has also confidently predicted than in ten years more environmental disputes will be mediated than litigated. This optimistic view is also shared by one of the leading scholars and practitioners of environmental mediation, Lawrence Susskind of the Harvard Law School Program on Negotiation, who has argued that "if the current trend continues, many of the important resource allocation decisions made each year could depend on the successes of the independent mediators."[15] Whether or not environmental mediation will live up to such high expectations will be one of the questions explored in this book. But nevertheless, it is clear that mediation already has become a significant development in the area of environmental politics, and thus merits some careful analysis.

NEEDED: A MORE BALANCED
AND CRITICAL ANALYSIS

As indicated above, a great deal of enthusiasm has been generated by environmental mediation. And by and large, the popular and scholarly writing has been very positive. Most books and articles have extolled the virtues and advantages of this new approach to environmental decision making.[16] This is understandable: the idea of old enemies now cooperating makes good press; and most of the writing on this topic has been done by mediators or by those who openly champion mediation. And yet, as we will see, not everyone involved in environmental politics is so enthusiastic. In particular, many members of the environmental community have expressed a number of suspicions about this new cooperative approach. For example, some fear that compromise is often inappropriate in important environmental issues; and others are concerned that what proponents describe as "cooperation" may actually be "cooptation." Even Michael McCloskey, the executive director of the Sierra Club who participated in some early efforts at dialogue, has now become somewhat skeptical of the process, suggesting that mediation might primarily be an exercise in public relations and that so far it has had no real practical results.[17] However, while such suspicions clearly exist, there has been no attempt to systematically describe or investigate them. This book is intended, in part, to fill this gap. It will attempt to give equal weight to both the advantages and disadvantages of environmental mediation; it will explore the political promise and the political pitfalls.

This balanced approach is reflected in the organization of the book. The first two chapters describe and explain the various political advantages that have been ascribed to environmental mediation. Chapter 1 considers the advantages that mediation may have over the traditional adversarial approaches to environmental dispute resolution—especially litigation. In particular, it describes claims that mediation is cheaper, faster, and more satisfying than litigation. The second chapter examines in more detail how mediation actually works. It considers how face-to-face interaction and the techniques of the mediator help to generate effective dialogue and successful agreements. Chapter 3 begins a more critical look at this process. It attempts to separate myth from reality in environmental mediation by looking more closely at the claims that mediation is cheaper, faster, and less confrontational than litigation. These claims will turn out to be more problematic than they first appeared. Chapter 4 turns to the serious political problems than can afflict environmental mediation. It will be seen that the informal, face-to-face nature of negotiations may have some significant disadvantages, and that inexperienced participants may be seduced by the cordiality of the process into making undesirable concessions. Chapter 5 considers the role of power and how its maldistribution can encourage the cooptive uses of this technique. It describes several ways in which imbalances of power between developers and environmentalists can work to the advantage of the former in many mediation efforts. The sixth chapter explores a more subtle but equally important political problem in mediation—the way in which mediation can distort the nature of environmental disputes. It will be seen that mediation and mediators promote a particular view of environmental conflict and environmental issues—a view that may work to the disadvantage of environmental interests. Finally, chapter 7 offers an exploration of two of the larger political questions surrounding the use of environmental mediation: What role is it likely to play in environmental politics? And what role should it play?

RESEARCH SOURCES

The information used as the basis of the book's analysis came from a wide variety of sources. I extensively utilized the growing scholarly and popular literature on environmental mediation. Three areas of this literature were particularly helpful. First is the material written by environmental mediators themselves, including an increasing number of books, articles, and newsletters.[18] As a rule, this work tends to focus on questions of technique in mediation: what makes for an effective mediation effort, what steps are involved, what mediation tools are available, what are the best times to intervene, and so on. This material contributed greatly to my understanding of the inner workings of mediation efforts, but was less helpful in answering the larger political questions. As the authors of one of the leading books on environmental mediation admitted, their work emphasizes what they call the "microanalysis" of environmental disputes—incentives to negotiate and how deals can be made binding, for example—and "gives less attention to a broader set of questions that deal with the wisdom of making policy seriatim through the process of negotiation."[19] The limited scope of this analysis is understandable, however, given that much of this work is intended to be practical advice to other professionals.

A second area of literature about environmental mediation is the increasing number of case studies.[20] These chronicles of specific negotiation efforts tend to be heavy on description and light on analysis, but nevertheless they were an important source of data for this study. I relied heavily on these case studies in developing and illustrating the various arguments that I make about mediation in this book. This source of information was not without its problems, however. Given that most of these case studies were written by authors sympathetic to environmental mediation, it often was much easier to find case studies to illustrate the advantages rather than the disadvantages of mediation. Ironically, however, I was able to find some of the best examples of the political pitfalls in mediation in descriptions of mediation efforts that the authors seemed to consider very successful.

Another area of scholarly literature helpful in the study of mediation is the writing of legal scholars.[21] Their work proved particularly useful in beginning to address some of the more political questions surrounding this technique. Much of this work explores how informal dispute resolution techniques can serve as alternatives to our present court system. There has been an extensive analysis of the limitations of litigation and the comparative advantages of mediation. This work is of obvious relevance to this study, but it too has its limitations. Specifically, most of this analysis focuses on the use of mediation in resolving *private* disputes—such as those involving landlords and tenants—and thus is not always easily extrapolated to the use of mediation in public policy disputes such as those concerning the environment. Also of interest in this legal literature is a growing body of work that raises questions about the political role that alternative dispute resolution may play in American society.[22] Some scholars suggest that informal dispute resolution processes may work to the political disadvantage of traditionally powerless groups, and that these approaches may serve primarily the interests of political and economic elites. While little of their work is directly applicable to the study of environmental mediation—it too focuses primarily on private, not public, disputes—their critical analyses provided much food for thought in my own work.

Another useful source of information was the conferences

on environmental mediation that I attended over the last several years—especially the annual conferences sponsored by the Conservation Foundation. At these meetings, I was able to record and later transcribe a number of presentations by mediators, business leaders, government officials, and environmentalists. These were particularly helpful in documenting the views of people involved in environmental disputes, and in uncovering the different perspectives and assumptions that they bring to the mediation process. The informal conversations at these meetings also proved to be very illuminating.

Over the last five years, I have also conducted a series of interviews, both in person and over the telephone, with a number of mediators and environmentalists. The main subject of these interviews was the potential political abuses of environmental mediation—a topic that is rarely addressed in the literature on mediation. I found these interviews invaluable, not only as a source of information, but also as a way of using discussion to clarify and hone my argument.

Finally, I was fortunate enough to be able to utilize several new pieces of research conducted by other students of environmental mediation. Andrew Sachs kindly shared the research he did for his masters degree at MIT. It consisted of the transcript of in-depth interviews he conducted with a number of mediators concerning the role of power in environmental mediation. Also, Dorothy Lagerroos and Caryl Terrell of the Wisconsin League of Women Voters allowed me to use data collected in their study on the use of mediation and negotiation in policymaking in the Wisconsin State government.[23] They conducted a two-part survey of legislators, administrators, corporate lobbyists, environmentalists, and others involved in several negotiation efforts sponsored by the state legislature to try to resolve some conflicts over environmental legislation. I believe this study is the only systematic survey done of those who participate in or were affected by these kind of negotiation efforts, and it proved very useful in documenting and measuring how satisfied various interests were with the process and its outcomes.

THE PERSPECTIVE
UNDERLYING THIS STUDY

A few words are necessary about my intellectual perspective on environmental mediation. Being a political scientist, and not a dispute resolution professional or a legal scholar, I bring a somewhat different set of concerns to the analysis of mediation. My main interest is not in the techniques of mediation, or in its comparative advantages to litigation—though of course those are subjects that I address in this book—rather, my natural interest is in the politics of this process. By politics I mean the issues of power, equality, and democracy that are necessarily involved in any policymaking process. It is sometimes suggested that mediation is an alternative to politics—that it is something that exists apart from the normal adversarial struggles surrounding environmental policy. The assumption in this book, however, is that environmental mediation is not above politics, but is simply a new form of it. And this assumption—that environmental mediation is inherently a political phenomenon—has strongly affected the way I have approached the study of this process. For example, it led me to take seriously the possibility that there are political biases imbedded in the mediation process. As a rule, policymaking processes are rarely politically neutral—procedures for making decisions inevitably tend to favor certain kinds of policies and certain kinds of interests. Scholars of legislative processes, for instance, have long noted that the difficult and decentralized procedures by which a bill becomes law in the U.S. Congress tend to discourage dramatic policy changes, and tend to favor those interests that wish to preserve the status quo. And if it is the case that most policymaking processes have subtle but significant political biases built into them, it seems unlikely that mediation would be an exception to this rule. Accordingly, in my study of environmental mediation, I have tried to be sensitive to how this process may favor certain kinds of outcomes and certain kinds of interests. Indeed, the question of how fair this process actually is has always seemed a crucial one to me, and it is the consideration of this question that provided much of the critical analysis in the latter half of the book.

My approach to the study of environmental mediation has not only been affected by my training as a political scientist, but also by my continuing interest in citizen participation movements. I have long been interested in theories of direct democracy, and the question of how citizens might participate more effectively in making important political decisions. In fact, I originally was attracted to environmental mediation because of proponents' claims that this was a new and exciting form of direct citizen participation in environmental decisionmaking.[24] This interest in direct democracy has led me to examine carefully how environmental mediation measures up as a form of participation. Thus I have been greatly concerned with such questions as: How democratic is mediation? Can citizens really participate effectively in this process, or does it often function as a way to distract or coopt citizens? In particular, my familiarity with citizen participation efforts has led me to question whether mediation is being used for political cooptation. The history of citizen participation in the United States has shown that participatory techniques are often used for purely political purposes—to give the illusion of citizen power while actually serving more the interests of policymakers who desire to increase the legitimacy and public acceptance of their decisions.[25] This has clearly been the case, for example, in the use of public hearings. While they do give citizens a feeling of participation, they are often used simply to legitimize policy decisions that have already been made. Such examples have given me a natural suspicion of citizen participation techniques and have made me aware of the necessity of closely examining the political claims associated with them. It is that spirit of skepticism that animates much of this inquiry.

Also, given my interest in citizen participation, I am hoping that this analysis of environmental mediation will not only be of interest to legal scholars and political scientists, but also to those citizens who might be thinking of participating in these kinds of mediation efforts. I think that it is important that potential participants enter into mediation with a full understanding of the advantages and disadvantages that this strategy has to offer. As it stands now, the available literature is one-sided in celebrating mediation and encouraging its widespread use, and potential participants are largely left on their own to detect potential pitfalls. By providing a more balanced analysis, citizens will be able to consider the use of this option in a more careful and critical way. Mediation can be a useful political process, but only, I believe, if the participants enter into this process with fully open eyes, and with as few political illusions as possible.

SOME LARGER POLITICAL IMPLICATIONS

This exploration of the politics of environmental mediation also has some implications that go far beyond the area of environmental politics. Cooperative approaches like mediation are not simply being advocated for environmental problems, but for other kinds of public policy problems as well. In fact, many private mediation institutes who began by focusing on environmental issues have now begun to broaden their scope and offer mediation services for all types of public policy disputes. Thus, environmental mediation is not an isolated phenomenon, but part of a larger movement in American politics which seeks to promote negotiation and cooperation as a way of solving our pressing political, social, and economic conflicts. In recent years, an increasing number of modern political scholars and commentators have suggested that confrontations between competing interests in the modern state have produced a serious political malaise. Samuel Huntington has argued that the veritable explosion of special interest, single interest, and public interest groups during the last several decades has created a situation in which government has been overwhelmed with incompatible demands. He sees the federal government constantly being torn in several directions at once, slowly slipping into policy paralysis as it is unable to devise coherent policy plans that satisfy all interests.[26] Similarly, Mancur Olson, in *The Rise and Decline of Nations*, has argued that the political disease that helps to account for the economic decline of England is the debilitating stalemates caused by warring special interest groups. He suggests that so much time is spent fighting over the size of pieces of the economic pie, that too little time is spent on activities and policies would increase the size of the pie for all. He argues that the constant conflict between various groups—like labor and management—also threatens to turn the United States into a gridlocked society.[27]

Other political observers have suggested that the answer to this gridlock problem may lie in substituting negotiation and co-operation for the confrontation that usually characterizes interest group interaction. Many commentators have recently argued, for example, that increased cooperation between unions and managers is one of the keys to an economic revival in the United States. If we can only get over the traditional suspicions that have poisoned union-management relations and work together to increase productivity and product quality, then U.S. industry will be better able to compete against foreign competition. Cooperation and mediation are also being championed as the solution to many of the other conflicts afflicting our society. Felix Rohatyn has suggested, for example, that cooperation is essential in addressing such diverse problems as the federal budgets, the conflicts between the frost and sun-belt regions, our educational problems, racial conflicts, and international disputes. He has maintained that no politician, political party, or interest group has all the answers to solving all of these pressing social and economic problems, and that the only way to find workable answers is through increased cooperation between interested groups. In writing about the 1984 elections, he argued that "the question that deserves to be explored, and about which little is heard, is that of cooperation versus confrontation. . . . I believe that an attempt must be made at cooperation in almost every area of our society."[28] A Ford Foundation study came to very much the same conclusions, suggesting that dispute resolution techniques be tried in the areas of race relations, civil suits, consumer complaints, and educational opportunity.[29] And in fact, there have been an increasing number of attempts in the 1980s to use negotiation and mediation in many of these areas. Indeed, this political movement has advanced far enough now to acquire its own acronym, ADR—"alternative dispute resolution."

Clearly, then, environmental mediation is not an unique phenomenon, but part of a larger trend in American politics toward exploring more cooperative approaches to our social, economic, and political problems. Unfortunately, an analysis of the larger alternative dispute resolution movement is beyond the scope of this present inquiry; but a careful consideration of how mediation works in the specific context of environmental issues can shed some light on the more general phenomenon. In particular, a better understanding of the particular political benefits and the political problems associated with environmental mediation should tell us much about the potential for cooperation in other areas as well. If cooperative techniques like mediation are to become an important established part of the American political system, if they are to join litigation, administration, and legislation as ways of making crucial political decisions, then we had best ask the most probing and critical questions we can about this new process. This book is one effort to do so.

CHAPTER ONE

Mediation Versus Traditional Political Institutions

Mediated negotiation is appealing because it addresses many of the procedural shortcomings of the more traditional approaches to resolving resource allocation conflicts. It allows for more direct involvement of those most affected by decisions than other administrative and legislative processes, it can produce settlements more rapidly and at lower cost than the courts, and it is more flexible and adaptable to the specific needs of the parties in each unique situation.

Lawrence Susskind[1]

To understand the rise of environmental mediation and the appeal that it exerts, one must understand the problems inherent in the usual ways that our society has attempted to deal with environmental disputes. As one listens to proponents of this alternative approach, it becomes evident that much of their case for mediation is a negative one—one based on criticisms of the legislative, administrative, and judicial institutions that we have traditionally relied on to resolve these controversies. In the eyes of mediation proponents, these conventional institutions often have worked poorly: many environmental disputes go unresolved for years, continuing to fester and clogging our already overcrowded courtrooms. It is this perceived institutional failure that has motivated the interest in alternative forms of dispute resolution. As two proponents of mediation have explained: "additional methods of achieving consensus are generally sought when there is widespread dissatisfaction with existing mechanisms. Mediated negotiation of public disputes represents, quite simply, an attempt to overcome various inadequacies in the present American system for resolving public resource allocation disputes."[2] Accordingly, this chapter will be concerned primarily with comparing mediation to these traditional political institutions. The first part will catalogue and explore the main complaints leveled at our current dispute resolution mechanisms, with a special focus on the drawbacks of litigation. The chapter will then move on to consider a case study of an environmental controversy where traditional approaches failed and mediation succeeded. An analysis of this case will begin to reveal just what it is about this new approach that allows it to avoid the problems inherent in other approaches. It will become evident that it is the nonadversarial, participatory nature of environmental mediation that accounts in large part for its ability to resolve environmental disputes where other approaches have failed.

THE DRAWBACKS OF LITIGATION

Advocates of environmental mediation find fault with all traditional modes of environmental policymaking and dispute resolution. But the most concentrated criticisms usually are reserved for one approach in particular—litigation. The court system has become a target in large part because it seems that more serious environmental controversies inevitably end up there. For champions of mediation, this tendency to resort to the courts is a massive problem—for they believe that the court system is often one of the most undesirable and inefficient ways of trying to resolve environmental controversies. Their criticisms of the courts usually fall into two categories: first, that litigation is a poor mode of public participation in these important decisions; and second, that litigation is often appallingly ineffective in actually resolving the basic issues at stake in environmental disputes. Let us first consider the drawbacks that litigation has as a mode of citizen participation.

One of the reasons that litigation can be a poor way for interest groups to influence environmental policymaking is its sheer expense. Critics charge that the costs of a prolonged court battle and the inevitable appeals can be prohibitive—especially for small local environmental groups who typically are poorly organized and have few financial resources. But even for large national environmental organizations, the costs of litigation often can be a burden and can take away needed funds from other important activities like public education.[3] The result is that while some groups may see litigation as an effective and powerful means of effecting environmental policy, it may be largely unavailable to many others. This problem of limited access is not isolated to environmental cases, but is part of a larger problem of excessive costs that threatens to cut off access to the court system for large segments of the public. As a report by the National Institute for Dispute Resolution recently concluded, the prohibitive cost of litigation "means that the courts are generally inaccessible to all but the most wealthy parties and large organizations."[4] The suggestion, of course, is that informal approaches like mediation constitute a cheaper and thus more easily accessible source of justice for those involved in environmental controversies. One proponent of environmental mediation has speculated that this new process could cost, on the average, less than half as much as litigating a case in court.[5] Thus the hope, as expressed in the NIDR report, is that methods like mediation "will not only reduce the burden of the courts and the economy, but provide a more satisfying means to justice for a larger portion of the population."[6]

The long delays involved in litigation are also cited as a major drawback by proponents of mediation. Even in the best of circumstances, litigation tends to take place at a leisurely pace, but the crowded dockets of some courts often slow down the process even more. It is not unusual for environmental cases to take months simply to come to trial, and adding on time for appeals, it can often take years to resolve some of these disputes. Critics are fond of pointing to environmental cases that have been in the courts for decades. Inevitably the Storm King Mountain dispute in New York state is cited as an example of this problem.[7] This controversy has become a classic case for several reasons. First, it is celebrated by conservationists because it was one of the first federal cases that established the rights of citizens with no proprietary interests to intervene in environmental decisions. It began to open up the court system to environmental groups by sanctioning their standing in court cases involving environmental issues. But Storm King has now also become a symbol of the massive delays that can be the result of using the courts in such cases. In brief, the controversy began in 1963 when Consolidated Edison applied to the Federal Power Commission for a license to build a pump storage power plant at the base of Storm King Mountain on the Hudson River about forty miles north of New York City. The application sparked the opposition of several environmental groups, who eventually opposed the plant on legal, economic, and environmental grounds. But of particular concern was the threat the plant posed to the spawning grounds of the striped bass. It was alleged that most of the striped bass caught in the Atlantic between Cape Cod and New Jersey came from spawning grounds in the vicinity of Storm King Mountain. The dispute was in and out of the courts and regulatory agencies for almost seventeen years. Finally, in 1979, a mediator entered into the case and eventually helped the parties reach an agreement in 1980. The agreement was a complex one, involving concessions by both sides. Among other things, it provided for the abandonment of the plans for the Storm King plant, and the relaxation of some environmental restrictions on other Consolidated Edison plants on the Hudson River. The mediator was able to accomplish in a year and a half what litigation and administrative wrangling had failed to do in almost two decades.

Of course, most environmental cases do not take this long.[8] But the point still remains that litigation is a process full of delays, and those delays can be costly to both environmentalists and developers. These costs go beyond the expenses involved in the process of litigation itself. In the case of developers, while their projects are delayed, inflation can raise construction and capital costs, and they may also have to carry the costs of partially completed projects.[9] Of course, environmentalists sometimes file suit in order to cause just such costly delays for projects, in the hope that the developers eventually will become discouraged. But the delays involved in litigation can be a two-edged sword—one that hurts environmental interests as well. In some cases, delay can mean the continuation of environmentally destructive practices. For example, it was discovered in the late 1960s that Reserve Mining Company was dumping large amounts of environmentally destructive material into Lake Superior. But the company was able to continue the practice for over a decade as they fought the case through various levels of state and federal courts.[10] And such delays can be even more troublesome when they have irreversible effects, as may be the case in efforts to save unique habitats or species.

It is these costs and delays involved in litigation that have prompted some involved in environmental controversies to proclaim the need for a new approach. One of the most prominent spokespersons for this position in industry has been Louis Fernandez, chairman of the board of Monsanto Company. In a speech given to the 1983 meeting of the Chemical Manufacturers Association, he argued that it is now the time for business, government, environmentalists, and concerned citizens to "discard old, combative ways of thinking and acting" and "try cooperation instead of confrontation."[11] And why should industry adopt this new conciliatory approach? Because, he argued, "the alternatives of continued bickering, continued pulling and tugging at the regulatory agencies, and finally, continued litigation are simply more expensive than any of us can afford and more time-consuming than the public will tolerate."[12] On the environmental side, William K. Reilly, president of the Conservation Foundation, also has made a number of speeches with very similar kinds of arguments, and calling for more cooperative and less costly relations between industry and environmentalists.[13]

Besides noting that litigation is a costly form of participation, proponents of mediation also complain that court decisions often fail to resolve the basic conflicts between the parties. One aspect of this problem is the tendency of the courts to not address the real issues at stake in many environmental controversies. Often judges hesitate to get involved in the substantive dimensions of environmental disputes and prefer to make their decisions purely on procedural grounds.[14] Thus, although decisions are rendered, the underlying controversies go unresolved, and may only lead to more lawsuits. In addition, mediation proponents claim that the winner-take-all type of decisions rendered by the courts are often inappropriate and counterproductive. The adversarial nature of litigation assumes that one side is right and the other wrong, and thus often overlooks compromises that could fulfill the needs of both parties. The winner-take-all approach also encourages the losing party to keep pursuing the case, perhaps through appeals, thus adding to the delays and expenses that have already been incurred.

In short, for proponents of mediation, litigation is seen as a cumbersome, expensive, time-consuming, and frustrating way for interest groups to participate in the resolution of environmental controversies. And yet, since the early 1970s, it seems to have become one of the most common approaches to these issues. In part, this is because many of the environmental laws passed in the 1970s explicitly gave environmental and citizen groups the right to sue and thus opened the door for widespread litigation. But this is only part of the explanation. It does not explain why environmentalists have chosen to use that door. To understand this one must also consider the failures and the drawbacks that have accompanied the other traditional approaches to resolving environmental controversies—legislation and administrative decisionmaking. Environmentalists and industry have turned to the courts primarily because these other avenues of participation have proven unsatisfactory. As one commentator has explained, it is "the inadequacies of legislative and administrative processes that often lead frustrated stakeholders to seek redress in the courts."[15] Thus the appeal of mediation can only be fully understood by going beyond the problems with litigation and considering the failings of the policy-making system as a whole. Unfortunately, these other institutions also seem to suffer from the same two problems which afflict the court system: they often provide little opportunity for effective public participation, and they fail to actually resolve the basic issues at stake.

THE FAILURES OF LEGISLATIVE
AND ADMINISTRATIVE APPROACHES

Ideally, most conflicts over environmental problems should be effectively dealt with at the legislative level. But critics cite several problems with legislative approaches. First, it can be difficult for all of the interests affected by environmental decisions to be heard. It is thought that this is largely because "effective lobbying is restricted to organized interest groups with political know-how and considerable financial resources."[16] In practice, this means that environmental groups often cannot participate effectively in the legislative arena. Many environmental and conservation groups have limited financial resources and have difficulty funding the large professional staffs needed to be effective in state and federal legislatures.[17] Making this problem worse is the fact that many environmental groups are tax-exempt organizations and the Internal Revenue Act of 1969 prohibits the expenditure of "substantial" amounts of money by these groups for lobbying.[18] This perennial lack of resources inhibits environmental groups from competing effectively on the legislative level, and thus some have chosen to fight their battles elsewhere.

Even when there is substantial representation of affected parties, the legislative process often fails to resolve the basic environmental issues at stake. Many times, for example, Congress finds itself unable to manufacture a viable consensus on environmental policies. In this respect, 1983 was a typical year, with Congress deadlocked on many crucial pieces of environmental legislation. It was unable to reauthorize the Clean Air Act, the Clean Water Act, the Hazardous Waste Law (RCRA), the Toxic Substances Control Act, or the Pesticide Control Law—all of which were operating beyond their official expiration dates. Scholars of Congress have observed that this kind of deadlock and delay is not unusual when Congress faces difficult decisions. Its been noted, for example, that it is typical to find "inaction, delay, and long incubation periods for regulatory legislation."[19] In addition, when Congress does act, its decisions often tend to be vague and symbolic.[20] As political scientists have pointed out, controversial legislation often is made purposefully vague and ambiguous in order not to offend any important interests and to garner as much congressional support as possible. For example, in the case of the Outer Continental Shelf Land Act Amendments of 1978 there was great controversy over how the continental shelf should be used and whether the development of oil or the protection of fisheries and marine environments should have priority. But the legislation itself remained ambiguous on this all important question, speaking of the need for a "proper balance" between competing uses of the shelf, and stating that that criterion should be the basis for decisions in this area made by the Secretary of the Interior.[21] The problem, of course, is that this kind of legislation does not end disputes, it only sidesteps them and puts them off onto the agencies that must try to administer the legislation.[22]

Thus, the conflicts over environmental policy usually flare up again in the implementation phase, as administrative agencies like the Interior Department and the Environmental Protection Agency try to interpret their vague legislative mandates. But these organizations are also accused of functioning poorly as resolvers of controversies. The complaints are the familiar ones. First, it is argued that many affected groups often have little access to administrative decision making. In some cases, as in the Reagan administration, environmentalists may be deliberately ignored and left out of the process. But even relatively open administrative procedures do not ensure adequate hearing of all sides. Again part of the problem is financial, with some groups unable to afford the staff for extensive administrative lobbying efforts.[23] Of course, most agencies must receive public comments or hold hearings where concerned parties can voice their preferences—but mediation advocates put little faith in such procedures. Procedures like public hearings often only give the appearance of participation, while granting the participants no real say in policymaking. There is no guarantee that testimony will have any influence at all on administrators' decisions. Indeed, as one environmental scholar has complained, "hearings are not the basis for decisionmaking. Rather, project plans are placed on the docket as a *fait accompli* by agency managers who challenge the competence of laymen to find fault with their documents. The agencies have missions to defend and are not neutral hearing officers."[24]

The point about neutrality is important, for administrators rarely act as neutral mediators between the adversaries in an environmental dispute. They rarely see their roles as one of resolving conflicts, but rather see themselves as carrying out a particular vision of environmental policy. In the Carter administration, that vision was generally a pro-environmental one; in the Reagan administration, the vision has been more pro-industry. But given this commitment to a certain interpretation of environmental policy it is not surprising that the decisions of administrators often seem in the eyes of industry or environmentalists to be arbitrary and one-sided. As a result, administrative decisions often only alienate one side or the other, and the dissatisfied parties inevitably continue to pursue the dispute, usually in court. Sometimes administrative decisions even succeed in provoking both sides. Environmental groups and industry, for example, have challenged new environmental regulations from opposite points of view.

It is not difficult to see, then, why so many environmental disputes wind up in court. The frustrations and failings of the legislative and administrative process practically guarantee that many disputes will find their way into litigation. And not that long ago, this resort to the courts was thought to be a healthy development—at least in the eyes of environmentalists. In the early 1970s, Joseph Sax wrote his famous book, *Defending the Environment: A Strategy for Citizen Action*, in which he argued that the courts could act as a corrective to the failings of legislative and administrative environmental policymaking.[25] His criticisms of these traditional policymaking institutions in many ways presaged the points now being made by mediation advocates. He argued that environmentalists often had little participation or real power in the legislative and administrative decision-making processes. Moreover, the decisions made by administrative agencies charged with protecting the environment were often primarily influenced by political factors and failed to give sufficient weight to environmental concerns. The solution, he suggested, was for citizens to use litigation to force administrators and industry to pay more attention to environmental concerns. The courts could be a real source of power and leverage for citizens and environmental groups. For while administrators could easily ignore testimony at a public hearing, they could not ignore a court injunction against an agency ruling or project. Given this empowering characteristic of litigation, it is not surprising that it was quickly taken up as a major political strategy by the environmental community.

But as we have seen, although litigation does have some advantages over other forms of political participation, it can have its drawbacks as well; and advocates of mediation argue that it is far from an ideal way to resolve environmental disputes. And for them, the problems with litigation go beyond the time and expense involved. They also point out that the courts have simply become overloaded and incapable of processing all of these conflicts. As one environmentalist has complained: "The courts simply can't handle the load. When Professor Joseph Sax suggested in 1970 that environmental disputes be settled in court, there was no Clean Air Act, nor any of the other twenty-one environmental statutes spawned in the 1970s alone. In 1973, 47,000 cases were filed in Federal District Courts. In 1982 that figure rose to over 206,000. As more environmental "rights" are recognized, the potential for conflict increases. Courts simply do not have the time to be the exclusive arbiter of these rights."[26]

TABLE 1

Drawbacks of Traditional Dispute Resolution Institutions

Legislature	Bureaucracy	Courts
Expensive: effective lobbying requires large expenditures for staff, campaign contributions, etc.	Expensive: effective administrative lobbying requires funds for large staff and on-going research capability.	Expensive: prolonged court battles and appeals involve high costs.
Limited Access: not all groups have the funds and staff for effective lobbying effort.	Limited Access: not all groups have resources and staff for effective lobbying.	Limited Access: not all affected parties can afford high cost of litigation.
Delay: legislative process prone to delay and dead-lock on difficult and controversial issues.	Participation (e.g. public hearings, comment periods, etc.) often more symbolic than real.	Delay: postponements, appeals, over-crowded courts cause frequent time-consuming delays.
Legislators may under-stand little about local site-specific environmental disputes.	Adversial atmosphere produces win-lose deci-sions that rarely resolve conflicts.	Judges lack expertise on technical environmental issues.
Legislation tends to be vague. Basic conflicts are not resolved and tend to re-emerge in implementa-tion phase.	Unilateral, top-down decisions lack political legitimacy. Decisions frequently challenged in court.	Adversarial, win-lose approach fails to resolve controversies and en-courages losing party to continue conflict.

MEDIATION AS THE ANSWER

For all of these reasons, it is argued that an alternative to litigation and our other standard approaches to environmental controversies is sorely needed. (See table 1 for a summary of the disadvantages of these conventional approaches.) Can we not find a more efficient and effective way to resolve controversy? Is there not a way to create a more lasting and workable consensus on important environmental controversies? For mediation advocates, the answer to these questions is a resounding "Yes!" For them, environmental mediation is a new and constructive step away from the traditional adversarial approaches. "Mediated negotiation is appealing," explains one advocate, "because it addresses many of the procedural shortcomings of the more traditional approaches to resolving resource allocation conflicts."[27] When mediation works, it is argued, it can provide a timely and relatively inexpensive resolution to a controversy, a solution that may actually lay an issue to rest. But in order to fully appreciate why mediation advocates have gotten so excited about this new approach it is best to get beyond generalizations and consider the details of an actual case where mediation has worked its magic. Let us consider, then, one of the early cases of environmental mediation; a case in which mediation was able to fashion a resolution to a conflict where traditional political approaches had failed.

THE CASE OF PORTAGE ISLAND

Portage Island is 865 acres of beautiful forests and sandy beaches located in Puget Sound near Bellingham, Washington.[28] For fifteen years there was an ongoing controversy over who should own the island and how it should be used. Originally the island was owned by various members of the Lummi Indian Tribe whose reservation was adjacent to the island. In 1965, the Whatcom County Park Board paid $1.4 million, including $450,000 from the Interior Department, to buy the island from these owners. They planned to eventually develop it as a park. Originally the Lummi Tribe was attracted to the jobs and money that would be brought in by the park and had strongly supported the sale; but in 1970 the tribal council changed its mind and began to oppose non-Indian use of the island. Many of their objections were environmental and centered around the fact that the public could get to the island only by boat or by driving through the Lummi Reservation and then crossing a sand bar that is exposed at low tide. Both of these means of access were considered environmentally unacceptable by the council. They feared that marine traffic would interfere with the fishing nets and the shellfish grounds that the Indians had around the island. They also concluded that increased motor traffic through the reservation would be objectionable and disruptive. Lummi opposition to the use of the island as a county park was also fueled by their growing sense of sovereignty. It was a time when Native Americans around the United States were becoming increasingly sensitive to this issue. As one council member explained: "This is a small reservation, about 1,500 people living on 12,000 acres. A lot of our land has already been sold off to non-Indians. With Portage, we would be losing nearly another thousand acres. We began having second thoughts."

The conflict that ensued between the county and the Lummi Tribe was a classic example of the failure of traditional administrative and judicial approaches to resolve such disputes in a timely and effective manner. By May of 1970, the situation had deteriorated into a stalemate, with increasing polarization on both sides. Legally, the park board owned the island, but the Indians had put up no trespassing signs on the sand bar and were patrolling the waters to prevent non-Indians from reaching the island. Throughout the 1970s, this tense stalemate dragged on. Both sides appealed to the Interior Department to settle the issue, but this only ended up complicating the controversy, for one part of the Interior Department, the Bureau of Indian Affairs (BIA), supported the Lummi position, and another part, the Bureau of Outdoor Recreation backed the park board. In addition, the issue had already been before an administrative court once. The court had backed the tribe and the BIA on the question of whether the Lummis could deny access to the island. But that decision did not

resolve the basic controversy. The county was obviously dissatisfied with this ruling and appealed to the Interior Secretary to
decide in its favor. By the late 1970s, Interior Secretary Cecil
Andrus was anxious to settle the issue. But he was caught in a
dilemma: whichever way he decided, the losing party would be
infuriated and would inevitably appeal his decision in the federal
courts, and the dispute would continue. One disgruntled county
park board member even vowed to take the issue to the Supreme
Court if necessary. It seemed that this dispute, like many environmental controversies, was doomed to drag on for many more years
without a resolution.

     In 1978, seeking a way out, Secretary Andrus asked John
Hough, Director of the Western Field Offices of the Interior Department, to explore the possibility of getting the two sides together to negotiate a settlement. Hough quickly perceived that
one major stumbling block to negotiations was the role of the
Interior Department itself—it could not effectively oversee the
negotiations because it was too involved in the dispute to be seen
as impartial by either party. Fortunately, Hough had heard that
one of the first institutes for environmental mediation, Gerald
Cormick's Office of Environmental Mediation, was located in
nearly Seattle. The organization was contracted and agreed to
provide neutral third-party mediators to help resolve the dispute.
Andrus gave the mediators three months, from January 1, 1979
to March 31, 1979 to produce an agreement. If they failed, the
Secretary would step in and decide the issue himself.

     The two mediators, Leah Patton and Vern Huser, were
faced with an extremely difficult task. The dispute appeared to be
a classic zero-sum game. Each side wanted the island, and
whoever did not get it would be very dissatisfied. Thus there
seemed to be a very direct and basic conflict of interest between
the parties, with little chance of compromise. Moreover, years of
controversy and legal battling had embittered both sides of the
dispute. Members of the park board were frustrated and angry
and swore that making Portage Island into a park was a matter of
"pride and principle." At first, they insisted that they would only

meet with the Indians if the talks were limited to *how*, not whether, the island was to be used as a park. The Lummis had become equally adamant about their position. And to make matters worse, the two sides not only had conflicting interests at stake, there was also a large cultural gap which increased suspicion and made communication difficult. Clearly, finding a solution that would satisfy both of these very different, very suspicious, and very demanding parties was not going to be simple.

Undaunted, Patton and Huser began the mediation process. Three representatives from each side attended the first meeting at Fisherman's Cove, a restaurant on the Lummi reservation. The meeting began at six in the evening and ran into the early hours of the next morning. The first few hours consisted of dinner punctuated by awkward silences and stilted conversations about the weather and local news. For some, this was the first time they had had diner with an Indian or a non-Indian. The business portion of the meeting consisted primarily of formal statements of positions and concerns, with little give and take. There were six more meetings between January and March. They each had the same format as the first, an informal dinner followed by more formal negotiations, but each meeting was characterized by increasingly relaxed and spontaneous exchanges. No lawyers were directly involved in these negotiation sessions, a factor that the Lummi lawyer believed was instrumental in achieving a final agreement. "If I had been there or the park board attorney had been there," he said, "I don't think much would have happened." Between the meetings the mediators called the participants, asking questions, clarifying positions and suggesting areas of agreement. They also reported to the Interior Department on the progress of the talks.

Eventually, in March of 1979, an agreement began to emerge. The park board representatives expressed a willingness to sell the island back to the Lummis, if they would agree to let it be used as a park. The Lummis eventually agreed to this proposal, with the stipulation that no boat landings or marinas be included in the plan for the park, thus protecting their fisheries. They also insisted that the BIA provide the money to buy back the land. Secretary Andrus eventually agreed to this on the grounds that providing the funds was small price to pay for settling the dispute, and the fact that it could be justified as part of the BIA's program to solidify tribal land holdings. There were a few last minute hitches, but these were overcome and on April 19, 1979, the Lummis, the park board, and the county signed an agreement stipulating the terms on which the Lummis would buy back the island. On November 10, 1980, the county commissioners voted to sell the island for the agreed-upon price, and the next month the Lummis purchased the island.

As of this date, the agreement settling the Portage Island dispute has not been fully implemented. The island is back in the hands of the Lummi Tribe, but it has yet to made into a park. In this sense, the ultimate viability of this agreement is still open to question. Nevertheless, this case does serve to illustrate several of the claimed advantages of mediation. First, it was able to generate an agreement with a minimum of delay. With only a few months of negotiations, mediation was able to resolve a dispute that already had dragged on for almost a decade, and that threatened to take several more years of litigation. Moreover, this kind of speedy resolution not only saved the participants time, but also a considerable amount of money that would have been spent on court battles and appeals. But beyond being a more efficient approach in terms of time and money, what is perhaps most impressive about this case is that mediation produced a mutually beneficial decision where it appeared that none was possible. The final agreement was not only quicker and cheaper than a court decision, but also a *better* decision. Both the county and the Lummis were able to come away from the dispute with substantial parts of what they wanted. For proponents, it is this ability to fashion mutually satisfactory agreements to resolve controversies that gives mediation its most important advantage over more traditional approaches like litigation. And according to them, this ability is largely rooted in two unique characteristics of mediation: its non-adversarial nature, and the fact that it involves the direct participation of the affected parties.

A NONADVERSARIAL APPROACH

Most traditional approaches to resolving conflicts are adversarial in nature—each side attempts to win at the expense of the other. Institutions like the courts are designed for competitive, adversarial relationships, not cooperative ones. Even the participation that takes place in legislative and administrative institutions often is structured in adversarial terms. For example, in most administrative processes, like public hearings, the participants rarely talk directly with one another. As critics point out, "most administrative processes fail to provide sufficient opportunity for face-to-face dialogue among contending parties. Interested stakeholders are typically limited to expressing their concerns and registering their complaints through one-way communications. This, in turn, encourages groups to escalate their demands and exaggerate their claims."[29] It is thought that this kind of adversarial structure and adversarial atmosphere does little to encourage the search for true compromise solutions to these conflicts.

Importantly, these traditional adversarial approaches are not designed to encourage groups to *resolve* their differences, rather they are designed to *decide* an issue. This distinction—between resolving and deciding an issue—is a crucial one; one that helps to explain the success of mediation. Most judges, administrators, and legislators do not see their primary job as one of resolving controversies. Instead they see their job as making legal or policy decisions. As Richard Neely, author of *Why the Courts Don't Work*, has pointed out, "Courts are not primarily in the dispute resolution business; they are really in the business of making the wrong side pay up. Enforcement, not conflict resolution, is what courts largely accomplish."[30] Of course, judges and policymakers often believe that by making a decision they will resolve the controversy, but that is usually a mistaken assumption. Simply making a decision often does little to end a dispute. This is especially true when the decision is of the win-lose variety. For in practice, the side that loses has a strong incentive to continue its efforts to delay or obstruct the implementation of the decisions. This, proponents of mediation claim, is one of the main reasons that many of our environmental controversies drag on and on.

To his credit, Secretary Andrus realized that this would probably be the case in the Portage Island controversy. He could easily have made a decision in favor of the park board or the Lummis, but he understood that any such decision would have inevitably been challenged in court by the losing side. The result would have been additional years of litigation. Thus one of the common problems with traditional approaches to environmental dispute resolution is that the decisions rendered do not really end the conflict; at best they only drive it underground temporarily. In most cases, it will emerge again in a somewhat different form. Even the results of a final court appeal may not end a conflict. It is not unusual, for instance, for an environmental group dissatisfied with a court ruling to turn to other political strategies such as demonstrations, acts of civil disobedience, sabotage, and so on. When successful, mediation cuts off that cycle of continuing adversarial conflict.

FASHIONING WIN-WIN SOLUTIONS

In contrast to the traditional adversarial approaches, mediation explicitly aims to resolve environmental disputes to the satisfaction of all parties involved. In negotiating parlance, it attempts to fashion "win-win" solutions to these problems. (Many economists and social scientists refer to "win-win" situations as "positive sum games," and to "win-lose" situations as "zero sum games"; but I will use here the more colloquial terms preferred by many mediators.) In part it is possible to fashion win-win solutions because mediation is designed to be cooperative and nonadversarial, but it also is argued that much of what makes this kind of win-win solution possible is the fact that mediation is a form of direct democracy—where disputants participate directly in the decision-making process.[31] It is thought that without such direct participation and negotiation, win-win agreements would often be difficult, if not impossible, to fashion. But why should this be the case? Theoretically, there seems to be little reason why an insightful and well-intentioned judge or administrator could not fashion a win-win solution to a controversy. But in fact, there are several reasons why successful win-win decisions are unlikely to be made by unilateral policymakers. First, all of the posturing that takes place in traditional adversarial approaches makes it difficult for policymakers to fully appreciate which positions and claims are really important to the disputants and which are not. Even a sensitive administrator would have trouble understanding what options would satisfy which parties. For example, given the hardline positions initially articulated by the disputants in the Portage Island controversy, could Andrus have anticipated that the park board would give up its insistence on county ownership of the island, or that the Lummis would be more flexible on the question of access? Probably not. In practice, then, it is often impossible for policymakers to understand the complex motivations of the disputants or to anticipate exactly what trade-offs they would be willing to make.

Lawrence Susskind makes a related point when he argues that elected officials are often unable to legitimately represent both sides in environmental disputes. He maintains that elected officials are often ignorant of the "depth or intensity of concern that certain groups or interests have about particular issues." Moreover: "In controversial situations that are site-specific, in which my imme- diate neighbor and I disagree, no elected official can adequately represent both of us. Highly localized disputes probably would be better resolved by the parties directly involved. In community-wide and state-wide disputes as well, it might be better if the stakeholders represented themselves or chose special representa- tives to the particular negotiations surrounding the specific con- troversy. Then everyone would be assured of maximum representation."[32] In other words, it is unrealistic to expect elected policymakers to understand or faithfully represent all the interests of their constituents. Would conflicting interests be best repre- sented by the affected parties themselves? Such a process would not only assure that all interests were represented accurately, but would also increase the chances of finding a solution that all stakeholders could live with. Mediation certainly does not guarantee such an outcome, but it does increase the odds of its coming about.

The possibility of lone policymakers making successful top-down, win-win decisions is further complicated in environmental controversies by the large number of interests involved. Unlike two-party, labor-management disputes, most environmental controversies are multiparty. There are usually a whole host of business, environmental, and government groups that become involved in environmental disputes. For example, the controversy over the environmental impact of the expansion of Boston's subway system ended up involving the City of Cambridge, the Massachusetts Bay Authority, the Sierra Club, the Massachusetts Audubon Society, many local business groups, several Cambridge and Arlington residents' associations, and others.[33] When there is such a large and diverse number of interests involved, it becomes even more unlikely that a single authoritative decisionmaker could make a decision that would come close to satisfying all of these parties. Mediation, of course, does not rely on one person understanding all of the various interest involved. Instead it relies on the participants themselves, who are best qualified to understand and bargain over their own interests. In this sense, direct participation allows the fashioning of agreements that are much more complex and satisfactory than could have been created by a single decisionmaker.

Proponents also claim that direct participation also allows for a better understanding and treatment of the scientific and technical complexities of environmental controversies.[34] One of the ways that environmental disputes are different from many other kinds of political disputes is their complex technical dimensions. For example, disputes often involve disagreements over the exact effects of pollutants on the environment, and it is argued that judges and administrators are often unqualified to fully understand and deal with these kinds of issues. Administrators can at least appeal to their staff for help with technical issues, but judges typically do not even have that resource to fall back on. Not surprisingly, it is judges in particular who often are cited for their "lack of expertise" and their inability to "understand or consider pertinent technical information."[35] The suggestion is that the parties involved in the dispute often have the facts and expertise necessary to make the most sound decisions; and that this knowledge can better be tapped in open and cooperative negotiations than in adversarial approaches where information is usually hoarded.

DIRECT PARTICIPATION
AND THE PROBLEM OF LEGITIMACY

In short, it is argued that the direct participation of the affected parties is a key element in producing better and more equitable environmental decisions. But mediation's power to put an end to disputes lies not only in its ability to produce better substantive decisions, but also in the fact that its participatory nature increases the legitimacy of those decisions and therefore increases the likelihood that they will not be challenged in the future. One of the reasons that traditional approaches do not finally resolve disputes is because decision makers may have little legitimacy in the eyes of the disputants. Unilateral decisions made by administrators and judges are often perceived by either environmentalists or industry as being arbitrary. They are seen as decisions handed down by decision makers who have little appreciation for the merits of the case. This is particularly true in administrative decisions where environmentalists often feel excluded from the decision-making process. And fruitless participation in largely ceremonial participatory efforts like public hearings may only increase their sense of frustration and powerlessness. In such situations, they are likely to be highly suspicious and resentful of any final decisions that are made. For some groups, their exclusion from the process of decision making, may by itself be sufficient reason to oppose the decision—irrespective of its content. As one mediator has argued, even when the terms of a final decision are actually favorable to a party, they may reject the decision simply out of "suspicion born of their exclusion from the drafting process."[36] This is testimony not to the irrationality of the parties involved, but to the importance of the way that decisions are made. When groups feel that a decision is being forced on them, the natural tendency is to resist it. It is not hard to imagine, for example, the park board in the Portage Island case rejecting an Andrus decision that let the Lummis buy back the island. But since that idea came from negotiations that they participated in, they were much more likely to accept it.

Thus one of the major advantages of mediation is that no decisions are forced onto the disputants. The disputants themselves are the decision makers, and the agreements they make are purely voluntary. This kind of direct and real participation in decision making greatly increases the legitimacy of the final agreement. As one mediator has explained, it is important that the final agreement come from the parties themselves—not the mediator. "I won't make any formal recommendations; that is not my role. My role is to get the parties to reach agreement among themselves. This is important in that if you are a party in negotiation you are much more likely to see an agreement through if it is something that you had a hand in putting together. If it is your idea that is part of that agreement, then you are going to own it a lot more than if it is my idea. So I keep my mouth shut if I can and let the parties form their own agreement."[37]

Of course, the insight that direct citizen participation in policymaking increases the political legitimacy of policy decisions and smoothes their implementation is not something first discovered by mediators. Advocates of participatory democracy have long been making the very same arguments. Participatory theorists from Rousseau to more modern thinkers like Carole Pateman have always argued that when citizens participate directly in policymaking, they tend to see the resulting policies as their own. As Pateman has observed, one of the primary political advantages of direct democracy is that it "enables collective decisions to be more easily accepted by the individual."[38]

CONCLUSION

For advocates of mediation, this alternative approach has been made necessary by the many failings of our traditional political approaches to environmental controversies. And upon initial consideration, environmental mediation does seem to have a number of impressive advantages over more traditional approaches to environmental disputes. In theory, mediated agreements have the potential to be quicker, cheaper, more fair, more satisfactory, and more stable than those decisions produced by other approaches—especially litigation. Naturally, a careful analysis of the validity of these claims needs to be made—a task that will be taken up in chapter 3. In the meantime, however, we need to spend a bit more time understanding exactly how mediation works as a political process.

This chapter has only given a rough sketch of how mediation produces its alleged advantages over other political processes. It has been suggested that these win-win solutions can be achieved in part because mediation is a highly democratic and cooperative approach, but clearly more explanation is needed as to how these characteristics actually produce satisfactory resolutions to difficult environmental controversies. Accordingly, the next chapter will consider in more detail what goes on in mediation efforts, and explain more about how mediation is able to encourage the development of these win-win solutions to environmental conflicts.

CHAPTER TWO

The Advantages of Informality

Two sisters quarreled over an orange. Each wanted the orange and was unwilling to share it with the other. They argued and yelled and threatened violence. Only after their mother arrived and began asking questions did it become clear that the conflict was quite unnecessary. It turned out that one sister wanted the orange to make orange juice while the other sister wanted only the peel in order to make marmalade.[1]

If there is a secret of environmental mediation—a characteristic that most accounts for its ability to generate successful agreements—it lies in the informal nature of the process. What is special about mediation as a political process is not only that it allows for the direct participation of the disputants, but that their participation is relatively unencumbered by formal rules of procedure. In contrast to the courts and administrative processes, mediation allows the disputants to interact directly in a free and relatively casual manner. This kind of interaction is thought to have a number of major advantages. Most importantly, it enables the disputants in an environmental controversy to identify and discuss the real sources of their conflict. Environmental conflicts can never be finally resolved unless the parties have an opportunity to address the real obstacles that lie in the way of their agreement. But while this may seem obvious, advocates of mediation charge that this is exactly what traditional approaches often fail to do. It is argued that the formal constraints that characterize most administrative and judicial approaches often work to obscure or distort the true nature of environmental conflicts. Consider, for example, the public hearings held by administrative agencies concerned with environmental problems. Although they ostensibly are designed to solicit the views of the public, officials often restrict testimony only to that which addresses the specific law or regulation being considered. Thus in a hearing over the licensing of a nuclear power plant, opponents may want to bring in what they see a relevant issues, such as the problem of nuclear waste or the proliferation problems accompanying the plutonium fuel cycle; but such issues are usually ruled out of order because they do not pertain to the narrow question being considered at the hearing: the design and operation of the particular plant under review. In this way, formal hearings may only help to obscure rather than clarify the real nature of the disagreement between the affected parties.

Critics of the courts maintain that litigation also rarely addresses the real issues at stake in many environmental controversies. Again this is largely due to the formal requirements of the legal process, and the fact that the real source of a conflict often cannot serve as the legal basis for a court challenge. Environmentalists are not free to bring a developer to court simply because they disagree with a certain project. They must have some *legal* grounds on which to challenge the project. But often the only legal grounds available are quite different from the issues that are at the heart of the dispute. As one critical study concluded, "lawyers may have to reframe the issues separating the parties to fit a particular legal doctrine, and thus may change the nature of the dispute. As a result, the court is often not able to address the real issues and tailor an appropriate remedy."[2] For example, many of the suits brought by environmentalists must be based legally on the National Environmental Policy Act or the Administrative Procedures Act. The main feature of these acts is that they stipulate certain procedures that developers and government officials must follow. Thus to challenge projects in court, environmental groups must usually do so on procedural grounds. As one Justice Department lawyer observed, the majority of environmental cases she handles have to do with procedural issues—most commonly the failure of the government or a private developer to do an environmental impact statement, or to do an adequate one.[3] Of course the real issues are usually substantive—the adverse environmental impacts of a project—but the only *litigable* issues are procedural. Not surprisingly, these procedural cases usually fail to resolve the dispute. Even when environmentalists win their case, often all they actually win is a new environmental impact statement from the developer. What they usually want, of course, is to stop the project, and so the fight to block development continues.

In short, when environmental disputes are addressed in the context of traditional political institutions, they are often framed in ways that inhibit their resolution. In contrast, mediation can allow the parties to more easily address and resolve the issues separating them. Mediation efforts are relatively wide open and are not constrained by the formal rules that characterize traditional approaches. No issues are automatically excluded, and there is room to bring up any and all complaints or disagreements. As a result, proponents argue, the process allows the parties to come to a much better understanding of what separates them and what the real issues in the dispute are. These are the first crucial steps on the road to a true resolution of a controversy.

Of course this is not an automatic process, and it is not suggested that the disputants will come to these new understandings on their own. Indeed, proponents stress that the role of the mediator is crucial in getting the parties to address the real sources of their conflicts. It is thought that disputants often come into negotiations with exaggerated and distorted understandings of their dispute. In particular, disputants in long and bitter controversies often come to assume—like the sisters in the fable cited above—that their dispute is necessarily a win-lose one, that it is based on irreconcilable differences in interests. Good mediators use their skills to help the disputants see that the problem is often something much different and much less intractable than it first appeared. For example, the problem may be essentially one of misunderstanding or miscommunication—as was the case in the fable. Or as one leading environmental mediator, W. J. D. Kennedy of ACCORD Associates, has explained, the conflict may be a product of a confusing combination of issues and emotions; "Conflicts over natural resources are rarely exactly what they seem. What appears to be a simple collision of purposes is usually a combination of issues, past history, personalities, and emotions. One must analyze and untangle the muddle before trying to solve the problem."[4]

Much of the job of the mediator, then, is to help the disputants abandon simplistic and misleading conceptions of the problem and begin to address the real obstacles to agreement. Using their power to set the agenda and to define the issues to be discussed, mediators try to gently reframe the problem into a more negotiable form.[5] And in many ways, it is this process of reframing the issues that accounts for the ability of environmental mediation to work its magic—to generate mutually satisfactory agreements to difficult controversies. The informality of the process, combined with the guiding hand to the mediator, encourages the participants to look at their disagreements from a more fruitful perspective.

This chapter will examine this aspect of mediation in some detail; it will examine exactly how the direct and informal interaction that takes place in mediation allows the disputants and the mediator to address and resolve the various sources of environmental controversies. As we will see, mediators have begun to label and categorize these sources. Roughly speaking, they can be divided into (a) psychosocial disputes that revolve around such things as overheated emotions and negative stereotyping, (b) data disputes that center around scientific disagreements, and (c) interest disputes that involve competing or different interests. We will examine each of these sources of conflict and consider both how they contribute to environmental disputes, and how mediators have developed corresponding techniques to deal with each of them.

PSYCHOSOCIAL CONFLICTS

It is commonly assumed that all environmental conflicts revolve around substantive issues. But this is not always the case. One of the advantages of an informal, face-to-face approach like mediation is that it allows the mediator to get a good understanding of how such nonsubstantive factors as personal and group dynamics can play an important role in a particular conflict. What they have discovered is that environmental controversies, like most political controversies, are often complicated by what are called "psychosocial" conflicts—conflicts that have more to do with the social and psychological dynamics that exist between the feuding groups than with the actual substantive issues involved.[6] It is argued that this is a crucial dimension of conflicts and one that is often overlooked by economists and political scientists who typically focus on the substantive dimension of conflicts—like competing interests. To truly understand the real causes of environmental conflicts, it is suggested, we must also look at them as a psychologist would, "stressing the importance of emotional factors—many of them unconscious—in how people define their self-interest and interact with other groups and individuals."[7]

A typical example of these psychosocial factors is the "dysfunctional" emotions that participants bring to disputes and negotiations. Participants in environmental controversies do not always bring a calm and cool attitude to the dispute; they are often hot and emotional. They may be corporate executives, environmental leaders, or government officials, but they can be as angry, frustrated, depressed, irrational, vengeful, and neurotic as anyone else. And not surprisingly, these emotions can interfere with negotiations. It can be hard to compromise with someone when you feel like killing him. There are even times when these kinds of emotions may be the main barrier to an agreement. Donald Straus, president of the American Arbitration Association has pointed out that in many mediation efforts, "perhaps the hardest problem is that you're not dealing with a battery of high-powered lawyers and negotiators; you're dealing with activists who are not coldly logical."[8] Writing in *The Environmental Professional*, James Creighton, a specialist in conflict conciliation, makes a similar point. He argues that "there are a number of emotional motivations that lead to conflict on grounds other than disagreement on facts or values or interest differences. One group may feel insulted or oppressed by another. Individuals or groups may react to others based on emotional symbols such as hairstyle, dress, or language. A group or individual may feel resentful that they were not consulted."[9] And there are times, he maintains, when these kinds of emotional problems can actually overshadow the substantive dimensions of a dispute. A group may even "take actions at odds with their apparent self-interest if they feel insulted or tricked by their opponent."[10]

The detrimental role that emotions can play in disputes is a perennial problem in politics, and there is little in conventional policymaking approaches that seeks to address this problem. This is understandable, for at first glance there seems little to be done about this very human problem. Perhaps the only way to deal effectively with these uncontrollable emotions is to require all of the representatives of disputing parties to first go through several years of psychotherapy—an intriguing but unfortunately somewhat fanciful suggestion. However, in the context of mediation, this suggestion may not be as unrealistic as it first seems. For at times, environmental mediators do play a quasi-therapeutic role in the negotiations. Indeed, sociologist Susan Silbey and anthropologist Sally Merry, who have spent much time observing mediators at work, have labeled one major style of mediation as "therapeutic."[11] They found that therapeutic mediators typically fault traditional political approaches like litigation for ignoring or worsening the interpersonal dimensions of disputes. In contrast: "The therapeutic style of mediation is a form of communication in which the parties are encouraged to engage in a full expression of their feeling and attitudes. . . . Therapeutic mediators will typically ask, "How did this situation start?" or "What was your relationships before hand?" They rely more heavily on expanding the discussion, exploring past relations, going into issues not raised by the immediate situation, complaint, or charge."[12]

The mediators studied by Silbey and Merry primarily were

involved in community disputes, but the same therapeutic approach can be found among some mediators involved in environmental disputes as well. These professional often call themselves
"conciliators" rather than "mediators" and they see their main
expertise as "managing interpersonal relationships." But even
those environmental mediators who do not explicitly see themselves as conciliators or therapists will often resort to a variety of
techniques to short-circuit the damaging effects of emotional factors. For example, instead of trying to repress or ignore negative
emotions, it is common for mediators to encourage negotiators to
acknowledge and express their inner feelings. As Donald Straus
has suggested: "The mediator must let [activists] vent their emotions, their anger, their stored-up feelings, before he can get at the
issues."[13] The theory here is one that is common in psychotherapy—that letting disputants express their emotions encourages
them to release those feelings. In many conventional political
settings, such an outburst might only lead to a heated argument
between opponents and increase the polarization. But mediators
try to structure the situation to prevent it from getting out of hand.
For example, they may separate parties into different rooms before
encouraging them to vent their frustrations. Or as in one mediation
effort, there may be a rule that only one person at the table can
be mad at one time, thus ensuring that no serious quarrels
developed.

Of course, some emotional factors may prove too strong or
too complicated to be dealt with in this way. James Creighton
cites two examples of this problem: "Psychologists have observed
that there are individuals who have a strong need to express
aggressiveness, almost independent of the target of their aggres-
sion. It is almost impossible to resolve a conflict with such an
individual, since the basis of opposition does not lie in current
interest or behavior and cannot be "satisfied" by compromise. . . .
If an individual emotionally defines himself as a "revolutionary,"
he will have extreme difficulty accepting compromise even if his
apparent self-interest would dictate it. Many people react to government agencies based on reactions to authority learned from
youthful experience."[14]

In such extreme situations, even a good conciliator may be

unable to overcome the psychosocial barriers that are blocking agreement. However, mediation may still offer a more constructive alternative than most conventional approaches. First, mediators are often urged to spend time becoming familiar with the motivations of the negotiators.[15] Thus they may be more likely to become aware that it is a personality factor, not a substantive issue that is blocking a settlement. More importantly, the mediator is often in a position to suggest a change in the negotiator, where they believe that emotions and personality have become a large part of the problem. Substituting a different representative can sometimes be a key step toward facilitating an agreement.

OVERCOMING STEREOTYPES

Another common example of the psychosocial barriers to the resolution of environmental conflicts is negative stereotyping. When groups become enmeshed in prolonged adversarial relationships, they usually develop stereotypical views of each other— reassuring oversimplifications which emphasize the negative aspects of the adversary. Thus environmentalists are seen as "environmental crazies" or "no-good, long-haired hippies"; governmental officials are portrayed as "insensitive bureaucrats"; and businessmen as "greedy capitalists" or "environmental rapists." Such stereotypes usually only get in the way of a compromise agreement. They fuel adversarial approaches by exaggerating the differences between the parties and increasing the polarization. Who wants to negotiate with a "rapist" or compromise with a "extremist." Without some kind of basic trust between the parties, no voluntary agreement is possible—and stereotypes make trust seem irrational.

In addition, stereotypes tend to justify the use of the most manipulative and deceitful political tactics. In its essence, stereotyping is a way of dehumanizing one's opponent, a way of turning them into objects. And it is much easier to coerce, manipulate, deceive, or mistreat objects than real human beings like oneself. As innumerable generations of soldiers have learned, it is much easier to kill and maim "gooks" and "krauts" than it is to kill and maim human beings with real names. The same dehumanizing process is often at work on a lesser scale in environmental disputes, where stereotyping of the opposition may help to justify or legitimize personal attacks, lying, violence, and other "hardball" political tactics. A particularly good example of this process was found by Mark Dowie, a journalist who attended a conference of utility and nuclear industry executives. The purpose of the meeting was to discuss strategies for dealing with the antinuclear movement. As Dowie related, at one point in the conference, "the pace quickened when it was decided that the appropriate label for the (anti-nuclear) movements leaders should not be 'crazies' or 'revolutionaries' but 'destroyers'—describing people, who, after all 'really just want to destroy America and the system.' Emotions ran higher when the primary objective for the new strategy became 'to destroy the destroyers..'"[16]

Stereotyping and adversarial approaches are mutually supporting, each feeding the other. Mediation seeks to break this cycle by undermining these dysfunctional images. It does so in two ways. First, direct discussions provide a better means of communication and clear up many of the misunderstandings and misinterpretations that fuel stereotypes. As Silbey and Merry points out, this kind of improved communication is seen by therapeutic mediators as being crucial, for they "assume that misunderstandings or failures of communication, rather then fundamental differences of interests, are the source of conflict."[17] When interest groups only relate to each other at a distance, as is typical in American politics, it is difficult for them to get an accurate and objective picture of the opposition. Groups often only relate to each other indirectly, through third parties like lawyers or the media. This distance allows each group to interpret (or misinterpret) the actions of their adversaries in ways that merely confirm their original suspicions. An incident that took place in the Portage Island controversy illustrates how this typically takes place. At one point, during early maneuverings over the question of access, the director of the park board was quoted in a local paper as declaring that the island was open to any county resident who wanted to use it. The Lummis interpreted this as an act of bad faith by the park board, and saw the statement as merely confirming their suspicions that the county was not trustworthy. Their reaction was immediate and strong: they put up no-trespassing signs and began patrolling the waters around the island. It later became clear, however, that the intentions behind the director's comments were quite different than what they seemed at first. He thought he was merely responding to a reporters *legal* question concerning the right of access, and stated that *in principle* all county residents had a right to use county property. As one park board member commented later, "The answer that [he] *had* to give was that since the public owns the island, the county cannot keep the public off of it."[18] Clearly, the director had not intended to encourage people to use the island at all. These kinds of misinterpretations and misunderstandings may be common in many environmental disputes, and to the extent that direct negotiations can minimize them, they will undermine simplistic stereotypes.

It is thought that mediation undermines stereotyping not only by clearing up misunderstandings, but also by enabling the parties to meet and experience each other as real human beings. It seems that it is difficult to maintain a simplified, stereotypical view of one's opponents after one has prolonged discussions with them. Of course, the breakdown of long-held stereotypes is by no means an automatic process. The skills of the mediator are often useful in this effort. They often encourage the negotiators to get to know one another and call each other by their first names. A typical technique is for the mediators to get the conflicting parties together in an informal setting apart from the negotiating table. They may, for instance, arrange for them to have lunch together at a local restaurant before a negotiating session. The spontaneous conversations that take place may seem insignificant on the surface, but they can have a important impact on the attitudes that opponents have toward each other. Its hard to think of someone as a diabolical "destroyer" when it turns out that they too are dedicated fans of the Boston Celtics.

As one mediator explained, "people tend to get to know each other and to like each other. There gets to be a personal bond—it's a natural human reaction."[19] This human reaction is one of the most crucial parts of mediation. For as the parties get to know one another and understand each other's concerns, this may enhance their respect and trust for one another. Without this trust, meaningful negotiations are often impossible. Since mediation agreements are often voluntary in nature, they are unlikely to be entered into without some form of mutual trust between the parties. This kind of trust is best encouraged when parties are required to relate to each other as human beings, rather than abstractions.[20]

To talk about developing respect and trust between long-time environmental adversaries inevitably sounds a bit naive. And clearly mediation cannot always succeed in overcoming the deep psychosocial barriers that separate some adversaries. But mediators are always full of anecdotes about cases where something akin to "trust" and "respect" eventually developed between what had originally been embittered opponents. Consider again the case of Portage Island. It would be hard to find a conflict in which there was more initial distrust between the parties—distrust fueled by large cultural barriers. But after the negotiations, one of the Lummi negotiators reported that, "I grew to trust one of the park board members particularly. He listened. When he spoke he showed that he had heard us. This guy wasn't into control and power. He wanted the island to be a park, but in a way we could live with."[21] Even the park board negotiator who had a reputation for being a hardliner admitted that "We did learn to appreciate their problem a little more." "I could see," he said, "that the loss of an 865 acre island is a big thing if you want to preserve the reservation."[22] And as a reporter for the local newspaper concluded, one of the most important facts about the Portage Island negotiations was that "negotiators for both sides finished the bargaining with a great deal of respect, admiration and trust for those sitting across the table from them."[23]

The Portage Island case is not an exception. Similar feelings of mutual respect and trust have resulted from other mediation efforts, such as the negotiations that took place under the auspices of the National Coal Policy Project. One of the earliest examples of environmental negotiations, this project was jointly headed by the corporate energy manager for Dow Chemical Company and a former president of the Sierra Club. Their goal was a large one: to try to settle many of the disagreements over coal mining policy in the United States. The results of the project were mixed: the two sides did come to a number of significant new agreements in their meetings, but these agreements were largely ignored by Congress and subsequently never made any impact on official coal mining policy. However, what is interesting for our purposes is that these meetings were a psychosocial success—that during the process of negotiations, old-time adversaries were able to move from an attitude of scorn to one of mutual respect. As one commentator observed: "At first, the industrial members of the mining task force were horrified when they heard that one of the members picked for the environmental side was Robert Curry, professor of geology at the University of Montana. In the past, Curry's biting testimony before courts and hearings had lacerated the technical competence and the motives of his industrial opponents. But by the time the mining task force had completed is first field trip through the lignite fields of the Gulf States, Curry's expertise and evenhanded attitude had earned the industry men's profound respect. "If I wanted to open a mine in the West," says lawyer John Corcoran, co-chairman of the mining task force and a former board chairman of Consolidated Coal, "Bob Curry is the first man I would go to about the environmental problems."[24] What is particular interesting here is that Robert Curry was first seen in a negative light when the opponents met in a formal adversarial setting; but once thrown together in the informal atmosphere of the field trip, "Bob" became seen as a real and reasonable person, worthy of respect.

One of the most important jobs of mediator, then, consists of repairing the dysfunctional psychosocial relationships that have developed between disputing parties. It is not without reason that some call themselves "facilitators" or conciliators"—words that emphasize that their role is not merely to find answers to a problem, but to smooth the hostile relationships between the parties. For these conciliators, it is this ability to deal with the psychosocial dimensions of environmental controversies that helps them succeed where traditional approaches have failed. As one mediator summed it up: "Most of what we do is simple human relations."[25]

DATA DISPUTES

Naturally, not all environmental disputes are primarily psychosocial in nature; many center on substantive disagreements between the parties. But again, it should not be assumed that these substantive disputes always involved intractable conflicts of interests. Mediators point out that many times the substantive disagreements between environmentalists and developers are primarily factual disagreements—what they sometimes call "data disputes."[26] The ability to address these kinds of disagreements is particularly important in environmental controversies—for it is thought that one of the characteristics that separates environmental disputes from many other political disputes is their tendency to revolve around complex technical and scientific issues. It is not unusual, for instance, for an environmental controversy to center on a disagreement over the exact nature of the impacts of a particular developmental project. Indeed, some mediators have suggested that such disagreements are at the center of *most* environmental disputes. "At the heart of most environmental controversies lies a dispute over the likely future consequences of a proposed action. . . . Although we can predict the operation of a few natural systems quite accurately—the rise and fall of the tides is a good example—our understanding of how most ecosystems operate is fairly limited. As a result, our predictions are necessarily approximations of reality. . . . This produces a situation ripe for conflict."[27]

Consider, for instance, a utility proposal to build a new coal-burning power plant. The factual questions surrounding such a project are almost endless. What kinds of environmental impacts will be caused by the plant? Will it contribute to the acid rain problem? How much? Where will the environmental impacts be felt? How severe will they be? What kinds of pollution control devices would be most effective? How much will electric bills go up if devices are installed in the plant? And so on. There are usually great disagreements over even such relatively straightforward questions as these. Typically, developers accuse environmentalists of exaggerating the negative environmental consequences, and environmentalists argue that developers underestimate these consequences and exaggerate the costs of ameliorating them.

Proponents of mediation suggest that it can be quite helpful in resolving these kinds of data disputes. Again, much of this has to do with mediation being an informal process that often brings the disputants together for face-to-face exchanges of views and information. When environmentalists, developers, and government administrators are left to themselves, or only interact in formal ways through intermediaries, they rarely question the quality or accuracy of their own research. But in mediation they are required to expose and defend their findings in front of each other and the mediator. In the process, each side is exposed to new information developed by the other side, and becomes more aware of the inadequacies of their own data and methods. As a result, according to one mediator, it is not unusual to find that both sides end up revising some of their initial factual claims. Howard Bellman, an experienced labor and environmental mediator, cites as an example a fish management case he mediated between an Indian tribe and a state fisheries commission. The dispute was characterized by a number of different technical disagreements, mostly concerning what would be the most effective method for rehabilitating the fisheries. But after two years of negotiation, "both of them changed their minds about some of the specific facts." They changed their minds and came to an agreement over such technical issues as what kind of equipment should be used to stock fish, which tagging techniques should be employed, what kind of law enforcement would be most effective, etc. Bellman concluded that: "The fact of the matter is that both of them learned about the merits of the other's position during the negotiations and both of them changed their positions on the merits. They found weaknesses in their own positions. There was an open-minded exchange."[28]

Naturally, simply bringing disputed parties together in the same room does not guarantee this type of agreement. Mediators must often play a very active role in structuring negotiation efforts in ways that encourage the resolution of these data disputes. One important technique employed by mediators is to get the disputants to view the negotiations as a "joint problem-solving effort" rather than a confrontation between opposing parties.[29] Establishing this new, nonadversarial perspective on the dispute is considered crucial. In a confrontational atmosphere, data disputes become contests between two sets of analysis and information; each side insists that its figures are right and the egos and reputations of the negotiators very quickly become involved. To avoid this, mediators suggest that the participants not view each other as the problem, but view the technical questions as the problem, and seek to cooperate to solve that mutual problem. In essence, mediators seek to redefine the nature of the dispute itself. Instead of a political dispute involving conflicting interests, the problem is cast as a technical one amenable to rational analysis.[30] Sometimes mediators will even change the physical set-up of the negotiating room in order to promote this new approach to the situation. Instead of having the sides facing each other, which implies that the other party is the problem, the mediator may seat both on the same side of a table facing a blackboard on which the details of the technical dispute are written out, thus emphasizing that they are working as co-investigators seeking to solve a mutual problem. As Roger Fisher and William Ury of the Harvard Negotiation Project explain: "The physical reinforces the psychological. Physically sitting side by side can reinforce the mental attitude of tackling a common problem together. People facing each other tend to respond personally and engage in dialogue or argument; people sitting side by side in a semicircle of chairs facing a blackboard tend to respond to the problem depicted there."[31]

In addition to the co-investigator approach, mediators will sometimes recommend that the disputants agree on a neutral expert or a procedure that will settle what the real facts are in a case. There have been several cases, for example, where computer models have been instrumental in determining to the mutual satisfaction of the parties what the likely environmental impacts of a project will be. One of these cases involved the management of salmon fishing off the shores of British Columbia.[32] The controversy centered on how to permit fisherman a fair annual catch and at the same time to ensure that the salmon stock was not depleted to dangerous levels. Much of the dispute hinged on a factual disagreement over how various levels of fishing would affect the salmon population. In order to help resolve the dispute, the groups involved agreed to jointly oversee the construction of a mathematical model that could be used to forecast the impacts of various fishing schemes. After construction of the model was completed, they began to feed in various alternative proposals. One proposal that seemed to have intuitive merit to the fishermen was the idea of prohibiting the retention of all salmon under fifty-one pounds. But once the model was run, it was discovered that this approach would probably not work. It was found that this approach would greatly increase the catch of salmon over fifty-one pounds and that this would result in an even more negative impact on the salmon stock than was already occurring. After running various other fishing schemes through the model, the fishermen finally agreed that the best approach would be to restrict the total catch per fisherman to a limit of a certain number of pounds of salmon per annum, rather than to put a limitation on any category or size of fish.[33]

These kinds of examples have prompted some proponents of mediation to put great faith in this "joint problem-solving" approach to environmental disputes. A leading environmental mediation organization, ACCORD Associates in Colorado, has become one of the main champions of this approach, and has argued that it may be the key to solving many, if not most, environmental disputes. One of ACCORD's mediators, Susan Carpenter, has maintained that if disputants only had the opportunity to meet face-to-face and exchange information, many environmental controversies could be avoided. "At least half of the conflicts we see occur because people did not have access to accurate information, or had no mechanism for talking with the other side (or sides). These 'unnecessary' conflicts could have been avoided if people had had some mechanism for talking candidly with each other."[34]

INTEREST CONFLICTS

Of course, not all environmental disputes are rooted in personality conflicts or data disputes. Some inevitably involve conflicting interests—a point that most mediators will freely acknowledge. Some disputes are caused, for instance, by the fact that developers are interested in encouraging the exploitation of natural resources, and environmentalists are interested in preserving them. In addition, corporations are typically concerned with minimizing environmental clean-up costs, while environmentalists are interested in maximizing protection of the environment, and so on. In such instances, the interest conflicts seem direct and clear. Indeed, this seeming incompatibility between the interests of industry and environmentalists is much of what has contributed to the view that these conflicts are inherently adversarial and zero-sum—that if one side wins, the other must lose.

Naturally, proponents of environmental mediation do not share this pessimistic perspective on interest conflicts. They believe that mediation can be instrumental in overcoming these conflicts as well. Their optimism is based on a unique set of assumptions about the way that interests play a part in environmental conflicts. They argue that our adversarial political culture tends to promote a limited and distorted view of interests. When confronted with a controversy, we normally tend to focus almost exclusively on *conflicting* interests. But mediators point out that this focus can be misleading—that it mistakenly assumes that this is the only kind of interest at work in these disputes. In actuality, they maintain, there may be three different kinds of interests present in any controversy—conflicting interests, different interests, and common interests.[35] It is thought that the mediator's ability to differentiate between these three kinds of interests and to emphasize the latter two is one of the main reasons that mediation can successfully resolve these controversies.

Consider, for instance, the importance of drawing a distinction between interests that are different and interests that are conflicting. This distinction is not an obvious one. It is common to assume that different interests are the basic cause of disputes, that if two groups have different interests then they will necessarily be in conflict. But logically speaking that does not always have to be the case.

To illustrate this, consider another fable told by a mediator, this one concerning two men quarreling in a library. One patron wants the window in the reading room to be open and the other wants the window closed. They argue back and forth and try various compromises—such as leaving the window half-open or just cracked—but they cannot reach an agreeable solution. At this point the librarian comes in. She asks why the one man wants the window open and he replies that he wants some fresh air. The other says he wants the window closed because he cannot stand drafts. The librarian ponders the different desires of the men and then arrives at a solution. She opens a window in the next room, bringing in fresh air without a draft.[36]

The point, of course, is that just because two parties have different interests that does not mean that those interests are incompatible. We may be able to find a solution that actually satisfies both sets of different interests. This simple but crucial insight is a large part of what accounts for mediation's ability to settle disputes. Much of the mediator's time is spent encouraging the participants to create solutions to the dispute that allow each of their different interests to be fulfilled. This approach is the source of the win-win solutions so celebrated by proponents of mediation. The case of Portage Island, described in the last chapter, is a good example of how valuable this approach can be. The eventual solution to the conflict was made possible because the mediator was able to convince the two sides that while they had quite different interests at stake, those interests were not necessarily in direct conflict. The conflict at first appeared to be a zero-sum game with each side wanting the island. But in fact the real interest of the park board was not in the ownership of the island, but in its becoming a public park. And the major interest of the Lummi tribe was not in stopping the park but in not losing ownership to a large part of their reservation. The final agreement where the Lummis got the island and the county got its park is a classic example of how to dovetail two sets of differing interests into a mutually acceptable settlement.

In order to facilitate the search for these kinds of win-win options, mediators will sometimes encourage the participants in a conflict to make another important distinction: between their position and their interests. As Fisher and Ury have explained, participants in a dispute tend to be preoccupied with their specific position on an issue, which is usually in direct conflict with their opponent's position.[37] In the library story, one man's position was that the window should be open, the other that it should be shut. Often positions are directly incompatible and focusing on them only leads to an impasse. Fisher and Ury suggest that more attention be paid to what lies underneath these positions, the interests that caused the parties to adopt their particular positions. Once one looks at interests, one may find that they are not incompatible at all. Again, this is part of what happened in the Portage Island conflict. Agreement was not possible until both sides quit focusing on their initial incompatible positions (who should have the island) and began to explore the reasons and interests that were underlying these positions.

This ability to get beyond initial positions and explore underlying interests is thought to be another great advantage of the informal, face-to-face style of interaction that takes place in mediation. The informal dialogue allows the mediator and the participants to ask questions of each other that can begin to uncover the underlying interests and motivations at work in the dispute. In many formal policymaking institutions, this does not take place.

In fact, in most traditional policy approaches, the focus of any discussion is usually on the legal or policy issues involved—not underlying motivations. Policymakers are typically concerned with specific policy proposals—a piece of proposed legislation on water development, a new antipollution regulation, or a law concerning logging practices. But putting specific policies at the center of the process inevitably encourages a focus on the positions that groups take on the policies—positions that are usually directly conflictual. Thus a focus on policy may only encourage an adversarial atmosphere, and obscure the fact that the underlying interests of the disputing parties are not incompatible. One of the first conflicts to go into environmental mediation was a disagreement over the building of a dam on the Snoqualmie River in Washington State.[38] The county and local residents supported the dam, while environmental groups opposed it. As long as discussion centered on whether one was for or against the dam proposal, it seemed impossible for the groups to agree. However, during mediation it was brought out that what the county and local residents were mainly interested in was flood control, and the primary concern of the environmentalists was that the dam would interrupt a freeflowing river and open the flood plain to urban sprawl. They were eventually able to integrate these different concerns by developing a proposal to build a dam on a different fork of the river and to establish a basin planning council to control development. The point, of course, is that the search for these kinds of innovative solutions is inhibited when attention of the parties is centered on a specific policy proposal. In mediation, the focus can become interests rather than policies. This can introduce more flexibility and creativity into the process, and this greatly increases the chances of settlement.

NEGOTIATION AS A LEARNING EXPERIENCE

Not only does the informal dialogue of mediation enable parties to move beyond their initial positions and uncover their basic interests in a dispute, it can also prompt participants to reflect upon and even change their minds about what those basic interests are. This is an important point, because many mediated agreements are made possible by one or both parties reassessing what their real interests are in a case. In much the same way that direct discussions can lead participants to reexamine their data and scientific analysis, discussions can also lead them to reexamine their basic needs and goals. In other words, negotiations may not simply be a process of trying to find a middle ground between two sets of competing interests, it may also be a learning experience in which the parties are forced to confront real questions about just what their interests are. And sometimes, this reevaluation process leads one or both parties to move away from their original conception of their interests, thus paving the way for an agreement. To go back to the Portage Island example, it is revealing to note that one of the reasons that the Lummi Tribe agreed to develop the island as a park was their realization that this use of the island might actually have certain advantages for them. According to one observer, the Lummis came to realize that having the island be a park actually would be in their interest because it "meant that the Tribal Council would never have to deal with the politics of determining its future use. [The] fear within the Tribe that some future Tribal Council would sell off Portage Island for commercial development was one of the biggest reasons why the Tribe was willing to accept its permanent status as a park."[39] Thus, during the process of negotiation, the Lummis came to a new understanding of what interest they might have in the island becoming a park—something they had not considered before. And this new understanding played a key part in their accepting the final agreement.

The fact that direct dialogue encourages this kind of helpful self-reflection comes as no surprise to advocates of participatory democracy. They often argue that direct participation not only is the best way to protect one's interest, but it also gives one a better understanding of what those interests really are. The political theorist Peter Bachrach has written extensively about the "value of participation as a way of understanding one's own position," and he has observed that a "man becomes aware of his political interests only as he becomes a communicative being" and participates in "democratic structures that facilitate political reflection."[40] Thus again we see a unique advantage that comes from direct participation and informal dialogue. Typically, interest groups are homogeneous organizations that are relatively isolated from other groups. As a result, the members' perception of their interests are continually reinforced by those who share their assumptions and concerns. Within such groups, serious challenges to shared positions rarely take place. It takes direct contact and discussions with opposing groups to force interest groups to reconsider and learn more about their own positions and that of others. Mediation, it can be argued, is an institution that is explicitly designed to encourage just this kind of discussion and reflection.

DEALING WITH TRULY OPPOSED INTERESTS

As we have seen, apparently conflicting interests may sometimes turn out to be only different interests, but it would be naive to believe that this is always the case. In many environmental controversies, discussion and self-reflection may only reveal that there is a very real and direct conflict of interests between developers, environmentalists, and the government. But even in such apparently win-lose situations, it is argued that mediation can still be useful in generating approaches to the problem which may satisfy both parties. But how is this possible? There are several approaches that mediators have available. One of the most innovative is the suggestion that the winning party compensate the losing party for their loss. Such an approach admits the win-lose nature of the situation, but attempts to create a mutually acceptable solution by mitigating the damages suffered by the losing group. Understandably, this idea, often called "negotiated compensation," has attracted much attention. For example, it has been of particular interest to state governments who are trying to find locations for hazardous waste treatment and disposal facilities.[41] State agencies around the country have found themselves in prolonged battles with local officials and environmentalists whenever they choose an area in which to locate a facility. The conflict of interests between the state's need to find someplace to dispose of these wastes and the community's desire to prevent such facilities from being built in their area is clear and strong. Where states have tried to simply override local authorities and locate facilities in a community, they have invariably run into stiff local opposition in the form of legislative challenges. court fights, and civil disobedience. However, some states, like Massachusetts, have tried a more negotiated approach to these controversies. Among other things, the Massachusetts Hazardous Waste Facility Siting Act provides for compensation to abutting communities that are likely to be affected by new hazardous waste facilities. Builders of such facilities are required to negotiate with these communities over how the company can compensate the community for any increased costs or risks associated with the facility. For example, a company might agree to purchase for the town special fire-fighting equipment designed to be used in chemical accidents. It will become clear later that this approach does have some potential problems and may not be desirable or effective as proponents have hoped. But clearly the basic idea of negotiated compensation is an intriguing one. It demonstrates, at least theoretically, that win-lose conflicts involving directly opposed interests may not be hopeless—that even in these cases, direct negotiations may yield an agreement that at least satisfies some of the interests of all the parties involved.

EMPHASIZING COMMON INTERESTS

Another approach that mediators use to encourage compromise in situations where interests are in direct conflict is to emphasize the third kind of interests present in these controversies—the common interests that exist between the parties. Just because there are opposing interests, this does not mean that there are not also important interests that the parties share. But again this is something that is commonly overlooked in controversies. As we have seen, attention is naturally focused on interest differences, not interest commonalities. But mediators emphasize that "in many negotiations, a close examination of the underlying interests will reveal the existence of many more interests that are shared or compatible than ones that are opposed."[42] Moreover, it is argued that changing the focus of the negotiations to those interests that are in common can be helpful in encouraging the parties to compromise—to give a little in their positions in order to promote their common concerns. An often cited example of how this process works is labor-management negotiations, where both parties clearly have large overlapping interests. It is thought that one of the reasons that labor and management tend to reach agreements is that both have a basic interest in avoiding strikes and in promoting the prosperity and smooth operation of the firm. Proponents of environmental mediation often suggest that similar kinds of common interests also underlie environmental controversies.

Indeed, it has been argued that underneath their squabbles, government officials, developers, and environmentalists share the some basic societal goals—a healthy, growing economy with adequate environmental safeguards. This was the position argued by Interior Secretary William Clark in a speech before the National Wildlife Federation in 1983. This was Clark's first major speech before an environmental group and clearly he was trying to begin his job by mending fences with environmentalists and moving beyond the intensely adversarial approach of former Secretary Watt.

[W]e believe that Russell Train of the World Wildlife Fund was correct when he spoke of the need for what he called "convergence." Russell put it this way, and I quote: "Over the long run, there is no inherent conflict between our major goals and concerns, environmental, economic, energy, agricultural, social." He said, "the major task for environmentalists is to push for convergent strategies which enable us to move over the long term to simultaneous achievement of these goals, strategies that will enable us to move to a long term sustainable relationship between people and resources." . . . As Russell Train noted, the greatest mistake that environmentalists can make is to forget that housing, agriculture and industry are also part of the environment. Only a strong nation can protect its customers and its environment. To achieve convergence strategy is essential to coping with the nation's and the world's vital resource issues. All those involved must avoid partisan snares that, I'm afraid, polarize us and make it really difficult to promote the common good. It should be recognized with all concerned that without wise economic development of resources we cannot provide the jobs and products to meet social and environmental goals.[43]

The logic of this argument is clear: that while environmentalists and industry do sometimes have competing interests, they also have some important shared interests as well; and emphasizing those common interests may be a useful way to encourage parties to sit down and negotiate resolutions to environmental controversies. Disputants are encouraged to step back and look at the big picture and realize that in the long run many of their disagreements are not due to conflicting ends, but are due to disagreements over the best way to achieve those ends. The implication is that we all share a basic commitment to such basic societal goals of economic development and environmental integrity and that most conflicts actually involve questions of how best to balance out those goals—thus they are primarily questions of means, not ends. If disputants can be encouraged to look at controversies in this way, then they will be able to enter negotiations not as immutable enemies, but as people who share much in common. It is thought that this attitude would greatly increase the chances of generating reasonable compromises over the issues involved.

CONCLUSION

Much of what is intriguing about environmental mediation is its ability to generate breakthroughs in what seem to be hopelessly deadlocked controversies. As we have seen in this chapter, what enables mediation to accomplish this feat is its ability to bring the disputants together in a relatively informal atmosphere. It is thought that this approach allows the participants—who are often considered to be confused initially about the nature of their disagreements—to recognize and address the real sources of their dispute. As one mediator has emphasized, "conflicts over natural resources are rarely exactly what they seem"—a phrase that could easily serve as the motto of this profession. As we have seen, much of the work of the mediator involves using various techniques to reorient the parties, to encourage them to look at their conflict and each other in a new light. By emphasizing that environmental disputes are often rooted in personality conflicts, misunderstandings, and data disagreements, and by stressing that disputants may have different but not competing interests, mediators seek to overcome dysfunctional preconceptions about the nature of environmental disputes and thus hopefully increase the chances that a win-win solution can be found. It should be pointed out, however, that not all observers endorse the way that mediators seek to reframe the issues involved in environmental controversies. Some environmentalists fear that in reframing the issues, mediators may manipulate the participants and give them a misleading understanding of the nature of their dispute—a possibility that will be explored later in chapter 6. For now, however, the main point is that the informal nature of environmental mediation allows for the examination and reframing of environmental disputes, and that this attribute seems to account for much of mediation's ability to generate mutually satisfactory agreements.

CHAPTER THREE

Separating Myth from Reality

People think the mediator comes and says, "Let's stop suing each other. Let's stop yelling at each other. Let's relax. Here is a comfortable chair. Can I get you some sharp pencils? Don't you see this is just another human being? This is a reasonable person." That's bullshit. What I say to them is "Hey, I was just in the room with that guy and if you don't reexamine your position he is going to come down your throat." I go back and forth with threats.

Howard Bellman[1]

In earlier chapters, environmental mediation has been portrayed primarily through the eyes of its proponents. And understandably, what we have seen is a very rosy view of this process—a one-sided view that emphasized all the potential advantages of this new approach. And by and large, it is this optimistic view of mediation that has been promulgated in the media. The notion that there is a creative new technique that can resolve long standing environmental disputes has made good copy; and so many proponents and journalists have promoted an image of mediation as a new procedural wonder drug that will finally cure us of many of these vexing conflicts. Needless to say, this image of mediation is an exaggerated one. The purpose of this chapter and those following is to balance out this overly optimistic view, and to offer a more realistic political evaluation of environmental mediation.

This chapter will begin this "reality therapy" by taking a critical look at several of the most common claims made about mediation. For example, proponents often claim (a) that mediation is made necessary by an increasingly overcrowded court system (b) that mediation is faster than litigation (c) that mediation is cheaper than litigation and (d) that there is a great deal of public dissatisfaction with litigation. As we have seen, much of the case for mediation rests on such assumptions—but are they true? It will be shown that all of these claims are quite problematic and little reliable evidence exists to confirm them. Also to be examined are several other persistent myths about mediation, including the claim that mediation heralds the emergence of a new cooperative approach to environmental politics—that it is a step away from the confrontational and adversarial style of politics that currently dominates most of our traditional political institutions. It will be seen that this depiction of the politics of mediation can be misleading, and that mediation is best understood as an extension of traditional adversarial politics, rather than an alternative to it.

ARE THE COURTS OVERWHELMED WITH ENVIRONMENTAL CASES?

Much of the case for environmental mediation is a negative one, resting on the alleged failings of traditional approaches like litigation. For example, as was seen in the first chapter, proponents of mediation usually argue that the ever-growing use of litigation as a remedy in environmental controversies has resulted in overcrowded courts, long delays, and exorbitant expenses. But just how accurate are these claims? Let us begin by looking at the first claim—court overcrowding. Advocates of mediation frequently suggest that this new process is needed because the judicial system is becoming increasingly flooded with environmental cases, and will soon be unable to cope with them all. As one proponent warned: "The courts simply can't handle the load [of new environmental cases]."[2] It is easy to understand where this fear comes from; during the last decade a long list of legal scholars and court critics have suggested that America has become a litigation happy society.[3] A large number of books and articles have lamented the American preoccupation with litigation—one author even invented a label for this legal disease, calling it "hyperlexis."[4] Even Chief Justice Warren Burger has spoken out about the severity of the problem, and has publicly complained that Americans have "an almost irrational focus—virtually a mania—on litigation as a way to solve all problems."[5] Given this general alarm about the problem of excessive litigation it is easy to see why advocates of environmental mediation assume that this is a serious problem, and that mediation can help to solve it.

But the facts say otherwise. Recent studies have shown that the problem of excessive litigation has been overblown. A $2 million study completed by the Wisconsin Civil Litigation Research Project has been the most extensive empirical study done on this problem to date, and it has served to puncture the myth of America as an overly litigious society. It found, for example, that relatively few disputes actually make it into the courts. Only one out of ten people involved in a dispute go to a lawyer. Moreover, half of the people who do seek lawyers never file suit, and of those who actually file suit, 92 percent settle out of court before the case goes to trial.[6] Hardly the signs of "litigation mania." These findings are also reiterated in a study done by the National Institute for Dispute Resolution. Even this promediation organization has admitted that, "Contrary to popular belief the problem [with the courts] does not seem to be excessive litigation. . . The number of cases litigated does not appear to be increasing faster than the population is growing. This increase is rather modest in a country that is experiencing as much social and technological change as is the United States."[7]

Given the evidence that we are not suffering from a general plague of excessive litigation, we need to look more carefully at claims that we are suffering from excessive growth in environmental litigation. And indeed, the evidence here suggests that this problem too has been largely overblown. Again, it is easy to understand why there appears to be such a problem. In the early 1970s there was a virtual explosion of new environmental litigation. In the year between 1970 and 1971, environmental suits begun in the federal district courts increased a staggering 142 percent—from 35 to 85; and the next year they increased another 65 percent to 129 cases.[8] But these early figures are misleading. First, this large jump was clearly a one–time phenomenon, sparked by new pieces of environmental legislation like the National Environmental Policy Act (NEPA) that established for the first time the rights of citizens to sue developers on environmental grounds. Second, as figure 1 indicates, after this initial rise, the number of environmental suits initiated in federal district courts has remained relatively steady over the years. This leveling-off phenomenon was also observed by Charles Warren, former Chairman of the Council on Environmental Quality, who noted in 1978 that "it *appears* to us that the amount of litigation related to NEPA issues is leveling off: we found a slight increase last year, but the number was so slight that we suspect the real trend is toward a plateau, not toward a rising slope."[9] And this lack of substantial growth in environmental suits becomes even more significant when it is considered that the number of environmental laws were growing dramatically during the 1970s. Between 1970 and 1979, over twenty new environmental laws were added to the federal books, and there are now eleven statutes that specifically encourage citizens to sue over environmental issues.[10] But despite this, there has been only a modest growth in the use of litigation. Such figures suggest that fears of the courts being increasingly overwhelmed with environmental cases have been largely exaggerated.

IS MEDIATION FASTER?

One of the other frequent justifications for environmental mediation is that it is faster than litigation. As we saw earlier, court cases are often criticized as being excessively time–consuming, and it is thought that mediation can be a great help to overcome this important institutional drawback. But the problem with this claim is that there is little systematic evidence to back it up. Usually the evidence that is invoked by advocates of mediation is anecdotal in nature: they cite an example of a environmental suit that took many years to resolve and then tell of a mediation effort that wrapped up a difficult dispute in a matter of months. Naturally, this kind of evidence can be highly misleading. What is needed is systematic studies that compare the length of environmental suits to environmental mediation efforts. Unfortunately, no such studies exist. There is, however, one study done by Gail Bingham at the Conservation Foundation that does begin to shed some light on this question.[11] Although an enthusiastic promoter of environmental mediation, Bingham has been disturbed by the frequent unsupported claims that mediation was faster (and cheaper) than litigation, and she set out to try to find empirical data to illuminate the discussion of those questions. As we shall see, she was only partially successful. But though her study does not finally settle these questions surrounding the time and expense of mediation, its findings do suggest that the claims made by some advocates in this area may be exaggerated.

In her research, Bingham first compared environmental suits to civil suits in general. She found that environmental litigation did take somewhat longer, on the average—but that the median durations of both were relatively short. She compared the length of environmental cases and other civil cases in the United States District Courts during the twelve–month period ending June 30, 1983, and discovered that the median number of months from filing to disposition for environmental cases was ten months, while the median for all civil cases was seven months. Similarly, for cases that actual went to trial, the medial for environmental suits was twenty–three months, while the median for civil cases was nineteen months. She found that some environmental cases do take a very long time to settle, but that these constitute a small percentage of the total environmental cases. Only ten percent of environmental suits took more than forty–two months from filing to disposition.[12] This data suggests that the few long cases are the exception and that environmental suits do not take appreciably longer than other kinds of litigation.

But, of course, the real question is whether court cases take longer than mediated settlements. Unfortunately, that is a question that Bingham was unable to answer with any confidence. At one point in her report, she declares that from the information she has collected about mediation efforts, the median duration of the environmental mediation case is between five and six months; but she hastens to add that "not only is this information incomplete, it is definitely *not* comparable to the statistics on litigation cited above."[13] Clearly this is an area where more research is needed to finally settle these questions. It does seem likely, though, that the notion of mediation as appreciably faster than litigation has been exaggerated. It seems to be based largely on the perception of litigation always being a long and drawn—out process—a misleading image derived primarily from the excessive publicity focused on a few protracted environmental suits. And indeed, this is the very point made by Bingham when she concludes in her report that "it is likely, therefore, that it is the *threat* of protracted litigation, not the length of the standard case, that creates the popular conception that mediation is faster than litigation."[14]

IS FASTER BETTER?

Of course, underlying all of this discussion of which approach is faster is the assumption that faster is better. Mediation advocates typically assume that the delays caused by litigation are undesirable. But is that necessarily true? If we consider cases that have dragged on for decades, the answer is probably yes. In such cases, the issues never seem to be resolved and the expenses for all sides can be enormous. But such interminably long cases are unusual—most environmental suits rarely take more than one or two years to resolve. More importantly, it could be argued that these relatively modest delays may in fact serve an important political purpose. For example, it may often be in the public interest to delay development projects in order that their environmental impacts may be carefully considered. And indeed, this is often the purpose of the injunctions sought by environmental groups. Such reconsiderations can be vital, for an important characteristic of environmental impacts is that they are often irreversible. Once a unique habitat is destroyed, a rare species becomes extinct, or an old ethnic neighborhood is destroyed by a freeway, there is no going back. And when dealing with such irreversible impacts, it is not clear that speed in decisionmaking is a virtue. In such environmental issues, as with the death penalty, the rush to an irreversible judgment may only result in decisions that will later come to be greatly regretted. Thus, in this policy area, it may be only prudent to delay questionable development projects long enough to allow for a serious reconsideration and possible redesign. In other words, delays can often be desirable—and often, such delays are only made possible by court injunctions.

Of course, critics of the courts assert that the delays created by environmentalists often go beyond allowing a careful reconsideration of the legal and environmental issues and are only frivolous attempts by diehard environmentalists to block any development whatsoever.[15] Such delays, it is suggested, are usually based on no real evidence of environmental threats, and thus only serve to unnecessarily frustrate development projects that are clearly in the public interest. To see whether this accusation is true or not, one would have to go through a great number of court challenges and try to assess whether they were warranted or frivolous—a difficult task that no one has yet taken on. And yet there may be good reason to believe that the charge that most delays tend to be frivolous has been exaggerated. Joseph Sax, a leading environmental law scholar, has suggested that the nature of the courts themselves works to insure that this kind of abuse is unlikely to occur.

Delay is never imposed simply because some dissatisfied citizen desires it. Only a judge can convert a plaintiff's desire for an injunction into an

enforceable order. And judges . . . do not simply grant injunctions because they are sought; they must be persuaded that important issues are
at stake and that there is a reasonable likelihood of ultimate success by
the plaintiff. Thus agencies and industrial enterprises who have carefully
done their planning homework are in a very strong position to persuade
a judge that no impediment should be placed in their way. Experience
thus far with all the environmental cases litigated suggests very strongly
that judges are most reluctant—as any sensible individual would be—
to restrain important and extremely costly projects. They must be persuaded that something is wrong and that haste is undue.[16]

If Sax is right, if private and public developers often hurry
decisions without due concern for the environmental impacts, and
if the courts can weed out frivolous attempts at delay, then it may
be that the modest delays caused by litigation are desirable. This
is not to say that such delays are not frustrating for developers.
And when suits are used by corporations to delay the implementation of environmental statutes, environmentalists can become
quite frustrated as well. But in such important decisions, delay
and reconsideration can sometimes be a virtue. It should not be
forgotten that the main criterion for judging a political process
should be whether it produces the best decisions possible, not
whether it produces the fastest ones possible.

IS MEDIATION CHEAPER?

Another major claim made by proponents of mediation is that it
is consistently and significantly cheaper than litigation. It is argued
that the expense of litigation can be a great burden to the disputants, and may even serve to deny access to justice to those with
limited financial resources. But again, there is reason to believe
that this problem has been exaggerated. Litigation is certainly not
cheap, but neither is it always prohibitively expense. For busi-
nesses, attorney's fees in environmental disputes are likely to be
smaller, relative to the amount at stake, than other typical court

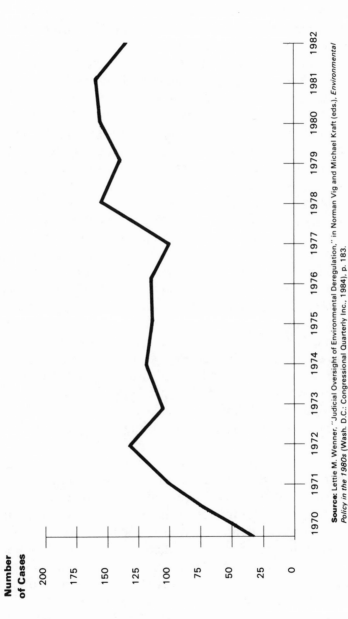

FIGURE 1

Number of Environmental Cases Introduced into Federal District Courts

Source: Lettie M. Wenner, "Judicial Oversight of Environmental Deregulation," in Norman Vig and Michael Kraft (eds.), *Environmental Policy in the 1980s* (Wash. D.C.: Congressional Quarterly Inc., 1984), p. 183.

cases in which they become involved.[17] In addition, on the environmental side, it is important to note that the possibility of court awarded attorney's fees can often make litigation an affordable option for these groups as well.

Moreover, it is not clear that mediation is always an inexpensive option. There is certainly little evidence to support this claim. Again, the only attempt to systematically investigate this claim has been by Gail Bingham in her study. But she encountered a number of difficulties in trying to collect reliable figures about the comparative costs of mediation and litigation. For instance, although she spent considerable time investigating over 150 cases of environmental mediation, she was forced to conclude that "information about the costs of these cases is too sparse to report with any confidence."[18] Moreover, she encountered considerable conceptual and methodological problems concerning this attempt to measure costs. For example, she notes that although mediators usually charge less than attorneys, one cannot always substitute one for the other. In a mediation effort involving complex legal issues, all sides may find that they need to employ lawyers to help them with their case. In addition, if groups are to be adequately prepared to debate complex environmental issues, they will often have to employ scientists, economists, and other experts. Thus, as Bingham has observed, "It is also important to consider other costs associated with resolving disputes. The costs of preparing for negotiation, for example, may be as high or higher than the costs of preparing for some kinds of litigation, particularly for public interest groups."[19]

And these are not the only problems. Bingham also notes that "a simple comparison of the costs of litigating a complex dispute that later was mediated, although striking, can be misleading. First, it is unrealistic in many situations to begin counting the costs of mediation from the time that parties agreed to negotiate, if the previous period of contention, litigation, and/or clarification of relative power contributed to the parties' willingness to negotiate a voluntary settlement."[20] In other words, there are times when mediation would not take place without the case first going to court; and in those situations, it might be most accurate to include these costs of litigation as part of the overall costs of arriving at a mediated settlement. And this of course would greatly change our conclusions about how inexpensive these negotiated settlements are. As one environmental lawyer observed, "If you have to wait for litigation, then many of the [monetary] benefits of negotiation are gone."[22]

In short, the issue of expense in environmental mediation is a complex and murky one, and this makes it quite difficult to confirm claims that mediation offers a significant financial advantage. And it is revealing that even when a strong proponent of environmental mediation set out in a yearlong attempt to find reliable data to support these claims, she was unable to do so. Thus, while it widely agreed that the expense of litigation is a serious problem, it is not clear that mediation is the solution. Expense may well be a significant problem in mediation as well.

THE LOW DEMAND FOR MEDIATION

To sum up, important questions can be raised about many of the alleged advantages that mediation efforts have over the courts. And unfortunately, there currently is little reliable empirical evidence to resolve these questions. However, there may be another way to shed light on these questions concerning the comparative advantages of mediation versus litigation—an approach that does not require elaborate statistical studies. One could use the market as an indicator of the relative advantages and disadvantages of these alternative approaches. The logic here is straightforward: if litigation indeed suffers from the massive problems that critics ascribe to it, we would expect to see substantial numbers of disputants flocking to environmental mediation. In other words, the demand for mediation should give us a rough idea of the level of dissatisfaction with current approaches, which in turn should give us an indication of the perceived disadvantages of the courts. We can begin with a consideration of how often disputants have chosen mediation. The best estimates to date indicate that during the last decade there were only 162 examples of mediation efforts throughout the country.[22] Considering that these are spread out over a ten year period, this number hardly indicates a ground swell of public demand.[23] Indeed, the demand for mediation is so low that many of the environmental institutes that were set up with foundation money in the 1970s are finding it extremely difficult to support themselves on the small number of cases that come their way.

Proponents of mediation have an explanation for this small demand. They argue that it is primarily due to the lack of public awareness. It is thought that few people know about environmental mediation, and that as knowledge of this option grows, its use will dramatically increase. But there are several factors that undermine this explanation. First, although it is true that mediation was a relatively obscure phenomenon in the mid-seventies, during the last five or six years, it has received considerable publicity in environmental publications. Moreover, various foundations have poured millions of dollars into promoting mediation: funding research and the publication of reports and studies, sponsoring mediation conferences and workshops, and directly subsidizing mediation institutes and mediation efforts. It would be difficult for anyone seriously concerned with environmental issues to be unaware of this option.

This explanation is also contradicted by the results of a recent study that indicate that even when disputants in environmental controversies are made fully aware of the option of mediation, the vast majority tend to reject it. This study, conducted by Suzanne Buckle and Leonard Buckle of MIT, had as its subject the work of an prominent environmental mediation institute in the northeast. The institute was concerned about their poor record in mediation efforts. The demand for their services seemed low, and when they did engage in mediation efforts, they felt that their record of success was disappointing. This was particularly problematic because the institute was getting large foundation grants, but having difficulty showing substantial results for the dollars being invested. The Buckles' study confirmed the extent of these problems. They found that in the 81 cases of environmental disputes in which the institute contacted the disputants and explained the nature of their services, 70 percent (57) rejected the option of mediation outright. Even more disappointing was that of the 30 percent (24) who began the mediation process, two–thirds of them dropped out of mediation after the initial session! In the end, only six groups of disputants signed an agreement as the result of mediation, and only three of these agreements turned out to be stable—which was generously defined as lasting at least six months.[24]

Interestingly, the Buckles tried not to be too pessimistic about these findings. When they presented their results at the 1984 Law and Society conference in Boston, they chose to emphasize the fact that in those cases where mediation was rejected, 34 percent of these eventually were resolved by out–of–court negotiations (while 24 percent were resolved by unilateral action and 23 percent were resolved by a formal adversarial process). They took heart in these figures and speculated that even though most of the parties rejected formal negotiations, their exposure to this option may have increased their willingness to try negotiations on their own. In this sense, the efforts of the mediation institute may have had an indirect effect of encouraging negotiated settlements in some of these cases. That is possible. But a more straightforward and realistic interpretation of these findings would suggest a much more pessimistic set of conclusions. The figures clearly suggest that there is no great public demand for mediation, even among those parties who are made aware of how it works and what its alleged advantages are. And despite the criticisms of litigation made by proponents of environmental mediation, most disputants seem satisfied enough with this and other traditional approaches to reject the option of mediation.

MEDIATION AND THE BALANCE OF POWER

What all of this means, of course, is that some of the advantages of environmental mediation seem to have been exaggerated; and that its usefulness, at least in the eyes of environmental disputants, may be considerably less than some proponents have claimed. As one mediator recently lamented, mediation is being "oversold and underutilized."[25] There may be a relatively simple explanation for this—which is that disputants are not very interested in negotiation and mediation if they think they can win all of what they want through other approaches.[26] For example, if developers or environmentalists believe they can easily win in court, they have little incentive to seek out negotiations. The same is true if they think they can achieve their goals through their influence on legislative or bureaucratic decisionmakers. It may be, then, that the low demand for mediation merely reflects the disputants' perception that they can win their cases in other dispute resolution contexts. This conclusion is supported by the work of Gerald Cormick, Leah Patton, and Howard Bellman—leading mediators who have been associated with the Mediation Institute in Seattle. Their experience and research has led them to believe that disputants are only likely to embrace environmental mediation when certain favorable political conditions exist. They have concluded that mediation only tends to be seen as appropriate when the circumstances of a controversy fulfill the following criteria: (1) there is a relative balance of power between the disputants; and (2) an impasse has been reached in the controversy.[27] They argue that mediation only becomes a viable alternative when these two characteristics of a conflict are present; otherwise, the parties are unlikely to negotiate in good faith. The logic of their argument is simple: once a balance of power exists between the disputants, then the possibility of a political stalemate is greatly enhanced; and once the stalemate makes it clear that neither party can win on their own, then they will be willing to negotiate in good faith and to compromise. As Cormick explains it *"Mediation requires some relative balance of power between the several parties.* The parties in a dispute will be willing to enter with "good faith" into the mediation process to the extent that they are unable to act unilaterally in what they perceive to be their own best interest. Therefore, unless the parties directly involved in a dispute have some relative ability to exercise sanctions over one another, there is slim possibility that good faith mediation will occur."[28]

In other words, disputing parties are only willing to negotiate and compromise when a balance of power prevents them
from getting what they want on their own. The Portage Island
conflict described in chapter 1 can be used to illustrate this principle. Recall the situation that had developed. For several years,
each party had enough power to create a virtual stalemate. Because of increasing Indian militancy, the county could not easily
develop the island as a park. Conversely, the tribe could not easily
regain title to the land, which remained firmly and legally in the
hands of the county. Given this situation of stalemate, negotiation
became a very attractive alternative. It presented the possibility of
both parties getting at least part of what they wanted.

Similar situations have existed in other successful mediation efforts. In the Hudson River/Storm King controversy in New
York, the Environmental Protection Agency (EPA), Consolidated
Edison, and several environmental groups were locked in battle
over the impacts of various utility plants on the fish population of
the Hudson River. Eventually a stalemate developed: the hearings,
studies, and law suits dragged on for years with no clear end in
sight. Neither side seemed able to get what it wanted. The utilities
were frustrated in their attempt to build a new plant, and were
faced with the possibility of the EPA forcing them to build $350
million worth of cooling towers for existing plants. On the other
side, the EPA and environmentalists were faced with seemingly
endless delays in their efforts to remove existing threats to the
river's fish population posed by already operating utility plants.
In short, neither side was getting what it wanted, and there seemed
little hope that either side would win out in the foreseeable future.
This situation of mutual frustration was a fertile one for negotiation, and eventually, with the help of a mediator, the parties were
able to work out a compromise agreement that was acceptable to
all of them.[29]

Understanding the crucial role that power and stalemates
play in mediation can help to shed some light on why mediation
is not being used more often. The demand for mediation may be
relatively low because the particular political circumstances that
encourage negotiation may be relatively rare. It may be that true

balances of power between disputants are not very common.[30] It may also be the case that even when stalemates and delays are created, they are not always *mutually* frustrating. A court injunction on a development project may frustrate the developer, but it may delight environmentalists, who would have little interest in breaking such a deadlock. It is Cormick's belief that these necessary antecedent conditions for mediation are often not present in many environmental disputes. After reviewing sixty environmental controversies over a period of three years, he estimated that only about 10 percent (6) of the cases actually fit his criteria of balanced power and stalemate.[31] It seems, then, that the use of environmental mediation may be seriously constrained by the absence of power balances and political stalemates, and that this helps to explain why mediation is not as popular an option as some of its proponents believe it should be.

IS MEDIATION REALLY NONADVERSARIAL?

Understanding the importance of power balances and stalemates in encouraging negotiations also sheds some valuable critical light on another one of the common myths about mediation—that it is a purely cooperative, nonadversarial approach. As we have seen, some advocates of mediation celebrate this characteristic of mediation. They point out that what is new and exciting about mediation is its ability to create cooperative instead of competitive relationships, to create true dialogue where only name calling existed before, and to replace animosity with trust. And this portrait of environmental mediation as an entirely different approach, an alternative to litigation and other adversarial processes is much of the reason that it has garnered so much attention. Mediation seems to be a process that addresses the yearning on the part of many Americans for a less belligerent and confrontational approach to our problems. The decades of 1960s and 1970s were a time of almost constant social, racial, and economic conflict. Many

Americans are now weary of hearing about all of these problems—
a mood that Ronald Reagan effectively exploited in his optimistic
and upbeat campaign for President in 1984. For those who have
grown tired of our unrelenting adversarial politics, mediation has
an obvious appeal. It embodies the hope that we can transcend
our current political fragmentation and begin to work together to
solve our pressing national problems—in this case, our environmental problems. Thus, in larger terms, environmental mediation
is often seen as signaling a break with the politics of confrontation,
and the emergence of the politics of reconciliation.

Often a communitarian vision of politics underlies nonadversarial approaches like mediation. As Jerold Auerbach has
pointed out in his history of alternative dispute resolution mechanisms in America, this communitarian theme has always been a
strong concern to those who advocated this approach.[32] Histor-
ically, these nonadversarial approaches flourished first in the early
colonial religious communities set up by the Puritans, the Quakers,
and the Shakers. This interest in conciliation as an alternative to
the courts emerged next in the religious and political utopian
communities that proliferated throughout New England and the
Midwest during the early part of the nineteenth century in communities like Oneida and Brook Farm. What all of these groups
had in common was that they were tightly–knit, intentionally
isolated from the surrounding "competitive" society, and had an
overriding commitment to communitarian values. Most explicitly
shunned the common legal forms of dispute resolution. They
viewed litigation as an expression of the individualism and com-
petitiveness that characterized the corrupt mainstream society. For
them, the purpose of dispute resolution was not to find out which
individual was legally right, but rather to reassert their shared
sense of justice and to reintegrate the disputants back into the
community. As Auerbach explains, "communal order was secured
through a variety of controls that were designed to eradicate conflict or eliminate 'discordant spirits.' The framework for resolving
disagreements was mutual and consensual, not individual and
adversarial."[33]

Interestingly, one sometimes finds similar communitarian

themes in modern writings about mediation. For example, proponents of mediation often lament what they see as the breakdown of community in our postindustrial society, and they sometimes look back nostalgically on days gone by, when the bonds of community, family, and church were much stronger in America. Consider, for example, the following passage from a Ford Foundation pamphlet on the need for more nonlegal dispute resolution mechanisms in the United States. "When the population of the country was smaller, less urban, less affluent, and more homogeneous, fewer disputes arose and established institutions dealt successfully with most of them. A much larger population, more closely in contact and engaged increasingly in activities requiring interactions, finds itself having to deal with conflict and divisiveness on an unprecedented scale. At the same time the cultural forces that arranged relationships in the past—that structured, guided, and connected behavior and prevented, mediated or arbitrated disputes—have lost much of their influence. The family, the church, the social club, the political association, and broadly based organizations of many kinds have witnessed an erosion of their peacemaking roles."[34]

The hope of course is that techniques like environmental mediation can now start to play that peacemaking role and can begin to reestablish the feelings and bonds of community that are so sorely needed in our society. This hope was explicitly expressed, for instance, in many of the comments made after the signing of the agreement that resolved the Portage Island controversy. A local paper hailed the mediated agreement as "the first step forward in improving relations between the tribe and non-Indians living in Whatcom county. And at the signing ceremonies, both Lummi and county authorities expressed the hope that from then on their relationship would be informed by what they called "the spirit of Portage Island."[35]

Of course, most working mediators would hesitate to list the reestablishment of cooperation and community in America as one of the goals they seek in mediation efforts. Out of necessity, their attention is focussed on smaller and more immediate goals, like producing a workable agreement for a specific controversy.

But one can still see elements of this communitarian vision of mediation in the practice of many mediators. For example, as we saw in the last chapter, some proponents identify one of the most important results of mediation as being the establishment of cooperative and trusting relationships. Indeed, mediators who primarily view themselves as conciliators (or therapists) see the creation of such bonds as one of the keys to a successful mediation effort. This nonadversarial approach that emphasizes reconciliation is sometimes called, appropriately enough, the "hot–tub" school of mediation. As the name implies, the hot–tub school places considerable importance on the more "touchy–feely" aspects of mediation and especially the process of overcoming the psychosocial barriers that interfere with generating agreements. Indeed, some who are "into" this approach to mediation even characterize it as a process that can be used to encourage a "higher form of consciousness." In this regard, it is revealing that a recent catalogue from the Omega Institute of Holistic Studies in upstate New York includes, under the heading "New Frontiers for Social and Personal Growth," a course on the win–win style of negotiation developed by Roger Fisher and William Ury. Negotiation is described as "a better way . . . [that] enables people to maximize mutual gain as well as create sustaining relationships." Like the other courses at the institute ("Therapeutic Touch Workshop," "Dance of Tennis," and "Creating and Running a Humanistic Business"), the negotiation course is thought of as an alternative approach that represents the workings of an enlightened consciousness. This, of course, is the hot–tub approach taken to an extreme. Yet it is indicative of the extent to which the view of mediation as a cooperative, communitarian, and even spiritual alternative to adversarial politics is often an integral part of the dispute resolution movement. One sees this aspect of mediation expressed in the views of Ted Becker, a political scientist at the University of Hawaii, when he describes what he feels is the revolutionary nature of this new cooperative approach to conflict. "The contemporary American mediation movement," he says, ". . . is part of a network of changes in social, economic, and political values conceptualized by terms such as 'third wave,' 'new age politics,' 'the aquarian conspiracy,' and 'mega-trends.' The mediation movement is only one manifestation of how people in the postindustrial, information age are trying to cope better with one another in all walks of life including families, personal relationships, the workplace, and the marketplace."[36]

THE HARD–BALL SCHOOL OF MEDIATION

The nonadversarial, communitarian vision of environmental mediation is a very seductive one—especially for those who feel uncomfortable with confrontational styles of politics. But while this vision is appealing, one must still ask whether it is true. Is mediation really primarily about establishing trust and cooperative relationships? Is it really the harbinger of the end of adversarial politics in environmental matters? There are some who would answer an emphatic "no" to these questions—and interestingly, they are some of our most experienced environmental mediators. Those mediators who appreciate the role of power in mediation, like Gerald Cormick and Howard Bellman, see the nonadversarial, hot–tub understanding of mediation as misleading and naive. For them, mediation is a form of power politics, not an escape from it. And this more confrontational understanding of mediation infuses the approach that these mediators take to negotiations. Bellman, for example, has little time for the kind of cooperative and conciliatory techniques that some other mediators believe are so important. As his quote at the beginning of this chapter illustrates, he is cynical about the worth of those techniques, because for him, power and threats are the basic elements of negotiation— they are what eventually force the parties to compromise.

For Bellman, environmental mediation is not an encounter session but an intensely adversarial and combative process, where each side tries to get the most for itself and only compromises when it is forced to. Instead of the hot–tub approach, this might be called the "hard–ball" approach—one that emphasizes the continuing importance of power politics in mediation efforts.

Like many of his colleagues who share this more adversarial view of mediation, Bellman came to environmental negotiations from a background in labor relations. Schooled in the trenches of labor–management warfare, Bellman has few illusions about the role that benevolence plays in mediation. Nor does he put much stock in the touchy–feely techniques or the psychological ploys used by some mediators to facilitate agreements. Indeed, when Bellman discusses mediation, he frequently makes a point of saying, "I am not a psychologist," and "I don't know anything about psychology."[37] Gerald Cormick is another leading environmental mediator whose perspective was also informed by involvement in labor–management disputes. He also puts little importance on establishing friendly, trusting relationships between adversaries; and he suggests that the nonadversarial nature of environmental mediation has been exaggerated. In fact, he went out of his way to puncture this myth in a paper presented to the American Association for the Advancement of Science in 1981. In that piece, Cormick warned that many of those who are tying to popularize mediation have made exaggerated and misleading claims. He pointed out that one of the most frequent misconceptions about environmental mediation is the belief that "successful mediation is where negotiators learn to like, trust, and agree with each other."[38] For Cormick, successful mediation efforts do not require congeniality, and can easily take place in an atmosphere of mutual hostility. All that is required, is that each party have a strong incentive to negotiate and compromise—and that can be provided by political stalemates.

ARE MEDIATORS THAT IMPORTANT?

This power-based analysis of mediation also gives us a very different perspective on the role and importance of the mediator in the negotiation process. As we saw in the last chapter, another common assumption in mediation is that the mediator plays a central and all–important role in generating agreements. It is thought that mediators should be skilled in facilitation techniques, and that they be able to act as quasi-therapists who are trained to help the parties overcome the psychosocial and other barriers that stand in the way of agreement. Thus the focus is very much on the creative techniques that mediators use at the bargaining table to encourage cooperative behavior. In contrast, practitioners like Bellman put much less emphasis on the mediator's conciliatory skills. They argue that the success or failure of mediation depends not simply on the techniques of the mediator, but also on the presence of certain characteristics in the conflict situation itself—such as power balances. Given the right potential circumstances, the skills of the mediator may not be crucial to the success of the negotiations—indeed a mediator may not even be needed. Bellman argues that this is especially true when the political situation is one of high risk—another condition he sees as conducive to serious negotiations. By high risk he means a situation in which the stakes involved are large, but in which neither party can be assured of winning. When this high level of uncertainty is present—and there is the possibility of losing everything—the disputing parties are much more likely to seek compromise and thus ensure that they get at least part of what they want. And in such situations, Bellman suggests, the skills of the mediator become less relevant. "When [disputants] get into that atmosphere of not knowing how it's going to come out, and they are so invested in the situation that it is important to them how it comes out, it's really easy to get it over with. They are fearful. They are looking into the jaws of losing. They are coming to the mediator and saying "Can you cut our losses?" [In such situations] the mediator doesn't have to be a powerful person, the mediator doesn't have to be a seductive person, the mediator doesn't have to be smarter than everyone else. He just has to be there, and not be one of them."[39]

It is just this kind of high–risk situation that existed in the Portage Island controversy. Recall that Secretary of the Interior Cecil Andrus was threatening to make a unilateral decision about the fate of the island. Given the division that existed in the Interior Department over this issue, it was far from clear which side Andrus would eventually support. So neither side could be confident of victory. Indeed, there is reason to believe that both sides were fearful that they could lose everything that they had fought for during the last decade. Given this situation of fear and uncertainty, both parties were more open to negotiations, because this process held out the hope that they could be certain to get at least part of what they wanted. Thus it could be argued that it was not the ploys of the mediators but the characteristics of the political situation that were the crucial factors in encouraging a successful negotiation. This is not to denigrate the efforts of the mediators in this case, which were considerable, but only to observe that without this kind of favorable political atmosphere, even the most skilled mediators may not have been able to generate an agreement. It is in this sense that the hard–ball school of mediation gives us a more realistic and balanced appreciation of the role of the mediator. Once we fully appreciate the central importance of such things as power, stalemates, and high risk in encouraging serious negotiations, then we are less likely to succumb to another common myth of mediation—the mediator as "miracle worker."

ARE MEDIATION AND LITIGATION MUTUALLY EXCLUSIVE?

Yet another myth about mediation is that it and litigation are enemies or at least mutually exclusive alternatives. This misconception is largely due to the efforts of proponents to draw sharp distinctions between what are portrayed as two completely different approaches—a theme we saw in the first chapter. But this dichotomy can be misleading; and again, an understanding of the role that balances of power play in encouraging serious negotiations is helpful in cutting through this myth. For it can be argued persuasively that without litigation, mediation would be unlikely to be used as much as it is. In many cases, it is the ability to litigate that creates the stalemates that foster mediation efforts. It is not a coincidence, for instance, that interest in environmental mediation began in the mid–1970s—at exactly the time of large increases in environmental law suits. This increased litigation was fueled by the passage of environmental laws like NEPA, which for the first time gave citizens the right to take development projects to court on environmental grounds. By giving environmentalists access to the courts, NEPA helped to create more of a balance of power between environmentalists and developers than otherwise would have existed. Before this recourse to the courts, there were few reasons why developers should agree to negotiate with disgruntled environmental groups. In this sense, the increase in environmental litigation was the mother of environmental mediation.

From this perspective, litigation begins to look more like the friend of mediation, and less like its rival. Litigation is first helpful in creating situations of stalemate. Suits and countersuits can create the lengthy delays that frustrate everyone involved. But equally important, litigation usually creates the situation of high risk that is valued by mediators like Bellman. It is a win–lose process in which each party risks losing their entire case. Judges and juries are notoriously unpredictable, and even with a very strong case, it is difficult to be certain of victory. It is often this nagging uncertainty surrounding litigation, as much as anything else, that prompts a party to consider out–of–court negotiations. Ironically, then, the very disadvantages of the court system that many proponents of mediation love to criticize—its expense, its slowness, its risks, its win–lose decisions—are the factors that make mediation possible and attractive. Knowing this, the more politically sophisticated mediators usually do not agree with those who characterize litigation as an undesirable adversarial approach that needs to be replaced with a cooperative alternative. In fact, Bellman has argued that mediators may find it useful at times to encourage the parties to sue one another—for only then will risks and costs reach the point where they will be happy to negotiate seriously.[40] Mediators often speak of waiting until conflicts are "ripe" for mediation, and litigation often plays a useful role in encouraging that ripening process. Thus, it is perhaps more accurate to see litigation and mediation not as strict alternatives, but in many cases as complimentary approaches.

INTEGRATING THE CONFLICTUAL
AND COOPERATIVE VISIONS OF MEDIATION

Clearly, the hot-tub vision of mediation can be seen as overly romantic and politically naive. But while this cooperative view is an easy target, it should not be dismissed entirely. For even though environmental negotiations are best understood as an outcome of power politics, this need not necessarily imply that nonadversarial qualities like trust and mutual respect do not sometimes play an important part as well. It may be true that it takes stalemates and high risk to get parties to the negotiation table, but that does not mean that they cannot then also develop new, more cooperative relationships as a result. Thus, these two different views of mediation may not be as incompatible as they first appear. Perhaps, they are best understood, not as competing descriptions, but as descriptions that each shed light on different stages of the negotiation process. The hard-ball school gives us the best understanding of the beginning stages of mediation—why mediation takes place in the first place, what motivates adversaries to sit down and negotiate. In turn, the hot-tub school sheds light on the possibilities that are present once negotiations begin, and highlights the cooperative interaction that can develop.

Thus, being politically realistic does not require us to dismiss the role that trust and reasoning together can play in mediation. Rather, it simply gives us a more practical understanding of how and when these factors can come into play. It makes it clear that this kind of cooperative political interaction is only likely to take place in situations where power is distributed relatively equally between environmentalists and developers. Only when the politics of power are exhausted can the politics of cooperation become a viable possibility. It is not necessarily naive, then, to expect people to learn to trust one another and to rely on reason and compromise to resolve their conflicts; it is only naive to believe that this can take place without there first being a balance of power and a political stalemate. After it is clear that adversarial approaches cannot satisfy the disputants, only then can the qualitative shift to a new and more desirable form of political relationship take place.

POWER AND REASON

The interrelationship between the adversarial and nonadversarial aspects of mediation is perhaps best illustrated in the way stalemates encourage parties to reason together to resolve their differences. Once a balance of power has been established, once the parties are unable to use coercion and manipulation to achieve their ends, the rule of reason becomes a viable option. Instead of a power struggle, the process becomes one of problemsolving using the best arguments and evidence. Even the most hard-boiled mediators, like Bellman, will admit power stalemates encourage parties to reason together. As he put it, "I think power and reason go together. People are very unlikely to reason with people who don't have power. Power promotes reasoning together."[41] Bellman also observes that power can promote reasoning together even when the parties involved never get over their animosities for each other. To illustrate this, he cites the controversy over fish management that he mediated between the Chippewa Tribe and the Wisconsin State Department of Natural Resources. In chapter 2, this case was used to describe the process of data mediation, where two parties get together and reason out their analytic differences. As Bellman explained, "the fact of the matter is that both of them learned about the merits of the other's position during negotiations; and both of them changed their positions on the merits. They had found weaknesses in their own positions. There was an open-minded exchange, [although] it took a long time to get to that." But importantly, Bellman also said of this mediation effort that the two parties "didn't necessarily change their minds about each other . . . People who were hateful at the beginning were still hateful at the end."[42] So here we have a successful negotiation in which many of the participants did not ever come to like each other, but which also arrived at an agreement in a rational and reasonable manner. This gives us a more complicated, but a more accurate view of how cooperative values like respect and reasoning together are produced in mediation. They can, but need not, grow out of the parties coming to like one another. More often, this kind of cooperative behavior is something the parties must be forced into by political stalemates.

It may sound a bit odd to suggest that cooperation and reasoning together are things that people must be *forced* into. It seems contradictory. But this paradoxical relationship between power and cooperation has often been noted by political theorists concerned with participatory democracy. These thinkers have long understood that a balance of power is a necessary precondition for many of the benefits that flow from direct citizen participation in politics. For example, democratic theorists have argued that one of the major benefits of direct participation is that it encourages individuals to consider and argue in terms of the public interest, instead of merely thinking in terms of their own private interests. Taking into account the public interest, however, is not something that occurs because of some altruistic motive on the part of the participants. Instead it is seen as something the participants are forced into by the process of direct democracy. This argument can be found, for example, in the work of Carole Pateman, a leading contemporary theorist of participation. In the following passage she discusses Rousseau's theory of the educational effects of direct political participation. Note the sense of coercion that reoccurs throughout the passage.

The central function of participation in Rousseau's theory is an educative one, using the term "education" in the widest sense. Rousseau's ideal system is designed to develop responsible individual social and political action through the effect of the participation process. During the process the individual learns that the word "each' *must* be applied to himself; that is to say, he finds that he *has to* take into account wider matter than his own immediate private interests if he is to gain cooperation from others, and he learns that the public and private interest are linked. The logic of the operation of the participatory system is such that he is *"forced"* to deliberate according to his sense of justice, according to what Rousseau calls his *constant will* because fellow citizens can always resist the implementation of inequitable demands. (Emphasis added)[43]

In Rousseau's view, then, citizens must often be forced to take into account such things as justice and the public interest. What forces them to do so, of course, is the fact that they cannot achieve their ends unilaterally. In a situation of direct democracy, where no one person has more power than another, one is forced to gain the cooperation of one's fellow participants to enact a policy. And to gain cooperation, one must suggest policies that benefit a wide range of participants. In other words, in situations of direct democracy, like a New England town meeting or a mediation effort, a process of reasoning goes on in which those arguments which take into account the public interest are the most persuasive. Rousseau was very sensitive to the fact that this reasoning about the public interest is only likely to become important in situations where the participants have relatively equal amounts of power. For him, that not only means equal amounts of political power—one man/one vote—but also relatively equal amounts of economic power. For example, he stresses in his *Social Contract* that the ideal society for democratic politics would be one made up of peasant proprietors, where each citizen would own enough property so that "no citizen shall ever be wealthy enough to buy another, and none poor enough to be forced to sell himself."[44] He realized that without relative economic equality, there could not exist the political independence and political equality that would ensure the proper workings of a direct democracy.

CONCLUSION

This chapter has examined a wide variety of common, but misleading, notions surrounding mediation. It has revealed a tendency for some proponents of mediation to exaggerate the advantages of mediation and to overromanticize it as a new form of nonadversarial, cooperative politics. Such exaggerations are perhaps inevitable—advocates of any new process have a natural inclination to inflate its advantages and overlook its disadvantages. The purpose of this chapter has been to deflate these claims a bit and to put them in a more realistic perspective. This is important, for if environmental mediation is to be used properly, participants must have no illusions about it—they must have an accurate idea of how it works and what can be expected of it. It would be a mistake, for example, for disputants to enter into mediation on the assumption that it will necessarily be significantly cheaper than litigation. Depending on the case, expense may pose just as large a problem in mediation as it does in litigation. It would likewise be a mistake for potential users to be seduced by the hot-tub view of mediation. They should not assume that mediation will provide an escape from the unpleasantness of adversarial politics, or that it will be a good substitute for litigation. As we have seen, without a real balance of power, such well-intentioned efforts to generate cooperation from one's opponents are likely to be fruitless. Only when potential users of environmental mediation are able to see it for what it really is, rather then what they hope it will be, will they be able to make intelligent decisions about its appropriate use.

CHAPTER FOUR

Mediation as Seduction

A hunter in the woods encountered a huge bear. As he took aim, he heard the soothing, beguiling voice of his prey: "Isn't it better to talk than to shoot? What do you want? Let's negotiate."

Cradling his weapon, the hunter said, "I want a fur coat."

"Good," said the bear agreeably. "That's negotiable. I only want a full stomach. Let's be reasonable."

So the two traditional adversaries sat down together and negotiated. After a time, the bear walked away alone. He had his full stomach and the hunter had his fur coat.[1]

Now that we have examined claims about how fast, cheap, and nonadversarial environmental mediation is, we need to turn our attention to an even more important set of claims about this process—that it is more democratic and more fair than many traditional approaches to these disputes. Many proponents celebrate mediation as an important new form of direct democracy, one that promotes a more equitable and just resolution to environmental controversies. Evaluating this claim is somewhat more difficult than the ones considered in the last chapter. Claims concerning time and expense are at least made in terms that are objectively measurable. Claims concerning justice and democracy are not cast in such convenient terms and so their evaluation is necessarily a much more complicated matter. But although the analysis is difficult, and will take up much of the next three chapters, these political claims are of such importance that they cannot be merely accepted at face value.

Another reason to explore these political claims is that not everyone believes them. A significant portion of the environmental community does not agree that mediation is an unmitigated political boon. Some suspect that mediation represents not so much a new effort at cooperation, but a new form at cooptation. For example, David Brower, president of Friends of the Earth, has been critical of efforts by environmentalists to substitute cooperation for a more adversarial stance toward developers. "Polite conservationists," he says, "leave no marks except the scars of the landscape that could have been prevented."[2] Mike McCloskey of the Sierra Club has also become a well-known skeptic of this more cooperative approach to environmental problems, and has seriously questioned whether environmentalists have gained anything meaningful out of many of these agreements.[3]

Part of what makes environmentalists nervous about mediation is the enthusiasm with which industry has embraced it. Business journals have been quick to herald mediation as the beginning of a new more cooperative relationship between business and environmentalists. *Fortune* hailed environmental mediation as "a refreshing example of applied good sense."[4] Corporations have also donated large sums to promote mediation efforts. Atlantic-Richfield, for instance, provided the seed money to start RESOLVE—one of the first centers for environmental dispute resolution. Other corporations, including Dow Chemical, U.S. Steel, and Union Carbide, have also invested money in promoting environmental mediation.[5] All of these companies, of course, have very poor environmental records, and have been involved in continual battles with environmental groups. This kind of corporate involvement in environmental mediation has understandably made some environmentalists skeptical of its worth. Mike McCloskey has noted somewhat nervously that "Few actions by the corporate world spring from public-spiritedness," and that "Atlantic-Richfield doesn't expect to waste its money."[6] Other environmentalists suspect that mediation may simply be another front in a new corporate political offensive against environmental laws. It is seen as a sophisticated industry ploy intended to pacify environmental groups and to distract them from pursuing more troublesome approaches to environmental problems like litigation.

Of course, a few environmental groups, like the Conservation Foundation and the National Wildlife Federation, have become heavily involved in promoting environmental mediation. But skeptics in the environmental community note that such groups tend to be the most cautious and conservative politically. And although they are reluctant to criticize the Conservation Foundation publicly, these critics will note privately that this organization has never been strongly activist and that it has always had unusually close ties with business and industry. It has never been a membership organization, and instead it has relied heavily on grants from foundations and corporations for its operating funds. In 1984, for example, almost 20 percent of the Foundation's revenues came from gifts from such corporate sponsors as Atlantic Richfield, Mobil, Conoco, Exxon, Gulf Oil, Shell, Standard Oil, IBM, Monsanto, DuPont, Crown Zellerbach, General Electric, R.J. Reynolds, Phillip Morris, Weyerhauser, Alcoa, Union Carbide, and others.[7] Hardly your typical environmental group. The other environmental organization exhibiting strong interest in mediation, the National Wildlife Federation, is a strong membership organization. However, it is important to note that its members are mostly hunters and sportsmen and have been identified as primarily conservative and Republican in political orientation.[8] Naturally, the fact that these two organizations are on the far right of the environmental movement has only raised suspicions about environmental mediation for more mainstream and activist environmentalists. In any case, it is clear that not all environmentalists are thrilled with the emergence of environmental mediation, and part of what will be examined in the next few chapters will be the political criticisms of this approach that have been raised by various critics in the environmental movement.

A final reason to examine the political claims surrounding mediation is the discouraging nature of past efforts to increase direct citizen participation in public policymaking. Scholars examining past innovations in citizen participation—including public hearings, advisory committees, and so on—have noted that these approaches often have given the illusion of participation without granting any real policymaking power to citizens.[9] Since cooptation has been on ongoing problem in the citizen participation movement, any new approach which claims to empower citizens must be approached with some skepticism. In addition, the work of other political scientists examining informal, face-to-face political interaction has raised significant questions about the political desirability of such approaches. Proponents claim great advantages from the face-to-face style of interaction in mediation, but scholars like Jane Mansbridge have found that such interaction can have substantial disadvantages as well. Mansbridge has done some extensive and intriguing work on the political interaction that takes place in such face-to-face meetings as New England town meetings and workplaces which are run democratically.[10] Her findings demonstrate that there are powerful social and psychological pressures at work in face-to-face political assemblies which work to produce consensus even when it does not actually exist. She found that in face-to-face assemblies, many ordinary people are reluctant to voice opposition because of fear of public ridicule and criticism. There is also a natural tendency to avoid open and direct face-to-face conflict in such assemblies. For example, voice vote or a show of hands tends to reinforce pressures toward unanimity. When votes can be heard or seen by others, there is a much stronger tendency to avoid conflict and go along with the crowd than there is with secret ballots. Mansbridge has concluded that these pressures toward consensus can have undesirable political consequences. For example, powerful groups can use this pressure toward consensus to obscure conflicts and maintain their position of advantage. As Mansbridge put it, "In moments of genuine conflict, face-to-face contact among citizens encourages suppression of that conflict . . . It therefore accentuates rather then redresses the disadvantage of those with the least power in society."[11]

There can be, then, a downside to informal, face–to–face political processes like town meetings. This suggests the need to explore whether such political pitfalls also exist in a face–to–face process like environmental mediation. Are there similar kinds of problematic psychological and political pressures at work in mediation efforts that can encourage unfair outcomes? This chapter will explore this question—focusing particularly on the possibility that the informality of the process and the conciliatory efforts of a mediator can work to seduce some participants into making excessive concessions. Some environmentalists have speculated that their cooperative colleagues may often find themselves in the position of the hunter in the fable above, who, in his efforts to be reasonable, found himself party to a "compromise" that was decidedly not in his interest. Naturally, proponents of mediation strongly disagree with this accusation, and much of this chapter will explore the debate over this issue.

TRICKS OF THE TRADE

One of the most seductive aspects of environmental mediation is its apparent straightforwardness. Litigation can often involve complicated legal maneuvering, and few people would think of getting involved without competent legal expertise on their side. But negotiations give the appearance of being something that any relatively intelligent person can do well. Indeed many proponents of mediation celebrate the fact that it is a simple and informal process that the common citizen can participate in—this is supposed to be one of its unique advantages. This view of mediation and negotiation, however, can be highly misleading. In reality, negotiating is a highly sophisticated and complicated art, and those who are good at it have spent years mastering a large body of knowledge and a set of practices that are not normally available to most citizens. Because of this, there is a danger that novices can easily be "taken to the cleaners" by more experienced opponents. This can be particularly a problem in negotiations over environmental issues where many of the participants are members of local citizen and environmental groups and thus are not likely to have extensive experience with difficult and lengthy negotiations.

For the inexperienced, it is easy to get the impression that negotiation simply involves sitting at a table and trading concessions with one's opponents in a relatively civilized manner. In fact, however, good negotiators often view the process as something akin to a long military campaign, where the side with the most resources and the best strategies and tactics will come out the winner. Importantly, experienced negotiators have at their disposal a large number of negotiating tricks and ploys designed to encourage their opponents to make poor decisions. Consider, for instance, some of the following less–than–ethical tactics that have been employed in negotiations:

The Good–Guy Bad–Guy Strategy

This is a classic strategy, also known as the "Mutt and Jeff" routine. The experienced side sends two negotiators to the talks. The first one to talk is tough and belligerent. He makes large demands and gives in on nothing. Next, however, comes friendly old Smiley, who takes over from the bad guy. For the novices on the other side, this comes as a great relief. It is a pleasure to deal with such a nice guy after being worked over by the mean one. Psychologically they become more receptive to what seems to be the more reasonable demands of the good guy. In reality it is all merely a ploy to make the real demands of the first group appear more reasonable and attractive.

The Four–for–One Strategy

Early on in the negotiations, the experienced negotiator makes a great show of reluctantly giving in on four points of importance to him. He then appeals to the innate fairness in the novice by arguing, "Look, I've made four concessions. Can't you at least make one to me?" The problem of course is that the initial four concessions were only for show and involved issues that the negotiator really cared little about. If he succeeds in getting a major concession out of the novice, he has then come out ahead.

The Snow Job

The snow job consists of giving the opponent so much information that he or she gets bogged down in trivia. A negotiator arrives with many boxes of documents to back up his or her points. The hope is that the opponent will be overwhelmed by the sheer quantity of information and be unable to look at it all carefully. Hidden in the masses of information will be deliberate errors, self–serving assumptions, and contradictory material. Unfortunately, the opponent may not have the time or diligence to find these things.

The Last–Minute Change

After a long and difficult negotiation, the two sides finally come to an agreement on all the issues. They are all happy and greatly relieved. But just before the final agreement is signed, the experienced negotiator reluctantly informs the novice that his superior has insisted he take back one particular concession. At this point the novice is psychologically committed to the agreement, and probably weary of haggling. He really wants to finalize the agreement, and may be easily convinced that this last point really doesn't matter that much. In all likelihood, the novice will give in at this point—though he will undoubtedly regret it later.

Bad–Faith Negotiating

Sometimes parties enter into negotiations without any intention of coming to an agreement. They may be simply stalling for time in order to develop other options, or they may be attempting to get important information from the other side, or they may be trying to delay a lawsuit, and so on. In any case, they will use a variety of tactics to string out negotiations endlessly, including changing negotiators, focusing on ir-relevant issues, constantly bringing up new alternatives to be considered, putting someone who is inarticulate and apparently a bit irrational in charge of negotiations, etc.

The All–Nighter Strategy

Experienced negotiators know that negotiating all day and all through the night can be an effective way to wear down the opposition. Such marathon sessions with little to eat can put novices at a distinct psychological disadvantage, making them tired, irrational, depressed, or error–prone. As one veteran negotiator put it, "Almost any deal can look pretty good at 3:00 in the morning."[12]

These, of course, are but a few of the tactics that can be used to trick and exploit opponents—the variations are essentially limitless. The point is that negotiations are far from the straight-forward process that they appear to be and are full of many psychological and political traps for inexperienced participants to fall into. Of course, not all sides in environmental negotiations are equally vulnerable to these traps. For example, most industry negotiators are professionals who are usually very familiar with negotiating tactics. After all, most business deals involve negoti-ations, and experienced businessmen soon become acquainted with the kinds of tactics and ploys that can be used. Government officials also tend to have some experience in negotiations. Poli-ticians often find that part of their job involves negotiating deals over public policy issues with various interest groups and political opponents. Thus it tends to be the citizen and environmental groups who are the novices in negotiations. This is especially true of local groups that consist mostly of part–time volunteers. As a rule, it is these groups that are most vulnerable to being tricked and exploited. To get an idea of how this can actually take place, consider the following example of how some local environmen-talists and local government officials found themselves up against a wiley opponent.

THE PERILS OF GROUNDWATER
NEGOTIATIONS IN INYO COUNTY

Since 1900, the Los Angeles Department of Water and Power (DWP) has been taking surface water from the Owens Valley 250 miles to its north to meet its expanding needs.[13] In 1970 it ex-panded its aquaduct and began to pump out groundwater from that area as well—at first only during droughts, but then contin-ually. The local citizens and government officials began to get concerned as the ecological consequences of this practice became obvious. The area is essentially an arid one, with little rainfall. It remains lush and green primarily because the roots of the vege-tation have been able to tap an unusually high water table. This ecosystem is relatively fragile, however, and as the DWP's ground-water pumping began to lower the water table, the vegetation quickly began to wither and die. The local officials of Inyo County took the DWP to court demanding an environmental impact statement (EIS). After several years, the DWP produced one and then another EIS, both of which were ruled insufficient by the court, which then proceeded to impose a pumping limit until an adequate EIS was forthcoming. Under increasing pressure, the DWP agreed to enter into negotiations with the county of Inyo in the hopes that some agreement could be worked out. The aim of the talks was to set up an arrangement whereby representative from the DWP and the county would meet every year and work out an agreement concerning how much water would be pumped and from which areas.

These initial negotiations, however, were not always the epitome of good-faith bargaining. For example, at one point the DWP agreed to make a concession to the county and to plant over an area near a major highway with alfalfa. Pumping had caused a loss of vegetation in that area, and the resulting dirt and dust began to blow over the road and created several multicar accidents. But while this offer to replant at first seemed like good news to environmentalists, it later became clear that the DWP was required to do this anyway by the state air pollution laws. Under this law, however, the DWP had to do it with *their* water—water that came out of the total to which they were limited. By including the replanting as a concession, the DWP hoped to get agreement to use water over and above their limit to do the replanting—which could prove quite advantageous to them. This is a relatively small example of negotiation trickery—and one that was easily detected—but there were some others in this case that were much more serious.

While these negotiations were going on, a bill came up in the California State Assembly that would formally give the counties the right to regulate groundwater—a right that the county of Inyo was already claiming in the absence of legislation stipulating otherwise. The lobbyists for the DWP, a considerable force in the assembly, worked hard to change the bill so that the counties of

Inyo and Mona would be exempted. Thus, if the bill were passed, Inyo County would lose control over their groundwater and the DWP could pump without negotiating with local officials. In effect, the DWP was trying an end-run around the negotiations. DWP lobbyists assured assemblymen that this modification would not hurt the interests of Inyo County, and even when specifically asked about this by the assemblyman from that area, they reassured him that it would do his area no harm. The bill passed the assembly and was sent to the governor. Naturally, when local citizens and county officials found out, they were outraged and confronted their local assemblyman, who happened to be up for reelection. Belatedly realizing his mistake, the assemblyman quickly appealed to his fellow Republican, Governor Deukmejian, who eventually agreed to veto this measure. What made the DWP's tactic even more questionable ethically was the fact that it lobbied for this bill while bound to an agreement of cooperation, signed by the parties in the negotiations, that explicitly stipulated that the parties would not support legislation that would change the current state of affairs! Later, when confronted with this contradiction, officials of the city of Los Angeles denied having any knowledge of the activities of the DWP lobbyists concerning this bill. In any case, without the timely intervention of the governor, the residents of Inyo County would have found themselves completely bamboozled by the DWP.

THE DISADVANTAGES OF INFORMALITY

What these kinds of problems indicate are the potential disadvantages of the informal nature of environmental mediation. Critics of litigation rail against the formal rules that dominate the process and the necessity of using lawyers to guide one through those complicated and esoteric procedures. However, what is sometimes forgotten is that many of these formal procedures are designed to ensure due process and to protect the interests of the participants.

For example, rules that limit what can be entered into evidence restrict what can be discussed in the courtroom, but the purpose is to ensure a fair trial and a just outcome. One large potential problem with mediation is that it incorporates no such procedural safeguards. Its very informality and lack of structure make it open to exploitation by unethical participants. This possibility of exploitation has been a matter of concern to some of those exploring mediation and other alternatives to litigation. Even in the report on alternative dispute resolution prepared by the National Institute for Dispute Resolution, which is generally positive about these new approachs, it was noted with some concern that the absence of lawyers increases the probability that some people will be taken advantage of. According to the institute's report, "These methods, which might reach settlements without the use of lawyers or counselors, may lead disputants to make choices they would avoid if they were better informed. This is an area of particular concern related to women, the poor, the elderly, persons for whom English is a second language, and other classes of disputants who are traditionally less powerful or less skilled in negotiations than their opponents."[14]

As an example, the report cites the possibility that a woman may be persuaded that mediation is a more reasonable and less painful process than litigation as a way of resolving property and custody issues in a divorce. However, if she does not have the benefit of counsel in those negotiations, a woman, "unused to asserting herself, may settle for less than she would be awarded through judicial proceedings."[15] It is this same general problem that exists in environmental mediation: less experienced parties— usually citizen and environmental groups—have few legal safeguards to protect them from being exploited in this process. As one scholar of environmental mediation has noted, this may be one of the largest disadvantages stemming from the informal nature of this approach: "Informal processes may offer greater flexibility and faster settlement. Yet the very strengths of informality— the ability to negotiate privately and to change procedural rules during the process—invite abuse. Any decision process can be used by parties to manipulate one another and the surrounding society; informal processes are less susceptible to review because they are less open and because the definition of fairness is less clear when rules are poorly (flexibly) defined or subject to revision in mid-stream."[16]

SAFEGUARDS AGAINST EXPLOITATION

Of course, environmental mediation is not entirely without safeguards to protect parties from unethical tactics. For example, it is often pointed out that the need for a stable and ongoing relationship between the negotiating parties will usually work to prevent one from trying to trick or exploit the other. In labor negotiations, for instance, the sides have an ongoing relationship in which their fates are interwined. Both have an interest in maintaining a smooth and viable relationship. Thus, an attempt to trick one's opponents, when it is eventually uncovered, is likely to poison that mutually valued relationship and make negotiations in the future much more difficult. This factor may also be at work in environmental negotiations where a good working relationship is of vital concern to both parties—for example, in negotiations between a government agency and an environmental group with which it constantly interacts. But unfortunately, many environmental disputes do not fall into this category; many do not involve important ongoing relationships. Often a battle between a local environmental group and a developer is a one-time interaction. In such situations, there is little to discourage one party from attempting to exploit the other—for it is unlikely that their tricks will come back to haunt them. So the tendency is to "take the money and run." At best, then, the need for an ongoing relationship may be only a partial safeguard against unethical negotiating tactics.

Sometimes it is suggested that the presence of a neutral, third-party mediator can play an important part in discouraging exploitation in negotiations. Familiar with most of these questionable tactics, a mediator could conceivably either discourage them from being used, or warn the inexperienced parties of their implications. And it is probably true that the possibility of exploitation is much higher in negotiations that take place without mediators to watch over the process. However, it is also possible that mediators themselves may become involved in "seducing" the participants in negotiations. And in fact, some environmentalists are very concerned about just this possibility. Their concern is that mediators may use a variety of sophisticated conciliatory techniques and pressure tactics to encourage participants to make concessions—even when those concessions may not be in their best interests. It is that possibility—that mediators can function as seducers—to which we next turn our attention.

CONCILIATION AS SEDUCTION

As we saw in chapter 2, much of the job of the mediator involves using a variety of conciliation techniques to smooth the relations between the disputants. They will usually try to break down the animosities and negative stereotypes that can interfere with effective negotiations. For example, a favorite tactic is to bring the conflicting parties together in informal circumstances (usually for lunch, dinner, or drinks) in the hopes that the parties will get to know and like each other better. And it sometimes works. Participants can sometimes develop not only polite, but positively cordial relationships. As one mediator explained it, during prolonged negotiations, "people tend to get to know each other and to like each other. There gets to be a personal bond—it's a natural human response."[17] But some critics of environmental mediation worry about this natural human response. They worry that inexperienced environmentalists will hesitate to be tough with their new found friends. They are concerned that the resulting agreements may be friendly, but not in the interests of the environmental movement. One environmental activist, James Benson of the Institute for Ecological Studies, puts the problem in this way: "All of a sudden you are hobnobbing with industry leaders you used to think of as enemies, and now you are sitting down having dinner and drinks with them. . . . Environmentalists are not really very feisty people, and when they get around a bunch of high-power corporate types they don't want to be unreasonable. They don't want to get into arguments. They want things to be peaceful and gentlemanly. . . . [They] get carried away, and really may lose sight of what it is they may be trading off. They may be trading off something in the negotiations that others may be unwilling to trade off."[18]

There may be a danger, then, in coming to know and like your opponent too much. And the problem is that some negotiators will not hesitate to exploit the cordial atmosphere created by the mediator—using it to personalize the negotiations. Personalizing is another ploy that is sometimes used to gain a psychological advantage over one's opponents. Herb Cohen, the author of a best-selling book on how to negotiate effectively, explains that personalizing is a commonly used approach in which you encourage your opponent to see you not as the representative of a remote institution or organization—but as a person. "You make the other party see you as unique, flesh-and-blood individual, someone who has feelings and needs, someone the other person likes, cares about, and somehow feels obligated to—at least someone the other person wants to do something for."[19] By creating this more personal bond, the hope is that you will be able to cash in on it at some important point in the negotiations. Cohen gives a hypothetical example of how such a relationship can be exploited.

"Didn't you promise me you were doing this? I was counting on you. I assured my boss about it. I told my family. I guaranteed the auditor. You aren't letting me down, are you?"

When the other party asks, "You aren't taking this personally are you?" you plaintively reply, "Yes!"

In other words, "lay it on" the other party. Get him or her emotionally involved. It is difficult for people to back off if you say the equivalent of, "I'd appreciate it if you'd do this as a favor for me." Such phrases are extremely effective in personalizing situations.[20]

Some critics, like Benson, believe that these personalized relationships may be exploited much more than environmentalists suspect. The negotiations that took place during the National Coal Policy Project are sometimes given as an example of how environmentalists can be seduced by the cordial relationships developed during prolonged negotiations. The project was one of the earliest experiments in environmental negotiation.[21] It began in 1976 and brought together sixty representatives of environmental groups, the coal industry, and the electric utility industry to work out their many differences concerning air pollution, strip-mining, and other aspects of coal policy. The project made headlines when it claimed to find agreement in over 80 percent of the issues considered. The *New York Times* heralded the project in a front-page article that observed that "probably never before have so many industrialists and environmentalists found common ground on such an array of issues."[22] *Fortune* described it as a "yearlong encounter session between businessmen and conservationists [that] has opened a new route to accord."[23] Importantly, the *Fortune* article went on to detail the "good fellowship" that developed between old adversaries. As industry and environmental representatives spent time together in meetings and field trips, many began to see each other in a different light. At the end, "project participants professed amazement not only at the number of issues they managed to resolve but also at the trust and mutual respect that developed."[24] And *Fortune* concluded that "the example of conciliatory behavior may be the project's most valuable contribution."[25]

However, some environmentalists were not impressed by the good fellowship and expressed fears that many of the environmentalists participating in the project had been seduced and coopted by the process. Louise Dunlap of the Environmental Policy Center and Richard Ayres of the Natural Resources Defense Council suggested that participants had been duped into compromises that industry could use to weaken present environmental laws.[26] For example, environmentalists in the project had agreed to allow tall smokestacks rather than emission controls on older coal-burning plants. Ayers saw this as a step backwards from the clean air laws already on the books. Tall stacks only disperse pollutants over a larger area and contribute to the growing acid rain problem, while emission controls reduce pollution at the source. Interestingly, environmental activists were not the only ones taken aback by such important concessions. Even industry was a bit amazed by the extent of the concessions that conservationists in the project were willing to make. As *Fortune* noted, "much to the surprise of the industry participants in the project, the environmentalists expressed considerable willingness to rethink—and perhaps give up—some of their hard fought legislative and judicial gains."[27]

MEDIATION AS EMOTIONAL PACIFICATION

Encouraging overfriendliness is just one of the ways that mediators may inadvertently foster the psychological seduction of inexperienced negotiators. And indeed, not all environmental mediators emphasize conciliation or encourage cordiality. There are other ways, however, that mediators may encourage overly generous concessions from participants. For example, mediators often put considerable pressure on participants to be "reasonable" and "responsible." Whether it is through cajoling or through threats, pressuring the participants to be more reasonable is one of the most important methods of the mediator. And this appeal to "reasonableness" can be quite seductive. Everyone wants to be seen as reasonable, and few feel comfortable being characterized as unreasonable or irresponsible. Thus, pressure to be reasonable can be very effective—especially against those new to negotiations. The problem, however, is that mediators have a very particular understanding of what it means to be reasonable—one that may not always be in the interests of all the parties involved.

　　Mediators often tend to see being reasonable as the opposite of being emotional. Emotions are thought to get in the way of the participants rationally addressing the substantive issues before them. So mediators may employ a number of techniques to encourage this move from being emotional to being more reasonable. For example, they may accuse participants who are expressing anger or resentment of being unprofessional or uncooperative. Or as we saw earlier, mediators may make an effort to get participants to harmlessly vent their anger and frustrations and thus get over these counterproductive feelings. But while in some circumstances this approach is appropriate, in others it may not be. In some environmental controversies, the emotional reactions of the participants are in fact quite reasonable. Consider, for example, negotiations that might take place about a leaking toxic waste dump. Nearby residents may harbor a great amount of fear and anger over the health risks to themselves and their children. It is far from clear that such emotions are irrational and unreasonable. And it is also not clear that it is in the interest of these citizens to get over their anger. Getting over such emotions is certainly in the interests of the mediator, who wants to eliminate any factor that makes agreement more difficult. But in doing so, there is a danger that it may work to undermine the legitimate emotions that are an important source of power and inspiration to some groups. In other words, mediation may act as a form of emotional pacification—preventing some participants from insisting on the very best deal that they can get. Most people can be hard-nosed negotiators only when they do not lose touch with their legitimate angers and frustrations.

MEDIATION AS THERAPY

To put all this another way, the quasi-therapist role for the mediator that was praised earlier in chapter 2 may have some undesirable effects as well. It may serve to pacify and coopt more inexperienced participants in mediation efforts. The questionable assumption in this therapeutic approach is that much of the dispute lies not so much in objective circumstances, but in the emotional and psychological problems of the participants. Importantly, this accusation of irrationality seems to be leveled at some groups more often than others—especially citizen and environmental groups. For example, opponents of nuclear power plants have often been accused of being victims of irrational and unfounded fears. The Department of Energy recently gave a grant to a Maryland psychiatrist to study and try to reduce public "phobias" about nuclear power. The assumption, as one observer pointed out, is that "critics of nuclear power might suffer from some kind of psychological disorder in their opposition to this technology."[28] The political ramifications of this view of the opposition to nuclear power are apparent: it serves to discredit opponents of these plants, making it appear that these critics have no rational basis for their concerns.

The point here is that mediation techniques may be used to discredit or dissipate supposedly counterproductive emotions, and thus serve to dull the fighting edge of some participants. This is nothing new. Scholars like Sherry Arnstein who have studied government-initiated citizen participation efforts have long observed that they are often intended primarily to serve as "therapy" for the public.[29] In public hearings, for example, citizens are allowed to voice their concerns and fears, and officials in turn have the opportunity to calm them down. As Arnstein points out, there is no real bargaining going on in such situations. Citizens blow off steam and feel somewhat better, while government officials get a chance to listen sympathetically and then educate the citizens on why the government's approach is the most reasonable one. The same thing may be true of mediation efforts. They may sometimes be used as a way of pacifying citizens without actually addressing their real concerns. Consider, for instance, a mediation effort that took place in Columbia, Missouri. This dispute involved a group of citizens and farmers who opposed a city park that would have intruded into their neighborhoods and farms.[30] This case will be examined in more detail in the next chapter, but what is interesting for us now is the way that mediation was used to pacify this opposition. A mediation team was called in to set up a series of public and private meetings in which opponents were encouraged to voice their objections and where city representatives patiently explained why they would push the project forward. In the end, the mediation was declared a success, in part because, as a representative from the city explained, "the farmers were and remain hostile to the concept of the project, but now have come to accept its inevitability."[31] In other words, the process of mediation emotionally disarmed the opponents. They were encouraged in mediation to vent their emotions, and they eventually became more reasonable, that is, reconciled to the project and willing to give in.

POLITICAL PRESSURE TO BE REASONABLE

Part of what makes the psychological seductions of mediation particularly problematic is the fact that the pressures and ploys of the mediator are often amplified by outside political pressures. During recent years environmentalists have been under increasing political pressure to be more reasonable in their policy demands. It has become common to see conservationists attacked by those in industry and the government for being "environmental extremists," and to hear it argued that the pendulum has swung too far in the direction of environmental protection—to the detriment of economic growth. These accusations have grown as the economic problems of the 70s have continued on into the 80s. The 80s have also seen the emergence of scholarly attacks on environmentalists like *Risk and Culture* by Mary Douglas and Aaron Widavsky.[32] One of the central arguments of their book is that the ranks of environmentalists are shot through with zealots and extremists who are irrationally sensitive to risks, and obsessed with creating the environmental millenium. Irrespective of whether such charges are true, they have taken their toll on the attitude of some environmental groups. In these increasingly conservative political times, environmentalists have become more sensitive to how they appear to the public and to policymakers, and some have made an increased effort to portray themselves as practical and reasonable.

Some environmental groups have also put themselves in a political position that makes them more susceptible to this pressure to be more reasonable. Some, like the Audubon Society, have chosen to define themselves as "nonpartisan," "public interest" groups. They say that they do not take political sides; that they are a politically neutral group that is merely seeking to defend the larger public interest. It is thought that the advantage in this approach is that it allows environmentalists to build a large bipartisan coalition on environmental issues and thus be more effective politically.[33] But the disadvantage is that it makes it more difficult for these environmental groups to take controversial stands. It makes it harder for them to be unreasonable and uncompromising when that is necessary. If they are too unyielding in their positions, they run the risk of alienating part of their bipartisan coalition—usually the more conservative elements. Thus these nonpartisan environmental groups tend to be wary of acting in a manner that could be described as unreasonable. And not surprisingly, it is these groups that have been most inclined to become involved in mediation efforts.

Outside political pressure can often make it difficult for environmentalists to oppose a mediation effort even when they believe it may be a waste of time. They fear that if they do not agree to negotiate, they will lose their hard-won political credibility with policymakers and the public. In one mediation effort coordinated by RESOLVE, environmentalists were initially reluctant to become involved, but as their spokesperson explained, when they found out that the governor and the Forest Service supported the effort, they finally "decided to participate, partly out of a fear they would look unreasonable if they didn't."[34] Thus there is the possibility that environmentalists might become involved in mediation, even when they are unsure that it is their best option. There are times when it may be in the best interest of an environmental group to pursue litigation as a solution to a particular problem—such as when an important legal precedent is at stake. But because of political pressure, they may find themselves sidetracked in a prolonged mediation effort. And once a group becomes involved in negotiations, this same political pressure makes it difficult for them to break them off. Patrick Parenteau, a former lawyer for the National Wildlife Federation, has observed that "if you are the one who gets up and walks away, you may be seen as the obstructionist in the process, and you may lose public support as a result of having to leave a negotiation or breaking it off."[35] There is the distinct possibility, then, that the political pressure to be reasonable can induce environmentalists to stick with a mediation effort even when it is not working.

IS SEDUCTION IN THE MEDIATOR'S INTEREST?

There are, then, a wide variety of factors both inside and outside of environmental mediation that can seduce or pressure some participants into undesirable positions. But naturally, most proponents of mediation deny that this problem is a significant one. For example, they point out that not all mediators are interested in getting participants to like each other—which is true. But nevertheless, there are reasons to take seriously the possibility of mediators acting as seducers. Specifically, it would seem to be in the interests of mediators to act this way. Mediators are often thought of as neutrals in these environmental disputes, who have no interest in the outcome. But this is not really true. Mediators may not have an interest in how the dispute is resolved, but they certainly do have an interest in whether it is resolved. Successfully resolving a dispute is personally satisfying and good for their careers. Thus it would seem in the interest of mediators to encourage parties to make as generous concessions as they can, for this would greatly enhance the chance of generating an agreement. It would be tempting for them to use any kind of psychological ploy or pressure to encourage agreement—even if it inadvertantly encouraged some groups to make excessive concessions.

However, some proponents of environmental mediation strongly deny the logic of this argument. They suggest that experience has shown that it is usually *not* in the self-interest of the mediator to seduce participants into excessive concessions. This kind of seduction, they argue, can easily backfire and actually interfere with getting a final agreement. The problem is that even if the mediator succeeds in seducing a negotiator into making overly generous concessions, those concessions would most likely be repudiated by the organization that the negotiator represents. This is the danger stressed by Gerald Cormick in his criticism of the hot-tub approach to mediation. He argues that mediators should be careful not to construct an atmosphere that is too congenial, because participants "often forget that the give-and-take of joint sessions, which can build understanding, trust, and even affection for those across the table, is not shared by constituents who may see accommodations as capitulation rather than as carefully developed positions." The likely result, he suggests, is that "solutions that are not politically viable may gain credence in the rarified atmosphere of cooperative negotiations, but be repudiated as a 'sellout' by constituents."[36] There have been a number of cases in which this very problem arose. It occurred, for example, during the negotiations over the Portage Island controversy described earlier, and nearly sabotaged the final agreement. When the park board negotiators presented the final package to the county commissioners for their approval, they were shocked to learn that a majority of the board balked at one of the major parts of the agreement—joint management of the park. This last minute disagreement greatly irritated the Lummi tribe and it was only with the hard work of the mediators that the project was brought back from the brink of failure.[37]

Cormick seems to admit that seduction is a real possibility, for he goes out of his way to warn mediators about it. But he also believes that it ultimately has little chance of working. For him, the constituents act as the ultimate safeguard against selling-out. Even when the negotiators have been seduced, the constituents are still able to see clearly and determine whether the agreement is actually in their interests. In this way, the seduction of negoti-

ators, even when it does occur, may not be the disaster that critics
suggest.

BLAMING SEDUCIBLE ENVIRONMENTALISTS

Another defense against the charge of seduction is the suggestion
that even though seduction may sometimes take place, it is a
mistake to blame mediation or the mediator for that problem.
After all, it is the job of the mediator to encourage the parties to
be reasonable, to make concessions, and to come to an agreement.
And though mediators may indeed pressure the negotiators, any
responsibility for any concessions must ultimately lie with the
negotiators themselves. As one mediator explained, those environmental activists who complain about the problem of seduction
are not so much pointing out a problem with the mediation process as they are pointing out the inadequacies of environmentalists
as negotiators.

Environmental organizers are wary of mediation because in mediation the grassroots types will be in a room with a bunch of corporate
executives; and they will wind up saying "Oh my God, the executives
are only people. They put their pants on one leg at a time. They are nice
guys. They buy me lunch. Gee, golf may not be such a bad game after
all." And so all of these environmentalists who were full of good character and right thinking are suddenly going to get perverted, because the
mediator is going to seduce them by putting them together with the big
shots. But that attitude is so naive, its so flimsy, it's so indicative of never
having done mediation. I can't change your character. If you have the
courage of your convictions, you have it before you get there and I'm
not going to take it away from you. If you are subject to being seduced,
you are going to be seduced. But there is nothing I do that changes your
character.[38]

In this view, then, seduction is only a problem if one is
seducible in the first place. Even if there is a tendency toward
seduction built into the conciliatory aspects of mediation, it is up

to the individual negotiators whether they are seduced by this process. If environmentalists cannot have dinner with their opponents without capitulating, is it fair to blame mediators or mediation for this? Perhaps it only indicates a weakness in the character or the negotiating ability of environmental representatives. And in fact, the comments of critics of mediation even lend some support to this interpretation of the seduction problem. As Benson explained earlier, much of this problem may be due to the fact that many environmental negotiators are simply too polite and not "feisty" enough.

But in the long run, this debate over who exactly is to blame for seduction may be largely irrelevant. The fact remains that inept or inexperienced parties in negotiations are more liable to be seduced and exploited—and this undermines the political fairness of this approach. But what is useful about Bellman's point is the implicit suggestion that a solution to this problem may lie not so much in changing the process, but in changing the nature of the participants. In particular, the possibility of seduction would certainly be minimized if environmentalists, citizen organizations, and other groups with little negotiating experience had more competent representatives at the bargaining table. This raises the possibility of employing professional negotiators, as is now the case in most labor-management negotiations. Presumably, trained professional negotiators would be more immune to the tricks of their opponents and the manipulations of the mediator. Perhaps, then, the problem of seduction could be avoided simply by having environmentalists and others employ professionals.

However, like all easy answers, this one may not be as simple or as effective as it first appears. For example, one major problem is that most local citizen and environmental groups cannot afford to hire professional negotiators. These groups are usually only loosely organized and often have trouble scraping together enough money for a good lawyer. But, for the purposes of argument, let us assume the best of all possible worlds, where all groups have access to professional negotiators. Even in this case, some serious questions can be raised about the effectiveness of this approach.

PROFESSIONALIZATION: A PROBLEMATIC ANSWER

How likely is it that professionalization will eliminate this problem
of seduction? To answer that question, it is useful to look to an
area where disputes are routinely handled by professional negotiators—labor-management relations. Labor-management negotiations have reached the high level of institutionalization and
professionalization that some would like to see in environmental
mediation. The two sides are virtually always represented by
professionals. Although typically there are negotiating committees
on each side made up of representatives from the local company
and the local union, each side usually brings in a professional
chief negotiator who serves as spokesperson for the committee
and does much of the negotiating. For management, these chief
negotiators are often attorneys from firms specializing in labor law
and labor negotiations; for unions, the chief negotiator is often a
professional from the national office of the union.

This high degree of professionalization, however, has not
entirely solved the problem of seduction. Indeed, some studies
have suggested that the role of professional negotiators in mediation can be very problematic. One of the most revealing studies
in this regard was recently conducted by Deborah Kolb. [39] She sat
in on a wide variety of labor-management negotiations mediated
by federal and state mediators. For our purposes, much of what
is interesting about the study is her focus on the relationships that
developed between the mediators and the professional negotiators—or "pros" as they are known in the business. What Kolb
found was a decided tendency for the mediator and the pros to
identify with each other. This occurs for many reasons. As Kolb
explains, the mediator and negotiators all shared the fact that (1)
they are professionals, (2) they are outsiders, and (3) they have
the same goal—the achievement of settlement.[40] As a result, the
mediator and the pros on both sides tend to form a "team" that
uses "collaborative and cooperative practices [to] manage the
process of mediation."[41] In particular, there are several ways in
which mediators expect the pros to help them construct an agree-

ment. Primarily, "[mediators] expect pros to share a similar definition about the components of a 'fair and reasonable' settlement and to support the mediator's efforts to convince their committees of its merits."[42] In essence, the professional negotiator is expected by the mediator to be the enforcer of reasonableness, helping to convince his or her committee to abandon "cloud nine" proposals and to accept a realistic settlement. As one reads through Kolb's descriptions of various mediation efforts, one senses that the mediators and the pros come to see themselves as a beleaguered enclave of calm and reasonable professionals who are working together to fashion an agreement despite the extreme and irrational stances of the various bargaining committees.

The ability to be reasonable and to sell a committee on the reasonableness of a package is considered to define a professional. This is evident from the way mediators speak of pros. As one mediator put it, "I like working with pros. They are realistic. They know settlements and bring reason to the case. They act as a steadying force and move their committees when the time is right."[43] When negotiators do not cooperate with the mediator in this way, this is usually considered to be unprofessional behavior. In one case where the negotiator for a union was acting to incite the union rather than to encourage them to compromise, the mediator complained that "He's not acting like a pro. I'm really concerned when a guy pushes his people to strike because he's upset at the company. He's not doing his job. He's not being a leader, and he's making matters worse with that rhetoric."[44]

Good pros, then, do not necessarily follow the lead of their constituent group, but act independently to fashion an agreement which they then sell to the client group. As one mediator put it: "The mark of a true pro is that he doesn't cofine himself to the parameters he is given but is willing to go further. He's willing to take a gambit [sic] on a reasonable package and then sell it."[45] But this raises an important question for those concerned about the cooptive potential in mediation: Do pros act as agents of their group or do they act as agents of the mediators? Kolb's findings suggest that pros sometimes play the latter role. She found that many mediators complain when pros are too loyal to their committees. For instance, one mediator was concerned that it was sometimes "difficult to get pros away from their committees. They only want to do what's good for their troops and that's not right."[46] But while it is understandable that mediators take this view of what constitutes a good pro, it is also clear that most constituent groups would not share this definition. Most groups want a negotiator who first and foremost pursued the interests of that group. But for negotiators there may be an important contradiction between professionalism and unswerving loyalty to their clients.

Moveover, the emphasis put on selling concessions to clients seems to undermine one of the main safeguards against mediation becoming seduction. Recall that Cormick argues that if a negotiator made excessive concessions, the client group could repudiate them later. But the likelihood of repudiation is greatly reduced if the negotiator is actively engaged in trying to convince the client group that this is the best settlement. Negotiators rarely just lay their suggestions out on the table for clients; they usually engage in vigorous selling campaigns. Sometimes, for example, the negotiators will conspire with the mediators to devise ways to sell packages to recalcitrant client groups. "Conspire" may seem like too strong a word here, but it is often quite accurate. Kolb found that it is not unusual for mediators and pros to meet for off-the-record discussions about how to get clients to agree to various concessions. In these meetings, the pros and the mediator will sometimes contrive little scenarios to be played out in front of the committee. For example, in a private meeting, a negotiator may tell the mediator he is having a difficult time selling some particular point to his committee and the mediator will agree to mention in his next meeting with the committee that the opposition will simply not budge on that particular point.[47]

Naturally, mediators are aware of the dangers in this kind of manipulation. As a result, they often go to great lengths to make sure that a negotiator retains the trust of his or her committee, and that the committee gets the impression that they are in charge of the negotiations. As Kolb describes it:

The mediators continually help the pro gain and maintain the trust of his committee. It is essential, according to the mediators, to convey to the committees the impression that they are integrally involved in making the decisions at each stage of the process so that a feeling does not develop among them that a deal is being made behind their backs. The mediators, therefore, explicitly use tactics to foster the committee's involvement. Names of committee members are learned and used. Off-the-record meetings [between mediators and pros] are rarely instigated by the mediator, except on procedural matters. Such meetings are held, of course (frequently at the behest of the pro), and the mediator offers plausible reasons to the committee to justify them. When "trust" is deemed a problem, a pretended phone call or other artifice may be used as a subterfuge to camouflage off-the-record meetings.[48]

This natural, conspiratorial relationship that often develops between professional negotiators and mediators casts serious doubt on whether professionalization is the answer to the problem of seduction. At best, using professionals may be a two-edge sword. On the one hand, it means that inexperienced environmentalists would probably have to worry less about falling for the psychological ploys of the mediator; but on the other hand, it seems that they would have to begin worrying about being manipulated and seduced by their own negotiators.

A POX ON ALL HOUSES?

Even if professional negotiators play a seductive role in mediation, it could be argued that this may not be a large problem because it affects all sides in the negotiations. Seductive pros could be a pox on all houses, affecting corporate, governmental, and environmental groups alike. If the effort to sell concessions is directed at all parties, it would even itself out. Unfortunately, however, there are several reasons to believe that in environmental mediation, seductive pros may be more of a problem for environmentalists than for industry. First, there is still the problem of inexperience, which may make environmentalists more vulnerable to the selling efforts of the negotiator. Second, environmental groups are more likely to have to rely on outside professionals who have less innate loyalty to the group; whereas corporations are likely to have in-house pros who are more strongly committed to the organization and its values. Third, and perhaps more important, there is evidence to suggest that this selling process is directed more at some parties in negotiations than at others. Kolb found in her study of labor mediation cases that the pressures to be reasonable and to make concessions was more often targeted at unions that at management. She discovered that many mediators view labor and management quite differently. Typically, mediators assume that management negotiators know exactly what concessions they will and will not agree to. They describe management as being "prepared," "well controlled," and "businesslike" in their approach to negotiations.[49] In contrast, unions tend to be viewed as more irrational, more demanding, and less clear about priorities. The result of these stereotypes, Kolb argues is a bias against unions, with mediators concentrating more of their efforts on convincing the unions to make concessions. She found that "mediators spend considerably less time with management encouraging them to make concessions. This is borne out in the meeting arrangements. Of the separate meetings held with the parties, on average 35 percent of these were with management and 65 percent with the union.[50] The frequent result was that while management rarely made more concessions than it had planned, unions often ended up giving in on dozens of their demands. Would environmentalists meet the same fate? It is not unreasonable to think so. Environmentalists are also often portrayed as overdemanding, emotional, and unbusinesslike, and thus could easily find themselves the target of selective pressure by the mediators and pros.

CONCLUSION

The most important political issue surrounding environmental mediation is not how fast or cheap it is, but how fair and just it is. And as we have seen, the possibility of seducing and exploiting inexperienced parties in mediation raises some serious questions. The proponents of environmental mediation claim that its innovations increase the chances of a better and more just resolution to environmental controversies. But ironically, it is these very innovations that also carry with them the potential for political abuse. The face-to-face nature of the interaction not only encourages trust, but also invites the abuse of that trust. The therapeutic role played by the mediator may not only overcome irrational emotions interfering with the settlement of substantive questions, it may also serve to disarm participants of their legitimate feelings of outrage and frustration. And the informality of the whole process, while granting flexibility to the negotiations, also does away with formal safeguards against such abuses. Thus, upon closer examination, what seem to be the sources of political strength in this new process, turn out to be sources of political weakness as well.

But while seduction is clearly a potential pitfall in environmental mediation, several important questions about their problem remain unanswered. First, how common is this problem? Obviously, more research is needed to assess how often seduction takes place. Unfortunately, however, such information may not be easy to obtain. There is a fine line between seduction and persuasion, and it is often difficult to establish the difference objectively. Also, those involved in negotiations are unlikely to admit that seduction has taken place. Certainly the seducers are unlikely to admit it; and those who are taken in are equally unlikely to come forward and advertise their naivete. For these reasons, it may be difficult to ascertain just how common this problem actually is.

Another key question surrounding seduction is whether it can be mitigated. First, it is important to see that it is unlikely that the problem can be eliminated altogether. As we have seen, the tendency toward seduction is built into the very methods and structure of mediation—it is inherent in the personal nature of the interaction and in the conciliatory role played by the mediator. In this sense, then, it is a potential that will always be present. Having said that, however, it should also be pointed out that this problem is likely to diminish as citizen and environmental groups become more experienced. Moreover, there are some identifiable factors that lessen the chances of some kinds of seduction. For example, outright fraud and trickery are likely to be lessened when negotiations are overseen by a trained, independent mediator. And it is probably the case that the use of professional negotiators would help overcome the naivete and inexperience of some participants. Of course, the use of mediators and professional negotiators bring with them their own risks of seduction. In the end, then, probably the only real safeguard against this problem is the participants becoming more aware of what seduction is and the various ways it can take place. Potential participants need to realize that the innovative, informal procedures of environmental mediation may do them as much harm as good.

CHAPTER FIVE

Mediation and Inequalities
of Power

Henry Kissinger invited several world dignitaries to tour a brand new zoo at which he had been acting as curator in his retirement. At the end of the tour, he assembled the entourage in front of a huge guilded cage. In the cage was a lion lying down with a lamb. The crowd gasped in amazement and admiration as they first applauded and then heaped compliment after compliment on Kissinger, the consummate mediator, the one individual who had developed a way to cause a lion to lie down with a lamb. Kissinger carefully explained to the awe-stricken crowd each of the steps that he took to bring about this incredible phenomenon. However, near the end of his lecture, his voice trailed off a bit as he noted that his approach was not, as yet, flawless.

"Why is that?" asked one of his guests. Kissinger sighed and replied, "During the day while we are working with them everything is fine, but each morning, after the long nights, we must replace the lamb."[1]

When evaluating any political process, it is crucial to consider the question of power. After all, how power is distributed and used in a political process largely determines how fair that process is and, ultimately, who will benefit most from the resulting policy decisions. It is important, then, to examine in some detail how power affects the negotiations that go on in environmenal mediation. The issue of power has already been touched on briefly in earlier chapters. It was observed that without a relative balance of power between the disputing parties, sincere negotiations were unlikely to take place. It was also seen that such things as dialogue, persuasion, and understanding are likely to play a central role in negotiations only when no party can easily overpower the other. In this chapter, we will consider the possible detrimental effects that imbalances of political and economic power can have on mediation efforts, focusing especially on how these inequities can bias the outcomes of negotiations.

But before we begin this examination, it is important to note that there is a disagreement over how common and important imbalances in power are in environmental controversies. Most proponents of environmental mediation subscribe to a pluralist theory of political power—which is to say that they believe that power is distributed relatively equally among the competing interests in environmental controversies.[2] Indeed, as one scholar of the field of alternative dispute resolution, Owen Fiss of the Yale Law School, has pointed out, this entire approach "implicitly assumes a rough equality between the contending parties."[3] One advocate of environmental mediation expressed this pluralist view of power in negotiations quite explicitly: "As in labor-management bargaining, each party [in an environmental dispute] holds high cards. Each can exert a certain amount of leverage on the other. The negotiation process becomes an art of balancing power against power to achieve acceptable compromise."[4] Usually it is argued that this kind of rough balance of power is possible because there are so many different sources of power available to participants in a dispute. Such things as money, organization, membership, legal expertise, scientific expertise, political influence, legal standing, negotiating skills, and favorable publicity all serve as potential sources of power. It is thought that with such a large variety of sources of power available, all groups must have access to at least some of these resources, and thus they will all have some leverage in bargaining. As one proponent explained:

Some people view negotiation as a power struggle, as a game where the strongest entity wins. But there are different components of power, those components are spread around the table, different parties have different components, and the distribution as a totality is fairly even. Even a party holding low cards—not much money and having not much scientific help—that is pitted against a multi-national corporation can still have a lot of power. If nothing else, an otherwise powerless party can throw sand into the works of business and government in order to gain power.[5]

This is probably an overly optimistic assessment of the power relationships involved in environmental controversies. Environmentalists usually do have some sources of power, but those tend to be the weakest ones. A local environmental group, for example, may have the ability to organize rallies and to gain some public sympathy, but such things are not particularly helpful if the group is faced with a well-financed corporation that has several prominent lawyers, an outside consulting firm, and much local political clout. In other words, there can be a crucial difference between having *some* power and having *enough* power to extract some significant concessions from one's opponents. As Howard Bellman, ever the political realist, has acknowledged, "Parties whose power yields only nuisance value will extract only small concessions."[6] And indeed, many environmentalists have concluded that their organizations consistently have trouble matching the economic and political resources of their adversaries in business and industry. And some are concerned that this basic imbalance of power will inevitably compromise the integrity of the negotiations that take place in mediation efforts. In a recent survey taken of participants and observers of a series of negotiation efforts in Wisconsin, three-quarters of the respondents believed that the negotiation process favored the most powerful interests and people. And it is interesting that while only two out of six business and industry respondents thought this was the case, ten out of eleven of the citizen and environmental representatives perceived this bias.[7]

Environmentalists' concerns about basic imbalances in political and economic power have found support in the work of a number of prominent political scientists and political theorists. Political thinkers as diverse as E.E. Schattschneider, Grant Mc-Connell, and Charles Lindblom have taken issue with the pluralist vision of power in American politics.[8] They have argued that there exists a persistent inequality between interest groups in American politics, with a decided bias in favor of large business and financial institutions. Other scholars, like Mancur Olson, have also noted that environmentalists and other public interests groups always face a number of unique and substantial obstacles in their efforts to balance out the political power of concentrated economic interests.[9]

Clearly, then, despite the assurances of some proponents of mediation, serious questions can be raised about whether there is equality of power between pro and anti-environmental forces in specific disputes. Accordingly, in this chapter we will consider what forms such imbalances of power can take, and examine the various ways in which these imbalances can undermine the fairness and legitimacy of mediation efforts. In addition, we will explore whether anything can be done about this form of political bias in mediation and in particular, whether mediators can and should take responsibility for trying to aid weaker interest groups in these negotiations. To begin, however, we will consider how imbalances of power can affect access to environmental mediation efforts.

POWER AND THE PROBLEM OF UNEQUAL ACCESS

Access is an important factor in any policy-making process. Access determines how representative these processess are, and this in turn determines how just and democratic the final policy outcomes are likely to be. Given these connections, it is not surprising that many of the complaints about unfairness concerning our traditional legislative, administrative, and judicial processes often center around a lack of equal access. Disgruntled groups argue that access to these institutions is biased in favor of those who have the most political and economic power. For example, some interests complain that because they cannot afford large political action committee contributions or expensive lobbyists, they do not enjoy the same direct access to legislators as better funded groups. Similarly, it is charged that access to the courts is often restricted to those who have the resources to fund long and complicated litigation efforts. At first it might seem that mediation, being a more informal approach, might be unafflicted with these problems. Ideally, it could be a process open to all interested parties, irrespective of their resources. In practice, however, unequal access can be a persistent problem in this alternative approach as well—and imbalances of power play a significant role in creating this problem.

      Part of the problem of unequal access stems from the fact that environmental meditation is not like labor-management negotiations where the appropriate participating parties are limited and easily identified. Environmental disputes are usually multiparty disputes, with a large number of affected interests. Moreover, at the initial stages of a dispute there is often much disagreement about which parties and organizations could or should be included in any negotiation process. As a result, it often falls to the mediator to determine who will participate. But this is not a question on which mediators are entirely neutral. They have an strong interest in keeping the number of participants as small as possible. There are a number of reasons for this. First, and probably most importantly, the larger the group, the more difficult it is to generate an agreement that satisfies everyone.[10] Bilateral negotiations between two parties often reach agreements easily. The more parties that are added, the more difficult it is to find a solution. There are other reasons for keeping a group small. Logistically, large groups are unwieldy and difficult to manage. Moreover, mediators often try to develop trust between the participants, and it is more difficult to develop this personal trust in large groups.[11] Finally, mediators might hesitate to include any party that might prove disruptive or obstructionist. Generating agreements is tough enough without inviting trouble by including difficult parties in the negotiations.

For all of these reasons, mediators often seek ways to limit participation. Sometimes mediators may let purely subjective criteria determine who is given access. They may only invite those parties who they feel comfortable with or who are likely to agree with their view of the problem.[12] Most professional mediators, however, seek to rise above their own personal biases and try to employ some more objective criteria to determine access. One of the most common criteria is the amount of power possessed by a group.[13] As a rule of thumb, the more powerful a group is the more likely it will be included in the negotiations. Usually the determining factor is whether a group has enough power to block or subvert any final agreement. For example, if a group can use the courts to block the implementation of an agreement, or has enough power in the legislature to overturn an agreement, the prudent mediator will include them in the negotiations. Otherwise, any mediated agreement may only be stillborn. Conversely, if a group does not have enough power to interfere with the outcome of a negotiation, the mediator has little reason to include them. As one mediator explains it: "One of the reasons that mediation works is that it is usually limited to people that have some impact on the situation. I don't ask people who don't have clout to participate in the mediation. This is not public participation, this is cloutful people's participation. That's a real important difference. I don't have anything to do with people without power because they can't affect what I'm doing. It's a pragmatic test.[14]

In this view, mediation is not intended to be a completely open process, and it is power that serves as the passport into these negotiation efforts. But while this is quite understandable from the mediator's point of view, it may not always be fair or in the public interest. This kind of unequal access means that politically weak groups that have legitimate interests at stake could be left out of the process—their interests unrepresented in the final agreement. Typically, there are several types of interests that fall into this category. First, there are unorganized interests. As Mancur Olson has pointed out, in public interest issues where the ill effects of policies are widely diffused among large numbers of people, those interest are often unorganized.[15] This is often the case with environmental problems, where large numbers of people may be affected by pollution but may have no organization to represent and promote their interests. Naturally, as long as these groups remain unorganized, they have no power, and will not be included in any negotiations. Perhaps more typical are situations where affected interests are organized, but they have little traditional political power. This is often the case with local environmental and citizen groups. They usually have difficulty amassing the resources to wage the prolonged legal and political battles that would establish them as "cloutful people" and thus worthy of inclusion in the mediation process. And when such groups are excluded, this obviously increases the chances that any agreement coming out of the negotiation process is more likely to only represent the concerns of the more powerful special interests.

WISCONSIN'S CONSENSUS PROCESS

Evidence that unequal access is more than just a hypothetical problem can be found in a study done by Dorothy Lagerroos and Caryl Terrell of the Wisconsin League of Women Voters. They studied a negotiation process in the Wisconsin State Legislature known as the consensus process. In this approach, informal study groups are convened consisting of legislators and representatives of various interest groups concerned with a particular piece of legislation. They negotiate and develop a piece of legislation that theoretically represents a consensus of the groups interested in the particular issue. This approach has been used for several environmental bills as well as other pieces of legislation. When a number of complaints began to surface about the process, the League decided to conduct a survey of past participants and observers in order to explore some of the political issues surrounding the approach—including the question of accessability. The survey polled over seventy participants and observers, and may be the only comprehensive survey of those involved in environmental negotiation efforts.[16] In regards to accessability, it was found that over half of those polled said that the process was closed to some groups. Less than a quarter saw the process as being open to all.[17] The following comments were typical: " 'Some with legitimate interests were left out of the process and denied genuine opportunity to participate'; 'It is too easy for some participants to be excluded from the consensus process, allowing disproportionate input from one side or another'; and 'At present, the so-called "consensus process" actually involves a select "inner circle" of players. Outside interest are either ignored or given little chance to make contributions.' "[18]

It is also revealing that several respondents commented on the crucial role that political power plays in determining who is going to participate. According to one observer, "Groups that have little political power are often systematically left (kept) out of the process." And as one legislative aide argued, "In effect, the consensus process disenfranchises some citizens. The more powerful groups 'slug it out,' leaving out minor fringe groups and weak issues or persons."[19] In addition, when one looks at the responses to questions concerning access given to various interest groups, some significant differences surface. For example, while two-thirds of the business and industry representatives polled described the process as being open to all, none of the local environmental and citizen groups in Wisconsin did so. And while only half of those from business and industry agreed that people who do not represent a politically significant power block are not included in negotiations, all of the local groups agreed with this proposition.[20] Such responses, along with local newspaper reports, clearly indicate that it is the weaker, local groups that were most likely to be left out of the negotiation process and that were most unhappy with the resulting consensus bills.

THE POTENTIAL FOR "SWEETHEART" DEALS

When certain groups are left out of mediation efforts, there is an increased chance that their interests may be inadvertently ignored in the final agreement. But there is also the possibility that those who do take part in the negotiation effort might *intentionally* conspire to violate the interest of those who are left out. This possibility is particularly disturbing to some environmentalists who suspect that out-of-court negotiations may become a common way for government and business to construct "sweetheart deals"—deals that leave conservationists out in the cold. This has become a matter of great concern during the Reagan years. In the name of deregulation, the Reagan administration has made a concerted effort to substitute negotiation for litigation in many regulatory areas, including the environment.[21] Environmentalists fear that this approach is simply an excuse for the admininstration to avoid vigorous and effective action against corporations that violate environmental standards—and that negotiations are used mainly to let violators off the hook. There is some evidence that this concern is justified. In a number of cases involving the dumping of toxic wastes, the Reagan administration abandoned litigation and pursued a policy of negotiated settlements with the offending companies. Numerous complaints arose, however, when local communities and environmental groups were deliberately excluded from these negotiations, and they charged that the government was going too easy on the polluters. This was the case, for instance, in the Love Canal controversy where the new Reagan administration quickly reached an agreement with the Hooker Chemical Company—an agreement that local citizen protested, claiming it would not guarantee a clean-up or protect their health and safety.[22]

Another example of the problem of sweetheart deals between government and industry was the informal negotiations that took place between the Environmental Protection Agency (EPA) and the Thriftway Company of Farmington, New Mexico, an oil refiner. As Alan Miller of the Natural Resources Defense Fund has pointed out, this case is a good lesson in what can go wrong when all relevant parties are not included in a negotiation effort.[23] In 1981, Thriftway went to the EPA to negotiate a waiver from EPA rules designed to limit the amount of lead in gasoline.[24] (Lead, which is known to cause brain damage in children, is restricted because of its high toxicity).[25] Corporate officials claimed that the lead standards were causing "a substantial operating loss" for the firm. The company had reason to believe that the EPA might be sympathetic to their plea, because EPA administrator Ann Burford had recently announced that the agency was going to reexamine its lead standards. On December 11, 1981, three representatives of the company meet with Burford, the top EPA air pollution enforcement official, Richard Wilson, another EPA staff member and an aide to New Mexico Senator Harrison Schmitt. Significantly, there were no representatives from citizen or environmental groups present during these negotiations. No transcript was kept of the meeting, but the Thriftway representatives came away from the negotiations understanding that Burford had agreed that the company could ignore the law while the EPA was studying the issue, and that they would not be prosecuted. Confident in these assurances, the company began to violate the federal lead standards the very next day.

When this alleged agreement came to light later in 1982, several members of Congress became incensed. Burford was called to testify on this matter and she maintained that she had not in fact condoned Thriftway's breaking of the law. And then, in December 1982, Thriftway was notified by EPA staff officials that it was being fined $126,526 for violating lead standards. In an angry letter to the EPA, Thriftway attorney Will Cockrell, Jr. responded that the refiner had violated the standards soley because of, and in complete reliance on Burford's "unequivocal commitment" not to prosecute. This apparent discrepancy was later investigated by Inspector General Matthew Novick. Again Burford denied having authorized Thriftway to ignore federal law. But the sworn affidavits given to Novick by the others present at the meeting (including the EPA aides) give a very different picture of the meeting. According to the affidavits, Burford told Thriftway representatives that they were free to ignore the lead standards; but when the Thriftway attorney had asked her to put those assurance in writing, Burford had refused. Moveover, as the negotiations had broken up, Burford had called the Schmitt aide aside and told him that she did not want to tell Thriftway explicitly to break the law, but added, "I hope they got the message." The aide assured her that they had. Burford then told another EPA employee that she had "solved one problem" for the company. Three days later, a Thriftway attorney called Wilson to confirm the understanding that had been reached. Wilson agreed that Burford had promised them immunity. The attorney pledged to "keep our lips sealed," and Wilson thanked him.

The Thriftway scandal is a somewhat unique case, but it does illustrate the kinds of dangers involved in informal negotiations where important interests are excluded. Clearly, had all interests in this matter been allowed to participate in the meeting, it is unlikely that Burford would have encouraged or agreed to Thriftway's violation of federal pollution laws. But given that environmental groups had little influence or power in the Reagan administration, there was little reason for Burford to include them in these negotiations. The inevitable result was an agreement which met the interests of the company and the Reagan administration, but that ignored the public interest. This should not be too surprising, however, because there is little room for any notion of the public interest in the mediation process. A good mediated agreement is almost always defined as one that satisfies those parties in the negotiations—with little reference to any outside public interest.[26] In part this is because any attempt to introduce this criterion would undoubtedly only complicate further the already difficult process of bargaining. But the tendency to downplay the notion of the public interest also reveals how mediation is again deeply rooted in pluralist political theory. Pluralist theorists argue that it is fruitless for policymakers to try to arrive at some objective definition of the public interest that could be used to evaluate public policy decisions. Instead, pluralists suggest that we simply redefine the public interest to be any policy that satisfies the interests participating in the decision-making process. We see this same kind of political logic at work in environmental mediation. The problem, of course, is that equating the bargainers' interests with the public interest is quite questionable—especially when significant parts of the public are left out of the bargaining process.

SOME PROPOSED SOLUTIONS

The problem of unequal access has been significant enough to garner some serious attention from politically sensitive mediators. Several suggestions have been made concerning how to guarantee sufficiently wide access. First, Gerald Cormick has suggested that a code of ethics for mediators should include the responsibility to ensure that all affected parties have an opportunity to participate. According to Cormick, mediators should broadly publicize mediation efforts, and actively encourage the participation of affected interests.[27] However, while these suggestions are clearly well intended, it is difficult to see how such a code of ethics could be a reliable solution to this problem. For as we have seen, mediators usually have a personal and professional interest in keeping mediation efforts as small as possible. An abstract commitment to the principle of equal access may easily buckle under the immediate pressures to keep the effort managable and to keep out disruptive influences. In practice, mediators seem to have a rather poor track record as protectors of equal access. Lawrence Susskind of the Harvard Negotiation Project surveyed a number of mediation efforts and concluded that "none of the mediators appeared overly concerned about the effects that the respective agreements might have on groups not directly involved in the negotiation."[28]

The other suggested safeguard of equal access is to codify the right to participate in mediation efforts in the law and thus to effectively take away the ability of the mediator to choose the participants. Timothy Sullivan has argued that the issue of equal access could be better addressed if environmental mediation efforts were mandated by law—much as labor-management decisions are now. As he points out, labor law "clearly delimits who participates in bargaining and establishes procedures for recognizing legitimate dispute participants. Once a union wins a majority of votes cast in a bargaining unit election, they gain the right to bargain on behalf of the workers."[29] The assumption here is that much of this problem of unequal access is tracable to the excessive informality of most negotiation efforts—an informality that allows the mediator to arbitrarily decide who participates. A more formal, legal process might mandate the participation of a wider variety of interested parties.

The idea of establishing legal rights to participate in environmental mediation efforts does sound intriguing, but just what that would look like in practice is less than clear. Moreover, citing labor-management negotiations as an example of how this might be done raises more questions that it answers. Labor-management negotiations are hardly the best model of how to include all affected interests in mediation efforts. Indeed, one of the most frequent complaints about labor agreements is that they do not always reflect the public interest, that they are inflationary, and so on. While unions are guaranteed participation, a number of other affected interests, including consumers and local residents are excluded.

Still, institutionalizing and legalizing mediation efforts could guarantee better access to this process. One example of how this might work is the way participation is structured in the negotiations mandated by the Massachusetts Harzardous Waste Facility Sitting law. This law is an attempt to resolve the many controversies surrounding the building of these plants by requiring negotiations between waste facility developers and local residents and officials over such things as location of the facility, safety measures, etc. The legislation mandates the creation of a local assessment committee that represents the interests of those in the affected communities. That committee consists of the local chief executive officer, the chairman of the local conservation commission, the chairman of the local planning board, the fire chief, four local residents, and four members nominated by the local chief executive officer and approved by the city council.[30] While this committee may not represent all affected parties, it at least guarantees the participation of a minimum number of local officials and citizens.

It should be noted, however, that for this more formal approach to substantially mitigate the problem of unequal access, there would have to be a basic change in the practice of environmental mediation. There would have to be a move away from ad

hoc, informal mediation efforts, which are now the rule, to more
formal and regulated ones mandated by legislation. As yet, this
movement toward more formalism is in its infancy—the Massachusetts case is one of the few examples of mediation efforts
governed by law.[31] And in as much as most efforts remain informal, the problem of unequal access is likely to persist.

IMBALANCES OF POWER
AT THE NEGOTIATING TABLE

But even if we assume, that the problem of unequal access can be
eliminated, imbalances of power between the participants would
still produce a whole other set of serious political problems in
environmental mediation. In particular, it is unlikely that the
bargaining process will be fair if one party has substantially more
power than another. Gerald Cormick and others have pointed out
that if negotiations are to produce just outcomes, they must take
place between parties with relatively equal power. As he pointed
out earlier, where the partries do not have sufficient power to
frustrate each other, good-faith bargaining is unlikely to take
place. It is sometimes assumed that when such large imbalances
of power exist, the more powerful party will simply avoid negotiation altogether, prefering to pursue its goals through conventional channels. But there is also the possibility that the more
powerful party might try to use negotiations to force a lopsided
series of concessions upon its opponent. Powerful groups may
easily prefer mediation over more formal approaches like litigation
in an attempt to save time and money. For these groups, mediation
may be the most efficient means to their ends—especially if they
are able to translate their political and economic superiority into
advantages at the bargaining table. In such imbalanced situations,
a compromise agreement may result, but there are real questions
about the fairness and legitimacy of such agreements. As one legal
scholar, Jerold Auerbach, has observed: "Compromise only is an

equitable solution among equals; between unequals, it inevitably reproduces inequality."[32] Let us consider some of the ways in which participants in environmental mediation may be unequals.

THE ADVANTAGES OF TECHNICAL EXPERTISE

When negotiators arrive at the table, they rarely have equal power and resources available to them. One of the most important sources of power within the negotiation process is expertise. Expertise can take many forms. One party may have better legal expertise, or as we saw in the last chapter, better expertise in negotiating itself. But a form of expertise that is perhaps of even greater importance in environmental mediation efforts is that involving scientific and technical matters. As we saw earlier, it has been argued that environmental disputes are often not so much a matter of conflicting interest, but the product of technical and scientific disagreements. And there is some truth to this: environmental policy is an area where technical data—especially concerning the exact environmental effects of certain pollutants and activities—plays a particulary large part. As a result, many me diation efforts concentrate a large part of their attention on tech nical issues. The approach, however, puts a premium on expertise and research, and this can be a powerful advantage for some groups. It is much easier for some groups to generate large amounts of research and analysis on a given environmental topic. As one environmental mediator has explained, this ability gives them a psychological as well as a substantive advantage in negotiations: "Knowledge is power. People who are able to present issues in a skillfully authoritative fashion—for example, those who can credibly claim to be in accord with current scientific thinking, or those who know what is practically achievable in some real world situation—are usually more convincing and thus more powerful in negotiations."[33] In practice, this advantage in expertise often goes to industry groups. They typically have the

economic resources, the in-house staff, and the outside consultants to produce volumes of research to support their position on
a particular dispute. Moreover, industry often has sole access to
proprietary technical information about industrial processes to
which even the government is not privy. The result of this imbalance of technical expertise is, as one conservationist put it, that
"environmentalists who get involved in mediation are certainly
outmanned and perhaps even intimidated. It is clearly a mismatch
when it comes to being able to counter the industries's side when
they have a wealth of information, computer models, and
analysts."[34]

Of course, many of the larger national environmental organizations have been developing in-house experts of their own, and
they sometimes get the voluntary help of sympathetic scientists
who help to narrow the expertise gap. But even so, environmental
organizations usually remain outnumbered and outspent in the
technical aspects of most environmental issues. Even such leading
environmental organizations as the Environmental Defense Fund
and the Natural Resource Defense Council run on shoe-string
budgets and have very limited staff. Often each environmental
issue is attended to by a lone staff lawyer, who must not only
grasp the legal aspects of the case and the political history of any
relevant government regulations, but must also become an expert
on the technical and scientific dimensions of the issue.[35] These
individuals will typically face a whole team of experts marshalled
by industry.

Patrick Parenteau, an attorney formerly with the National
Wildlife Federation, has pointed out that this imbalance in expertise may be one of the most important factors undermining the
fairness of environmental negotiations. Generally, he is sympathetic with efforts to expand the use of environmental mediation.
But as he said in a recent speech, "I am concerned about the
disparate technical resources available to the citizen organization
side in the mediation process. In the cases that our organization
has been involved in, and we have been involved in six or eight
negotiated or mediated settlements of a variety of issues, that has

to be the single greatest obstacle to an effective participation in the mediation."[36] And of course this situation is much worse for local environmental groups. With even smaller financial resources, they are almost always unable to compete effectively in the analysis of the technical dimensions of a dispute. This seems to be the case, for example, in Massachusetts, where as we saw earlier, communities are now required by law to negotiate with the private developers of hazardous waste facilities. Dana Duxbury, a hazardous waste specialist for the League of Women Voters, and a close observer of many of these disputes, has found that local officials and citizens often feel that they do not have enough information to negotiate effectively with the developers: "Citizens have been very frustrated by the limited technical information available early in the process about the proposed facility, the site, and potential social and environmental impacts. The law requires that a group of local leaders cope with a lengthy, politically charged, and highly technical process, and many believe that they are put at a disadvantage by the lack of information produced by the preliminary state review. Also, if the state played a stronger role in providing technical assistance to local communities, for analysis of a proposed facility and site, the environmental impact assessment and other matters, citizens might be better able to participate effectively in the process with waste disposal firms that can afford to pay staff and consultants."[37]

To be fair, this problem of lopsided access to expertise is not a unique affliction of environmental mediation. It arises in virtually every political process that deals with environmental problems. Lack of technical parity also works to the disadvantage of environmental groups in litigation and in legislative lobbying. But again, that is exactly the point: environmental mediation is no more fair than our traditional political approaches. In politics, information is power, and this is true even in such informal and apparently egalitarian political processes like mediation. As one environmentalist summed it up, the negotiation process "simply legitimates and reproduces the existing inequality in access to technical and legal expertise between public and private vested interests. While all participants are theoretically equal, some are in fact more equal than others."[38]

THE POWER OF OUTSIDE OPTIONS

As a rule, the amount of power a party has at the negotiating table is determined by the amount of power they have outside the negotiations. Usually this outside power is measured in terms of options. As negotiation theorists have pointed out, a party's strength at the bargaining table is directly proportional to the number of acceptable alternatives it has outside of the negotiations.[39] Those who are most powerful inside negotiations are those that have the most options if the mediation process fails. If, for example, a party has enough resources to mount an effective litigation effort, or an effective legislative lobbying effort, these options can give them a decided advantage at the bargaining table. Primarily this is because groups with viable options need the negotiations less and this allows them to bargain from a position of strength. It allow them to adopt a hard-line position and to not care if the negotiations fall through. Contrast this to a party that has few options outside the mediation process. Such a party necessarily bargains from a position of weakness, and may be forced to give concessions that are not in its interests—all because it has no viable alternatives.

In extreme cases, the lack of outside options may mean that a party's participation in the mediation process is less than voluntary. If a group cannot afford to take its case to court, for example, it may feel it has little choice but to accept a mediation effort—even if it knows it will be bargaining from a position of weakness. However, this lack of voluntariness may undermine much of the integrity and legitimacy of the mediation process. In environmental mediation, the question of voluntariness is a crucial one. Advocates often suggest that the fact that parties enter into mediation voluntarily and that all agreements are voluntary is part of what separates this process from more conventional approaches. More importantly, it is argued that voluntariness is much of what assures that the outcomes are fair and just. Since agreements are purely voluntary, no party would agree to one that is not ultimately in their interests. Voluntariness, then, is one of few institutional safeguards that help to ensure the fairness of this process.

It is not difficult to imagine a circumstance in which voluntarism is essentially absent from a mediation effort. Moreover, there is now empirical research in the field of alternative dispute resolution that suggests that voluntary participation may not be as common as it appears. While little such research has been done on the question of voluntarism in environmental mediation in particular, a great deal has been done on this question in other areas of alternative dispute resolution.[40]

For example, Christine Harrington found in her research on neighborhood justice centers, that there are often subtle threats of outside sanctions that make mediation less than voluntary.[41] She points out that local prosecuters sometimes "persuade" people to participate in mediation by dangling the threat of formal prosecution over their heads. It likely that similar kinds of outside pressures can also work to make participation in environmental mediation less than voluntary. When environmental groups feel out-manned and out-gunned in the conventional political institutions, they may be forced to turn to mediation as a last resort—even though they know they will be bargaining from a position of weakness. They may know that they will be forced to give up a lot and are likely to receive only a few token concessions, but they may decide that even those few concessions are better than losing totally. As one mediator has warned, "Agreements are sometimes reached because one party with substantial power holds out for what it wants while other parties with less leverage realize that they can either accept a small gain or wind up with nothing at all."[42] Some environmentalists fear that this happens in environmental mediation more often than not. As one put it, "basically, what industry is doing is giving crumbs to its opponents and walking off with pretty much what it wanted in the first place."

THE POLITICAL ILLUSIONS
SURROUNDING MEDIATION

It is clear that unequal power between participants in environmental mediation can undermine the extent to which this process is representative, fair, and voluntary. But what makes matters worse is that the appearances surrounding mediation often work to obscure the existence of these political problems. Mediation has a strong image of being voluntary and egalitarian, and this image may mask the fact that negotiation is biased in favor of the more powerful parties. Indeed, this was a common complaint voiced by some observers of the consensus process of negotiation that is used in the Wisconsin legislature. In one case, negotiation was used to draft a bill concerning the protection of groundwater in Wisconsin. Later, the president of a local citizens group wrote a local paper complaining that the description of this bill as a "compromise between industry and environmentalists" was deceptive. She pointed out that only one environmental group had been included on the negotiating committee that had drafted this legislation, and that even that group was opposed to the bill's final form.[44] Other environmentalists have made similar complaints about the presumed representativeness of mediation efforts. They argue that even when only a few environmentalists participate in negotiations, the final agreement is often portrayed as being endorsed by the "environmental community," which may not be the case at all.

Wisconsin environmentalists also complained that there was a deceptive appearance of egalitarianism in the negotiation efforts. They suggested that the way negotiations were portrayed to the press and the public hid the fact that powerful special interests often had substantial advantages over other participants. As one environmentalist explained: "Powerful industries are able to manipulate the process and give false impressions regarding agreements. Citizen groups have few resources and are unable to match the efforts of highly paid industry spokespersons. Yet media coverage makes it appear that all sides participated equally."[45]

In other words, the myths of egalitarianism and voluntariness surrounding environmental mediation lend an air of political legitimacy to these agreements—even when it is not deserved. And of course, this sense of legitimacy can prove very useful for those more powerful political interests. Indeed, this would help to explain why some powerful parties are interested in environmental mediation, even though they may be able to win through other strategies like litigation. For example, if a developer were able to achieve his objectives through mediation, his development project would be granted a degree of political legitimacy that would be hard to obtain otherwise. He could claim that even environmentalists support this project—irrespective of how voluntary or reluctant the agreement of the environmentalists actually was. Contrast that to a win through the courts. Even if the developer could prevail in a bitter court battle, the political costs and bad publicity might be large. The developer would risk being seen as a selfish special interest or as a "heavy" in the eyes of the public. But if he can achieve virtually the same goals (minus a few concessions) through mediation, he can achieve a major public relations coup. He now appears reasonable and flexible, and his project now has the seal of approval from environmentalists.

It seems, then, that the problem of unequal power in environmental mediation actually has several different dimensions: First, there are the biases in negotiations created by these imbalances in power. Second, there is the tendency for the mythology of mediation to hide the existence of these biases. And finally, powerful groups may be able to take advantage of this mythology to legitimize inequitable agreements.

GOVERNMENTAL POWER IN MEDIATION

So far, this discussion has focused primarily on power inequities between business and environmental groups. However, any analysis of the problems of power in environmental mediation must also take into account the power advantages enjoyed by governmental representatives who take part in these negotiations. To date, most environmental mediation efforts have involved some representative from local, state, or federal governments.[46] When these governmental representatives are involved, the dangers stemming from imbalances of power are probably at their greatest. The reason is simple: the government often has an enormous amount of legal power that it can bring to bear against the other participants. By definition, the government is charged with making policy decisions that groups in society are legally bound to obey. Thus it has a very effective form of power that is rarely available to other groups in a dispute. This power advantage can subvert the legitimacy of mediation efforts in several ways. First, the government may use its power to force parties to mediate. It can, for example, make mediation a mandatory part of the decision-making process. This is exactly what the Massachusetts state legislature has done with its new law governing the siting of hazardous waste processing facilities. The law requires local townspeople to negotiate with facility operators over the details of the facility. The problem, of course, is that this kind of mandatory mediation totally eliminates any voluntariness from the process. The Massachusetts law even forbids local towns from using their zoning laws to prevent the siting of a facility in their area. Thus these towns have virtually no choice but to mediate, and if they are recalcitrant and the mediation fails, the issues are simply decided by arbitration. In such a coercive situation, the towns are obviously at a disadvantage.[47] This law is only one example of what proponents call the "institutionalization" of mediation—where various levels of government formally incorporate the process into their policy-making efforts. The political implications of this movement toward institutionalization will be discussed in greater detail in chapter 7, but for now what is clear is that it certainly has the potential of increasing the level of coercion involved in mediation efforts and thus raises serious questions about the democratic nature of the process.

Perhaps the most troublesome aspect of government-mandated or sponsored mediation efforts is the possibility that they are being used simply as a way for the government to more efficiently implement it policies. At first glance, government sponsored mediation efforts appear to constitute a desirable new form of citizen and interest group participation in environmental policymaking. The government looks willing to sit down and negotiate over important issues. But as Jeffrey Miller, former chief of the EPA's enforcement branch, has argued, public participation is hardly the motive behind these efforts. What the government is primarily interested in, he says, is reducing court costs and speeding compliance with its policies.[48] Further evidence of federal government intentions to use mediation primarily for cooptive purposes is also found in a report done by Peter Clark and Wendy Emrich for the Interior Department. The intent of the report was to urge greater use of environmental mediation by federal officials. In the following passage, the authors describe to officials the potential political advantages of environmental mediation.

It is the thesis of this paper that Federal decisionmaking and, specifically public sector planning and regulation often can be improved by early involvement of all key interests groups likely to attempt to block a Federal action. Using conflict management tools like conciliation, facilitation, and mediation—which build consensus among constituents with a stake in proposed Federal actions—officials can in certain circumstances reduce unnecessary court delays, avoid regulatory stand-offs and move opponents to mutually acceptable settlements. Environmental conflict will be less disruptive to agency decisionmaking if officials learn to use conflict management tools . . . [Conflict management] should not be confused with more requirements for public participation. The key word is *management*. In cases where public groups are fighting with the Federal government, better conflict management means better control over the participation process. (emphasis in original).[49]

This passage is particularly revealing. On the one hand, it has a number of appealing political phrases like "participation," "consensus" and "mutually acceptable settlements." But on the other hand, the clear overriding purpose of mediation for these authors is to enable officials to implement their policies over the objections of opposing citizen groups. For them, the key word is *management*. They are not so much interested in furthering participation as they are in managing those groups that could "block" or "disrupt" the efficient implementation of government policy. In the case of hazardous waste siting, for example, early attempts by state government to simple preempt local authority and force the facilities on local towns have often only led to law suits, demonstrations, civil disobedience, and other forms of citizen opposition. Such situations might be managed better through mandated mediation, which occupies the time of opponents and gives them the feeling that they are having some influence on the decisions.

Later in the report, the authors make it clear that mediation does not require officials to actually relinquish any of their power to citizen groups. And they make a suggestion as to how officials can use mediation to give the appearance of negotiating with opposition groups while in fact maintaining for themselves the power to make the basic policy decisions. Some agencies "fear a loss of agency authority in the context of a group negotiation process. [But] a properly managed mediation process *guarantees* retention of agency authority: it does not challenge or weaken it. At the very outset, the mediator requires the agency to outline its specific constraints—regulatory, political, economic—under which it must operate and within which any final agreements must fall" (emphasis in original).[50]

It is this notion of constraints that allows an agency to retain control of the situation. By carefully stipulating its constraints, an agency is able to set the parameters of what is negotiable and what is not, and in that way retain its essential power. In essence, the government controls the agenda of the negotiations and predetermines the outcome. In practice this means that although an agency may be willing to grant concessions on details, the basic policy decisions remain nonnegotiable. This may be exactly what several states like Massachusetts are trying to do with their new hazardous waste siting laws. Although they are requiring negotiations between local towns and the site developers, the states have made it clear that the siting of these facilities will take place, and that normally the only issues up for negotiation are how a local area will be protected or compensated by the developer for the social and environmental costs of these facilities.

The process at work here is similar to the one describe by Peter Bachrach and Morton Baratz. They have argued that there are "two faces" of political power.[51] The first, and most overt, is the kind of power used to influence particular policy decisions. The second face of power is more subtle but equally important— the ability to prevent certain issues from ever making it onto the political agenda in the first place. Bachrach and Baratz call this process "nondecision making," which they define as "the practice of limiting the scope of actual decision making to 'safe issues' by manipulating the dominant community values, myths, and political institutions and procedures."[52] They argue that this approach is a common political tactic used by established political and economic powers. The way environmental mediation is being used in the Massachusetts Hazardous Waste Facility Siting Act would seem to be a prime example of this kind of nondecision making. The state has explicitly excluded from consideration in the negotiations certain issues that it finds threatening—such as the question of whether these facilities are even needed. This attempt to restrict negotiations to only "safe issues" has also taken place in Wisconsin. Their hazardous waste siting law also promotes the option of negotiations, but it, too, explicitly stipulates that the need for the facility itself is not to be an issue that is subject to negotiations.[53]

COOPTING ANTI-ENVIRONMENTAL FORCES

Importantly, the government may not only use its superior power to overcome the opposition of environmental groups, it may also use it to overcome the opposition of business groups as well. Jeffrey Miller explains that in the past, when the federal government was interested in enforcing environmental standards, it would often use its superior power to set the agenda when it was negotiating with corporations. "[The government] sets the agenda in an enforcement negotiation. It makes the demands while the company can only explain why a demand is unreasonable and why a counter-proposal might be better. Overall, however, the assumption of the private party in the enforcement negotiation is that it will have to pay penalties and comply with the government's wishes. The only questions that are open to companies are how much, how long, and to what extent government sanctions will apply."[54]

The government, in this sense, is an equal opportunity coopter. It may use mediation and negotiation to coopt either pro or anti-environmental forces depending on what its particular policy goals are at the time. In either case, of course, this kind of approach raises serious questions about the political legitimacy of the process.

Another example of how mediation may be used against anti-environmental groups is a case where a local government sought to use mediation to stifle opposition to a park development project. The dispute took place in Missouri and involved plans to turn an abandoned railroad right-of-way into a park. Railroads are abandoning an increasing number of rights-of-way in the United States. The Interstate Commerce Commission has estimated that more than 20,000 miles of railroads will be abandoned in the near future. Some local communities have been interested in converting these properties into "linear recreational facilities." The Interior Department has been authorized to make grants available to these communities for the acquisition of these properties and their development for recreation use. One such city was Columbia, Missouri.[55] Columbia was interested in acquiring an eight-and-a-half mile right-of-way being abandoned by the Missouri-Kansas-Texas (MKT) Railroad that ran from the downtown area out into the agricultural areas at the edge of the city. The city wanted to develop the tract as a linear park and nature trail that would be used for jogging, horseback riding, cross-country skiing, hiking, and bicycling.

There were several factors, however, that complicated the city's plans. First was the legal question of ownership. It appeared that the city would be unable to simply claim all of the land after MKT abandoned it, but that ownership of some of it would revert to the owners of the adjacent land. This meant that the city would have to find a way to acquire this land from the private owners. Unfortunately for the city, not all of these owners, which included suburban homeowners, suburban developers, and rural farmers, were willing to sell their land. Many were worried about the problems of privacy, litter, vandalism, and crime that might accompany the public use of the right-of-way. Fortunately for the city, the Interior Department (through the Heritage Conservation and Recreation Service) had asked the American Arbitration Association to assist communities in resolving conflicts associated with conversion of rights-of-ways. In the spring 1979, two mediators, Glenn Tiedt and John McGlennon, supervised two days of negotiations between the city and the individual landowners. During the meetings, the landowners were encouraged to voice their concerns, and in turn the city counselor's office outlined the options available to each landowner. The landowners' options were (a) to give the land to the city as a gift, (b) sell the title to the land to the city for an agreed upon price, or (c) have the city acquire the land through eminent domain proceedings. The mediators pointed out to the citizens that the gift option would be the best for all concerned. It would save the city money, and it would give tax benefits to the landowners. It would also allow the owners to include restrictive covenants in the gift requiring the city to provide such things as fencing. If the owner chose not to donate the property, the city would provide no guarantees concerning the development of the parkway, and any income from the sale of condemnation of the property would be taxed as capital gains. Unsurprisingly, eight out of the ten landowners agreed to donate or sell their title to the city. Condemnation was used only on one resisting farmer.

This case tells us a number of important things about how governments can use environmental mediation. The Columbia city officials controlled from the very beginning the terms of the negotiations. Their legal power—especially their ability to seize the land—allowed them to define the constraints within which a final decision would have to fall. As a result, whether or not the land would become a park was never up for negotiation. The only question on the agenda was how the city would acquire the land. The purpose of the negotiations was to allow the citizens to voice their objections, to try to accommodate them where possible, but to make it clear that the park would be built. The mediation effort was an attempt by the city to manage the opposition to the project, while retaining all the basic decision making power. And it worked extraordinarily well. As the mediators' report concluded: "Many citizens felt that for once their concerns were addressed rather than ignored by the public agencies. According to the city counselor, Scott Snyder, 'the farmers were and remain hostile to the concept of the project, but now have come to accept its inevitability.'"[56]

The report went on to compare the Columbia case with a similar case in Nebraska where the city officials did not have the foresight to bring in mediators. That city eventually had to abandon its efforts to create a park because of the threat of protracted litigation from the private land owners opposed to the project. Because Columbus was able to convince opponents not to pursue this litigatory strategy, their mediation effort was labeled a success. But while it was clearly a successful effort to manage and discourage opposition to the park, it is far from clear that it was a successful example of fair and unbiased mediation. It could be considered an example of reconciliation—but only in the sense that community organizer Saul Alinsky used that word. "When one side gets the power and the other side gets reconciled to it," he said, "then we have reconciliation."[57]

As these cases illustrate, there is a distinct possibility that environmental mediation can be used to give the appearance of significant public participation, while the essential decision-making power remains in the hands of the government.[58] In this way, mediation is no different from many of the other forms of so-called citizen participation, such as public hearings and citizen advisory panels. These techniques are often intended to be coopting—to allow citizens some symbolic participation, but to grant them no real power in the policymaking process. Mediation may simply be a new form of this very old government ploy.

CAN MEDIATORS BALANCE OUT
POWER INEQUITIES?

Can anything be done to reduce the insidious effects that imbalances of power can have on mediation and negotiation efforts? We saw earlier that it is at least theoretically possible for well-intentioned mediators to help remedy the problem of equal access. Is it also possible for mediators to help reduce the inequities in power that exist at the bargaining table? One possibility is for mediators to try to intervene in the negotiations to create more of a balance of power between the parties. One student of labor mediation, James Wall, has argued that mediators can sometimes come to the aid of a weak negotiating party. "To strike a balance between the negotiators' power positions, the mediators [can] provide the necessary power underpinnings to the weaker negotiator—information, advice, friendship—or reduce those of the stronger."[59] In the specific context of environmental mediation, Lawrence Susskind, who is sensitive to this problem of power inequities, has argued that there are times when mediators may be able to increase the bargaining skills of a weak negotiator. "Mediators may have to build the basic negotiating capabilities of one or more of the parties to ensure more equal bargaining relationships."[60] Clearly, any such efforts on the part of mediators would be helpful in beginning to redress these imbalances of power. But at the same time, one should have no illussions that this approach can actually solve the problem of power inequities in mediation. First, it is not clear to what extent these ploys on the part of the mediator could make up for a basic lack of political and economic power on the part of one of the parties. Giving information or advice to one of the parties may help little if that party does not have the resources necessary to bargain from a position of strength or to pursue other options outside of mediation.

In addition, this solution presumes that mediators are interested in balancing the power of the participants. But most have no such interest. Indeed, although mediators are clearly aware of this problem, most argue that it is wrong to try to remedy it in any way. For example, Susan Carpenter and John Kennedy have argued that despite these imbalances it is not the mediator's role to "encourage parties to strengthen their position outside of the bargaining table."[61] Howard Bellman has also made similar arguments, saying "I would not even try to improve the quality of a party's resources. For instance, I would never get a party a lawyer or an engineer simply in order to make them more powerful in the negotiation."[62] All of these mediators go on to say that they would make sure that a weak party was aware of its inferior position in the negotiations, but that their efforts would stop there. They seem aware that this is an apparently insensitive position to take, but as Bellman explains: "Mediators are not protectors, even when the issues are drastic or when people are suffering. Instead, the mediator allows the parties to protect themselves with their own resources. Mediators cannot protect one side because the party appears to be losing more than it deserves. That is a noble role to play, but it is a different role to play than a mediator's role."[63]

The key to understanding this position lies in understanding what it means for a mediator to be a professional. Interfering in any way between the power relationships of the negotiating parties is considered unprofessional. The professional mediator is one who remains scrupulously neutral. And any effort to remedy power inbalances would compromise this neutrality. This is the point made by Thomas Colosi, vice-president for national affairs for the American Arbitration Association. While he acknowledges that there is a "temptation to use the mediators 'neutral' position to attempt to change the power relationship," he argues that any mediators who do so risk being perceived as biased—and thus would undermine their legitimacy and that of the mediation process itself.[64] The assumption is that any mediator who helps empower a weaker party is actually taking their side in the controversy, furthering their cause. Such a biased mediator would eventually have trouble getting jobs. "The practice of empowering the underdog . . . may be successful a time or two, but it won't be very long before the [more powerful party] refuses to be involved with that particular mediator."[65] In other words, if mediators care about their careers, the should not get involved in trying to mitigate power inequities.

THE QUESTION OF POLITICAL CULPABILITY

The mediators' refusal to deal with imbalances of power is understandable from their point of view—this position serves to protect the neutrality of the process and is in their professional self-interest. But it also conveniently serves to absolve them of political culpability. They can feel that they are not responsible for any imbalances of power or the unfair effects these inequities might have on any final agreement. And indeed, there is some justification for this position. Why should mediators be held responsible for power imbalances they did not create? Is not their first obligation to keep the mediation process strictly neutral? The assumption, of course, is that it is possible for the mediation process to remain politically neutral, despite any inequities that may exist between the parties. Just as a finely made mirror neutrally reflects what is presented to it by the outside world, it is thought that mediation only reflects the imbalances of power that already exist in society itself. If we do not hold a mirror responsible for what we look like, why should we hold mediation responsible for what it reflects? In this sense, we could conclude that imbalances of power are not a *mediation* problem at all—but simply a fact of political life.

But one could approach this question of culpability in quite another way. One could argue that when mediators ignore substantial power imbalances they are not being politically neutral. For the unintentional effect of this neutrality may be to institutionalize and perpetuate the maldistribution of power that already exists. Environmental mediation may actually work to legitimize these imbalances of power by conferring an air of fairness to inequitable or cooptive agreements. To use another analogy, it is as if the mediator were a referee who comes upon some people playing an informal game of soccer. It is a curious game: the field is slanted in favor of one team and that team also has more and bigger players. The referee volunteers to oversee the game. But if the referee accepts the game as it is and merely attempts to ensure that the players act in a fair and sportsmanlike manner, the game still remains a biased one. And although the referee may congratulate himself on his impartiality in enforcing rules of fair play, he is inadvertently institutionalizing an inequitable game and confers upon it a sense of legality and legitimacy that it did not possess before.

Thus, mediators who act in a seemingly neutral way toward imbalances of power may in fact be acting in a politically biased fashion, in that they end up legitimizing biased and unfair agreements. In this way, they are inadvertently contributing to the reproduction of the inequalities that exist in society. If this is true, then mediators who participate in mediation efforts where one party has substantial power advantages over the others, can and should be held politically culpable for any unfair results. To be sure, they cannot be held responsible for the existence of substantial imbalances of political and economic power in American society, but they should be held responsible for perpetuating or legitimizing them.

It seems, then, that mediators are caught in a Catch-22. When confronted with a mediation effort in which there are substantial inequalities in power, they seem to face two equally unattractive options. They can either accept the situation as is and risk legitimizing an unfair agreement, or they can attempt to help balance out the power relations, and risk undermining their own neutrality and career. It seems as if we have a no-win situation. But there is one other option—to refuse to serve as a mediator in such situations. When the power relations are so unbalance that the chances are high that one party will take advantage of another, the only ethical choice for the mediator may be to not participate in such an enterprise. Of course this is easier said than done. It is often difficult to tell ahead of time the degree to which the power relationships between two parties are imbalanced. And most mediators would be understandably reluctant to give up an opportunity to mediate—especially with the demand for mediators being so low at the moment. But nevertheless, mediators who are interested in preserving the political integrity of their profession must be prepared to sometimes choose not to become involved in unfair bargaining situations. This approach will not actually solve the problem of power imbalances, but at least it will not contribute to it.

CONCLUSION

Proponents of mediation are often quick to point out that there are substantial power imbalances in traditional policymaking forums like the legislature and the courts. They are less quick to realize that such imbalances are also a substantial problem in environmental mediation as well—a problem that often can undermine the legitimacy of the process. The existence of these kinds of political problems really should come as no surprise. Environmental mediation operates within the context of the American political system, where large and often unjustifiable power inequities exist. Thus, as long as there are basic imbalances in economic and political power between pro and anti-environmental forces, these inequities will inevitably plague even new alternative political processes like environmental mediation. This is not to imply that such political problems as unequal access and unequal power can never be effectively addressed—but only that environmental mediation does not do so. Most mediators tend to ignore the problem of power, and even though there have been some suggestions for how the insidious effects of power inequities in environmental mediation might be mitigated, few of these promise to adequately address the problems.

It is important that potential participants in environmental mediation keep in mind that mediation can be no more fair than the larger political context in which it takes place. Participants can sometimes have the illusion that power relations are less important in informal negotiations—that just because they are sitting at the bargaining table with their opponents they have become equals. This, of course, is a serious political mistake. It not only obscures the inequitable power relations at work in the negotiations, but also may distract participants from activities that would help to rectify these power imbalances. In particular, environmentalists must be careful not to let the apparent egalitarianism of mediation distract them from the political organizing that would more effectively strengthen their influence in environmental matters. In the long run, the only viable solution to the problems caused by power inequities is the establishment of a more equal distribution of political and economic power between disputants in environmental controversies.

In the meantime, however, the only short-term safeguard against the problems of power in environmental mediation is a growing public awareness of their existence. In this sense, environmental mediation is a process that needs to be demystified. We need to begin to see through the misleading aura of equality and fairness that accompanies these mediation efforts. This political halo surrounding mediation may only legitimize what are actually inequitable agreements. So it must be made clear that as long as substantial and illegitimate power inequities continue to characterize American politics, environmental mediation can be as politically problematic as any other approach to policymaking.

CHAPTER SIX

Distorting the Nature of Environmental Conflict

Our society has mechanisms only for resolving conflicting interests, not conflicting views of reality, so we seldom notice that those perceptions differ markedly.

Amory Lovins[1]

There is another significant political problem in environmental mediation, one much less obvious than the problem of power. This one is related to the way that mediators and mediation redefine the nature of environmental disputes. As we saw in chapter 2, much of the work of mediators involves getting the participants to see each other and their conflict in a new light. They try to alter the participants' perception of their situation in ways that will enhance its resolution. As Thomas Colosi of the American Arbitration Association explains it: "The mediator's job is to get negotiators to doubt perceptions that block agreement. Those perceptions might be a view of an issue, an understanding of the impact of a proposal, a problem definition, an assumption, or a value."[2] Thus, the job of the mediator involves much more than merely increasing communication between the disputants, or offering innovative solutions. Rather, much of their most important work involves getting the disputants to abandon their own understandings of the conflict and to accept a new set of assumptions offered by the mediator. In this sense, environmental mediation is not simply a way of resolving environmental conflicts, it is also a way of redefining the way we think about them.

Importantly, this process of redefining the nature of environmental conflicts is not necessarily a politically neutral one—it can have subtle, but powerful, political implications. In restructuring participants' perceptions of a conflict, mediators may give them a distorted understanding of what is at stake in an issue, or a mistaken idea of what constitutes a good solution. Thus, as we will see in this chapter, defining the nature of environmental disputes is a political act, and the way in which it is done can work to the disadvantage of some disputants.

Ironically, proponents of mediation are well aware of the tendency of other political institutions to redefine and distort the nature of environmental conflicts; but they are largely blind to this problem in their own profession. They take great pains, for example, to point out the ways in which the court system encourages a misleading view of environmental disputes. Litigation, they charge, requires us to see all environmental conflicts as adversarial contests—win-lose contests—when in fact some are basically nonadversarial in nature. Mediators often accuse lawyers and the court system of forcing environmental conflicts into a certain category of conflicts even when they do not fit. There is obviously some truth to this charge. The court system, like all political processes, tends to reframe conflicts in a way that makes them easier to deal with by that institution. And lawyers have a clear self-interest in portraying disputes in adversarial terms. But what proponents of mediation fail to appreciate is that mediators too have an occupational self-interest in promoting a certain limited definition of conflicts. Mediators tend to redefine environmental conflicts so that their services are deemed appropriate. The problem, of course, is that while these redefinitions may be in the interests of mediators and mediation, they sometimes may not be in the interests of the participants.

It is important, then, to examine carefully the ways in which environmental mediation structures and colors our understanding of environmental conflict, and to consider how these understandings can be distorted and misleading. To do this, we will contrast several models of environmental conflict. The first two models are found in environmental mediation, while the third is radically different. Each of the models contains a particular view of what causes environmental disputes, what the best strategies are for resolving them, and what constitutes the most appropriate kind of solution. By comparing these models of environmental conflict, we will be able to better identify the political assumptions and biases contained in the mediation perspective on conflict, and also better understand the actual political impacts that these assumptions can have on environmental decisions.

THE MISUNDERSTANDING MODEL

One view of environmental conflict that is promoted by mediation is what will be called the Misunderstanding Model. This model assumes that environmental disputes are largely caused by misunderstandings and miscommunications, rather than by basic conflicts of interests, and that therefore many of these conflicts are unnecessary. Most of the elements of this view were discussed in chapter 2. To briefly recapitulate, it is argued that environmental conflicts are often rooted in a number of factors, including psychological problems, personality conflicts, miscommunication, and misinformation. Not every mediator gives great weight to these factors, but clearly some believe that they play the central role in many controversies. As one prominent mediator put it: "At least half of the conflicts we see occur because people did not have access to accurate information, or had no mechanism for talking with the other side. These 'unnecessary' conflicts could have been avoided if people had had some mechanism for talking candidly with each other."[3]

In this Misunderstanding Model it is assumed that environmental controversies are best characterized not as conflicts to be resolved, but as "problems" to be solved. And indeed, this model assumes that mediation primarily serves as a problem-solving mechanism. The presumption is that these problems almost always can be solved given enough communication and enough sharing of information. As one scholar, Kai Lee of the University of Washington, has concluded, "the problem-solving approach often portrays conflict as unnecessary," because "given expertise and participation, all conflicts are misunderstandings."[4] It is assumed that once we can see beyond these misunderstandings, we will see that there are few real or basic conflicts of interests between environmentalists and businessmen. While these two groups may have *different* interests, they are not incompatible. Indeed, it is assumed in this model that there is a consensus in society on the need for both economic development and a sound environment. And it is this assumption of the basic compatibility of developmental and environmental interests that makes possible the whole notion of a nonadversarial, win-win approach to environmental controversies.

The Model's Appeal
Obviously, stated in this extreme form, many of the political assumptions in this model strain credulity—even for some mediators. For instance, anyone who has experience in environmental politics is unlikely to agree that most environmental disputes do not involve basic conflicts of interest. But despite the fact that the assumptions in this model seem somewhat implausible, it is easy to understand why this view of environmental conflict is promoted by some advocates of mediation: it is the view of environmental disputes that best encourages the use of mediation. Thus, it may not be an accurate view, but it does serve the occupational self-interest of mediators. For if one assumes that many environmental conflicts are really a matter of miscommunication and misunderstanding, then mediation becomes the logical and preferred method for resolving them. There is an inherent link between a nonconflictual understanding of environmental controversies and the viability of mediation as a political institution. The more par-

ticipants come to believe that environmental controversies are merely problems and not disputes—the more environmental mediation will prosper. This link was explicitly acknowledged by one champion of environmental mediation when he suggested that the future of mediation was directly dependent on the emergence of a new perspective on our environmental conflicts. He suggested that the demand for mediators will increase only if the various sides in environmental controversies move away from seeing these conflicts in terms of " 'the environmental position' and 'the business position' and concentrate on underlying [common] interests."[5] Clearly, then, whether this model of environmental conflict is accurate or not, it can be seen as vital to promoting the acceptance and use of this new approach to environmental controversies.

But the existence of this view of environmental conflict cannot be entirely explained by the self-serving interests of mediators. This view persists also because it corresponds to positions being espoused by some significant actors in environmental politics. Indeed, much of what makes this Misunderstanding Model politically interesting is not its link with environmental mediation, but the fact that some of its assumptions have now become common themes in environmental politics. For instance, a number of business leaders, government officials, and environmental leaders have now begun to argue that the conflicts of interest between developers and environmentalists have been greatly exaggerated. Some in the business community have argued that there is no longer any fundamental incompatibility between the interests of business and those of environmentalists. It has been suggested that business leaders now realize that environmental safeguards are important. And this is thought to be especially true of that "new generation of corporate executives educated in corporate responsibility." This has led one leading business scholar to declare that the basic conflict between corporations and environmental groups over the need for environmental protection is a thing of the past. "In recent years, there has been a conspicuous 'reaching out' to one another by the environmental and business communities. The debate between the two groups no longer centers on whether the environment should be protected but rather on how best to do so most efficiently."[6]

This theme of common concerns between environmentalists and business has also been echoed by representatives of some of the less adversarial and more conservative environmental groups like the National Wildlife Federation and the Conservation Foundation. Spokespersons for such organizations have sharply criticized "those who doggedly attempt to portray environmental and economic interests as in fundamental conflict."[7] Instead, they have sought to emphasize the "common ground" that exists between environmental and business concerns. They consider the assumption of a fundamental conflict between business and environmental interests to be a relic of the 1970s—an outdated attitude unsuited for the 1980s. As William Reilly of the Conservation Foundation has argued, these adversarial assumptions may have been necessary in the 60s and 70s, but now that the necessary environmental legislation has been passed, and there is a national consensus on the importance of environmental values, it is time to adopt a more conciliatory and cooperative attitude toward the business community.[8] It is sometimes also suggested that many current environmental controversies are caused by environmentalists who refuse to change their old adversarial tactics and who have "a tendency to be rigid, unwilling to compromise or negotiate," and who "think the arguments made by industry are totally self-serving and exaggerated."[9] The call is for participants in these controversies to not see each other as enemies, but as "sincere and well meaning people who love their country and want only the best for it."[10] And of course mediation is often cited as an approach which exemplifies this new attitude of trust and cooperation.

Some important federal officials in the area of environmental policy have also endorsed the notion that there is no fundamental incompatibility between the interests of developers and environmentalists. This was one of the major themes of one of the first speeches given by former Secretary of the Interior William Clark. Speaking to the National Wildlife Federation in late 1983, he suggested that it was time to move beyond the "us guys, you guys" confrontations that characterized the stormy administration of Secretary Watt. Instead, he argued, we must recognize that the ultimate aims of developers, government, and environmentalists are basically the same.

Some Questionable Assumptions
The fact that many of the assumptions of this Misunderstanding Model of environmental conflict are being reiterated by leading figures in environmental politics makes the critical examination of these assumptions all the more important. It takes little analysis, however, to see that many of the central assumptions of this model are weak and questionable, and that they can give disputants a distorted understanding of the nature of environmental controversies. Consider, for example, the assertion that a basic consensus now exists among government, business, and environmental groups on the importance of environmental values. It is true, of course, that most people now pay homage to environmental values; but this commitment to environmental values usually is made at such an abstract level as to be almost meaningless. If one states values in an abstract enough way, no one will disagree with them. Everyone is committed to such abstractions as "peace," "prosperity," "freedom," and "family"—and of course "a clean environment." But as soon as one descends to the level of specific environmental goals and specific policy proposals, this encouraging consensus quickly weakens and falls apart. This lack of consensus has been made strikingly clear by the record of the Reagan administration and its effort to prevent the passage of stricter environmental regulations—such as those dealing with acid rain—and its attempts to slow down or frustrate the implementation of policies already in place—such as those concerning hazardous wastes. One could argue that there was an emerging consensus between government and environmentalists during the Carter administration, but the Reagan counterattack on environmental programs has relegated that notion of consensus to the realm of illusion.

Moving from the public to the private sectors, it is also far from clear that the corporate community now readily accepts the need for strong environmental controls. This would hardly seem to be the case given the way that many corporate and industry leaders eagerly joined hands with the Reagan administration in efforts to weaken controls over many areas of the environment. Nevertheless, a theory still persists among some environmental observers that we are experiencing a "greening of middle management." This theory postulates that in the 1980s many young middle managers in business and industry are closet conservationists, with a strong commitment to the environment. Whether or not this is true is of course very difficult to say. But even those who claim to see such a trend are careful to point out that it is hardly universal. As one leading environmental lawyer argued, while "a larger proportion of the middle management of major corporations does accept the notion of government control of pollution and the private obligation to limit pollution, it is by no means an effective consensus. There are so many individual industrial concerns that do not accept these notions."[11] More importantly, it is necessary to separate out the values that these Yuppies may hold privately, and those they act on while at work. Corporate managers may like to go hiking or cross-country skiing on weekends, but during the workweek their priorities must inevitably lie with promoting the prosperity and profits of their firms, even when these things conflict with environmental values.

But while the notion of a widespread consensus on environmental values is clearly exaggerated, this is not the weakest assumption imbedded in the Misunderstanding Model. That honor must go to the presumption that most environmental disputes are simply a product of misunderstandings or scientific disagreements and do not involve some direct and unavoidable conflicts of interest between environmentalists and developers. Clearly this effort to depoliticize environmental conflict strains credulity. It seems evident, for example, that most pollution disputes involve direct conflicts between the economic self-interest of the polluters and the environmental interests of the public. Likewise, other issues ranging from development of wilderness areas, to acid rain, to endangered species, to resource exploitation typically involve fundamental value and interest conflicts between developers and environmentalists. Indeed, it is difficult to imagine why there are such prolonged and bitter fights around these issues if they simply involved misunderstandings. These disputes become intractable precisely because they are zero-sum games with no easy solutions. Misunderstandings, miscommunications, personalities, and data uncertainties play a role in exacerbating these conflicts, but it is a mistake to assume that such things are a primary cause of most environmental disputes. Thus while the depoliticized view of environmental conflicts offered by the Misunderstanding Model may be appealing and comforting to some, it clearly flies in the face of political reality.

Political Ramifications
It is relatively easy to call into question the central assumptions of the Misunderstanding Model. These intellectual deficiencies, however, are not the greatest problem with this model. The more significant problem is the political ramifications of these assumptions—especially on unwary environmentalists. Take, for example, the claim of basic common interests between developers and environmentalists. Such claims can be used as a means of political manipulation. As Professor Jane Mansbridge has observed: "The claim that people have common interests can be a way of misleading the less powerful into collaborating with the more powerful in schemes that mainly benefit the latter."[12] It is not difficult to imagine such results in an environmental conflict. If environmentalists are led to believe that there are no basic interest conflicts, that everyone shares a commitment to environmental values, this could lead to a false sense of security. They may tend to trust their adversaries when in fact it is inappropriate, and they may be led into agreements that are disadvantageous to them.

Moreover, even when the assumptions of the Misunderstanding Model do not result in bad agreements, the mere fact that they encourage the use of mediation over other approaches may be a significant political problem in itself. Thinking that they merely have a misunderstanding, participants may opt for mediation instead of more adversarial approaches like litigation or community organizing. In this way, this model could distract disputants from more appropriate and effective political responses to an environmental problem. Advocates of mediation, of course, do not see this as a problem. Their view is: "No harm is done by trying mediation first. Try it, and if it does not work, if it turns out that the conflicts are too basic to resolve amicably, you can always turn to more adversarial approaches later." But there is a crucial fallacy with this argument—it neglects the harm involved in delay. When environmentalists get involved in mediation mistakenly believing that all they have is a misunderstanding, valuable time can be lost and valuable organization resources may be wasted. Serious negotiations could take months or even years—especially if one side is intentionally stalling—time during which more fruitful adversarial routes could have been pursued. The point here is similar to the one made by physicians who warn patients against quack cancer cures. Their warning is twofold. First, they warn that quack cures may be harmful to the patients health. But they also point out that even when these cures are not directly harmful, they nevertheless serve to distract patients from consulting with legitimate doctors who may be able to help them. Thus, to apply this analogy to environmental politics, mediation may sometimes function as a laetrile-like approach to environmental problems— a quack political cure that distracts environmental disputants from genuinely effective approaches to their problems.

THE CONFLICTING INTERESTS MODEL

To be fair, a large number of mediators do not hold to the basic assumptions of the Misunderstanding Model. As we saw in chapter 2, some are quite skeptical about this hot-tub perspective on negotiation and do not agree that the problems between environmentalists and industry derive mostly from misunderstandings. Many mediators are much more realistic and would freely acknowledge that fundamental conflicts of interests usually lie at the heart of many environmental disputes. Even Fisher and Ury of the Harvard Negotiation Project, chief practitioners of the effort to redefine disputes as almost anything else other than interest conflicts, will admit that in the end one cannot deny the existence and importance of these kinds of conflicts.

However well you understand the interests of the other side, however ingeniously you invent ways of reconciling interests, however highly you value an ongoing relationship, you will almost always face the harsh reality of interests that conflict. No talk of "win-win" strategies can conceal that fact. You want the rent to be lower; the landlord wants it to be higher. You want the goods delivered tomorrow; the supplier would rather deliver them next week. You definitely prefer the large office with the view, so does your partner. Such differences cannot be swept under the rug.[13]

Similar sentiments are also expressed by some directly involved in environmental mediation. Gerald Cormick, for example, has little patience for advocates of mediation who deny the existence of basic conflicts of interest, and who claim that mediation can eliminate the basic causes of disputes. "Those who would view mediation as a means by which society can forge a new consensus, making future conflicts unnecessary, are doomed to failure. Mediation is best seen as a process for *settling* disputes, not for *resolving* them."[14]

This perspective of environmental conflict forms the basis for a second model of environmental disputes—which will be called the Conflicting Interests Model. It is essentially a pluralist theory of environmental politics—one which assumes that interest conflicts in this area are natural and inevitable. It also presumes that often the best solutions to these kinds of conflicts are ones that split the difference between these equally valid interests—compromises in which each side gets some of what it wants. For many mediators, this model represents a much more realistic understanding of environmental conflict, and it is probably the most common professional perspective on controversy. And undoubtedly many environmentalists and industry executives would also see this model as being much more accurate than the previous one. It is a step away from the wishful thinking of the Misunderstanding Model, and an explicit acknowledgement of the inherently conflictual nature of environmental politics.

But while the Conflicting Interests Model does seem to be an improvement over the first model, it is important to see that this new model has its problems as well, that it is not neutral, that it also contains certain political biases. Like the previous model, it only tells part of the story about environmental conflicts, and it also has the potential to distort the participants' understanding of these conflicts. In order to see these potential distortions and to appreciate their political ramifications, it is necessary to examine in more detail the assumptions contained in this model.

Interests versus Values: The Basic Principles Model
The problematic political assumptions of the Conflicting Interests Model are most easily perceived when it is compared to a third perspective on environmental disputes, one that is not common in environmental mediation. Instead of seeing most environmental controversies as involving conflicting interests, one could see them as involving conflicts between basic values and principles. We will call this perspective the Basic Principles Model. The assumption in this model is that environmental disputes are rooted in the clashing principles and values of the disputants (see table 2). The principles may take various forms in different controversies—some may involve basic moral principles, others basic legal rights, and still others might involve what could be called "world views." It is clear that many participants in environmental controversies—especially environmentalists—tend to see the issues in this way. Indeed, many environmentalists become involved in these issues because of a strong commitment to a certain set of environmental, philosophical, and ethical principles. Often the specific policy concerns of environmentalists are rooted in a larger vision of how society and humanity should relate to nature. Some fear that industrial society is based on a commitment to dominate nature and a need to exploit it in ever increasing ways. They offer instead a vision of society that lives in harmony with nature, understanding and respecting its limits.[15] This kind of perspective

can strongly affect the way specific environmental issues are viewed. Consider, for example, a typical environmental controversy involving a proposal to dam a wild, white-water river in order to create a recreation area and an irrigation system. For some environmentalists, the issue involves much more than simply the interests of the individuals who would be hurt or helped by that particular dam. For them, a principle is at stake—in this case the importance of preserving wilderness areas. Does our society have a commitment to preserve our last sections of untouched nature—or should all areas be fair game for development? Does wilderness have a value of its own, or should human use always take precedence? In this view of conflict, the dam itself is not the only issue, what is at stake are the principles involved, and the kind of societal values they imply. One need not rely on hypothetical examples to see this point. In the 1970s, an interdisciplinary team of scholars spent several years studying the ongoing controversy over the proposal to build the Tocks Island Dam. In the end, they came to the conclusion that at the heart of the dispute over the dam was a series of clashing principles and values. They found that this dispute did not simply involve competing self-interests, but "a choice among alternative conceptions of the region's future, and at a deeper but still articulated level, among alternative conceptions of man's appropriate relationship with nature."[16] They concluded that one of the main reasons that the dispute was so hard-fought and prolonged was that it was essentially principled in nature—a notion that was eventually reflected in the title of their study *When Values Conflict*.

In any case, there is a real difference between seeing environmental disputes as conflicts of interest or as conflicts of principle. And it is clear that many environmentalists tend to see them as the latter. This is especially true of the more activist organizations, such as Greenpeace, Earth First! and Friends of the Earth, who tend to see themselves not so much as another interest group, but as part of a movement which is dedicated to creating an environmentally sane society. They do not see themselves as promoting simply their own self-interest—they may not even have the opportunity to personally enjoy the white-water river or park they are seeking to protect—rather it is the larger principles that are at stake. Thus, for these groups, their involvement in environmental politics is not a form of interest group activity at all, but more like a campaign or crusade to get certain basic ethical and ecological principles embodied in law.

Promoting Moral Relativism

In environmental mediation, however, there is a strong tendency to see disputes primarily as conflicts of interest, and the promotion of this perspective has a number of important political implications. For example, it can affect the way mediators and participants approach the moral and ethical dimensions of environmental issues. As a rule, mediators explicitly downplay the role of moral principles in environmental conflicts. They argue that conflicts are usually not a matter of one party being right and the other wrong, but a matter of competing interests. Indeed, they typically portray both sides as right and argue that both sides are pursuing equally valid interests. This amoral view of conflict is one of the central assumptions underlying environmental mediation and it is articulated even by the most politically sophisticated mediators. Gerald Cormick, for example, has argued that "there will be legitimate differences in priorities among persons with varying perspectives and divergent aspirations. These differences cannot be dealt in terms of 'right' and 'wrong'—all are 'right' or legitimate concerns."[17] Bacow and Wheeler make a similar point at the end of their book on environmental mediation. They stress that one of the main problems with the judicial process is that it gives the illusion that there is a "right answer" to these problems. The advantage of mediation, they argue, is that it cuts through this illusion. "The pulling and hauling that is the essence of bargaining," they say, "forces the parties to recognize that there are no right answers—only compromises worked out on intermediate positions. Instead of creating the illusion of truth, bargaining embraces the accommodation of competing interests. Moreover, the process of compromise forces each side to acknowledge the legitimacy of claims of the opposition."[18]

TABLE 2

Models of Environmental Conflict

	Sources of Environmental Conflict	View of Compromise	Appropriate Political Forum	Explanation of Emergence of Mediation
Misunderstanding Model	Since all share concern for the environment, conflicts are largely products of misunderstandings, miscommunications, personality conflicts, etc.	Since few basic interests are in conflict, compromise is unnecessary. Negotiation should reveal common interests and win-win solutions.	Mediation—because it increases communication and mutual understanding.	Industry and environmentalists now increasingly recognize their common interests and the importance of ongoing dialogue and co-operation.
Conflicting Interests Model	Conflicts are caused by inevitable conflicting interests of industry, environmentalists, and government.	Compromise is almost always necessary. The most realistic and just resolution is one in which each party gets some of what it wants.	Mediation—because the give and take of negotiation best facilitates compromise.	There is now a balance of power between industry and environmentals that creates stalemates and thus necessitates negotiation and compromise.
Basic Principles Model	Conflicts are fundamental and rooted in basic differences in values, principles, societal structures, worldviews, etc.	Compromise is usually unacceptable. Since environmental decisions involve choices between incompatible principles and societal structures, compromise is equivalent to capitulation.	Legislatures, bureaucracies, and courts—because these traditional institutions are better designed to address questions of basic principle.	Mediation is being promoted by some parts of industry and government as a new way to co-opt environmentalists and undermine their political power.

Again, one can easily appreciate why mediators would promote this extreme form of moral relativism. It is very useful professionally. First, it aids in their efforts to appear neutral. By avoiding moral terms, they also avoid appearing to favor any one side. More importantly, however, this view of conflict is essential in promoting the success of mediation itself. If mediation is to succeed, the disputants often must compromise their initial positions and meet somewhere in the middle. Promoting an amoral view of the dispute is an important part in laying the conceptual groundwork necessary to encourage and legitimate compromise. If disputes are seen in moral terms, where one party is right and the other is wrong, the attractiveness of compromise is minimized. Who wants to compromise with someone who is wrong? Such a compromise would probably be seen as immoral in itself. However, if one views environmental conflicts as clashes of different but equally valid interests, then compromise becomes a much more acceptable solution to the problem. From this perspective, splitting the difference becomes a fair and just solution to the conflict—each equally worthy party gets part of its valid demands met. In essence, then, the assumption of moral relativism contained in the Conflicting Interests Model helps to grease the wheels of compromise.

But while this amoral view of conflict is professionally useful for mediators, it is certainly questionable on other grounds. First, in denying that there are any serious moral issues involved in environmental disputes, it promotes a kind of moral irresponsibility. In American politics we all too often put interests ahead of ethics, and the amoral approach to issues promoted by mediators would only seem to worsen this problematic tendency in our political culture. Moreover, it goes against common sense to maintain that there is no right or wrong in political struggles. Indeed, it often seems that right and wrong, and such ethical principles as justice, equality, and freedom, are exactly what most serious political disputes are all about. Emily Yoffee makes a somewhat similar point in her critique of the use of mediation in international relations. She is critical of an approach that automatically assumes that the demands of every government and political group are equally honorable and just.[19] For her, this view only obscures the fact that some countries' policies and positions are morally wrong. And she chastizes mediators for failing to recognize this basic fact of political life. "In a world run by conciliators, methodology takes precedence over morality. . . . Central to the thinking of mediators is that everyone has the right to come away happy. To believe this is to suspend judgment of right and wrong."[20] Ultimately, Yoffee believes that it is naive and dangerous to deny that right and wrong exist in international politics—a point that applies equally well to environmental politics.

Obviously, any political process that turns a blind eye to moral questions runs an increased risk of producing decisions that are morally wrong—a drawback that must be taken very seriously. But this is not the only political ramification of this amoral approach to conflict. This approach may also have the effect of undermining some parties' political strength. For example, this view of conflict makes it difficult for environmentalists to occupy the moral high ground in a dispute. The moral high ground is often an important political resource for environmental groups— especially if they lack other traditional sources of political and economic power. It gives them a kind of moral power. But as soon as one accepts the Conflicting Interests Model of conflict, the whole notion of the moral high ground disappears altogether. Moral arguments become irrelevant. If environmentalists try to argue in a pollution dispute that the public has been wronged and deserves vindication, such arguments would most likely be dismissed by the mediator as adversarial, obstructionist, and inappropriate.[21] If effect, the moral relativism contained in this model works to morally disarm environmentalists. The fact that they may be right is of no political advantage to them at all in this process.

Indeed, the concept of a wronged party makes little sense within the Conflicting Interests Model. In this perspective, if any party is to blame, it is both sides equally. Each side is seen as responsible for perpetuating a damaging conflict because of their stubborn refusal to give in. Again moral judgment is suspended and it is assumed that both sides are equally at fault in the conflict.

The potential political biases promoted by this view become more evident when we apply it to another kind of political dispute—the conflict over apartheid in South Africa. Clearly the blacks in South Africa are a wronged party, subject to a particularly virulent and persistent form of racial discrimination and oppression. And yet when riots break out and lives are lost, we have seen some American politicians implying that both sides are to blame for the trouble, that the police were provoked, and so on. Clearly, this perspective on the racial conflicts in South Africa—that both sides are to blame—is not only inaccurate, but it also serves to undermine politically the cause of blacks fighting for the end to apartheid. The same point can be made about moral relativism and environmental conflicts. When the notions of morality and ethics become irrelevant, when there are no wronged parties, this works to the political disadvantage of environmentalists.

A Preference for Compromise

The tendency to promote an amoral view of conflict is not the only potential fault in the Conflicting Interests Model, there is also the problematic assumption that compromise is the most appropriate solution to most conflicts. This presumption for compromise at first seems to be eminently reasonable, especially given the assumptions of this model. If it is true that conflicts take place between two equally valid interests, the appropriate resolution is to allow each side to get some of what it wants—a compromise. Again, the vision of politics espoused in this model is a pluralistic and materialistic one—politics involves the competition between various groups over the distribution of resources and goods in society. Thus, environmental politics is assumed to be not so much about establishing correct principles as about bargaining over who gets how much of what. In this view, splitting the difference between the demands of the competing interest groups becomes the logical and desirable solution to most policy problems. And many advocates of environmental mediation see this predisposition toward compromise as one of mediation's greatest political assets. They believe that the best political path is usually a moderate one that lies somewhere between the extreme and polarized positions of the disputants. For example, one Wisconsin legislator praised the new efforts there to organize negotiations between interests groups and legislators as being politically desirable because the process "results in compromising whereupon radical positions are abandoned."[22]

But for other observers, this predisposition toward compromise is a serious political drawback. For instance, some political observers in Wisconsin have complained that the informal negotiation process instituted by the legislature encourages premature and inappropriate legislative compromises on important issues. The following comments about the process made by several legislators and lobbyists were typical:

> It promotes compromise when it is not in the public's best interest.
>
> Compromises are made when the votes might be there to pass stronger legislation.
>
> It may force compromise which could have a long term and devastating effect on resources, environment, economic or social welfare.
>
> The compromise, too often arrived at, is a watered-down version of a proposed policy which has the appearance of a solution without the substance and usually lacks the features needed to accomplish the objective for which the law or regulation is written.[23]

Clearly, then, not everyone is happy about this tendency to promote compromise. And this dissatisfaction is found not only among observers of the Wisconsin process, but among those in environmental groups around the country as well. It is often part of what makes them suspicious of environmental mediation. As David Brower of Friends of Earth has argued, if environmentalists enter into a dispute assuming that mediation and compromise are the way to go, this can ultimately work to their disadvantage: "It's important for environmentalists to be out near the edge in a conflict. If we begin as mediators, then the final decision ends up somewhere between the mediated position and the negative position."[24] These criticisms are easy to understand, especially if one views environmental conflicts as principled. If, for example, one believes that there are right and wrong positions in many environmental disputes—which is certainly not an uncommon nor an unreasonable assumption—then compromise between the two positions is hardly the most desirable outcome. Thus, on a theoretical level, there seems to be an inherent contradiction between seeing disputes as principled and seeing compromise as the preferred outcome. But in order to see more accurately why compromise is so problematic for many environmentalists, it is necessary to examine more carefully what compromise actually looks like in many environmental disputes.

Promoting ''Responsible Development''

What does compromise usually consist of in environmental conflicts? What does it mean, for example, for developers and environmentalists to split the difference between their positions? In practice, the result is often something called "responsible development"—a term used by Scott Mernitz in one of the first books on environmental mediation.[25] In responsible development, both sides get some of what they want. The developers get to go ahead with their project, but they agree to certain safeguards to protect the environment. For instance, in one controversy over a proposed shopping mall, the mediated solution allowed the mall to be built, but with concessions on the part of the developer involving such things as limiting the height of the buildings, putting in landscaping, treating their own sewage, etc.[26] For advocates of mediation, this kind of outcome is the hoped-for consequence. Indeed, Mernitz has argued that this is one of its main goals—that mediation is designed "to encourage responsible, planned, and progressive development."[27]

It is important to see, however, that for some environmentalists the practice of responsible development is not something neutral and desirable, but something that implicitly favors developers. This is especially true if the position of the environmentalists is one that opposes a certain kind of development in principle. Often environmentalists flatly oppose the building of a dam or a hazardous waste dump, and could care less whether the developer is willing to make some environmental concessions. Or to use another example, most environmentalists would strongly oppose drilling for oil on national park land, even if the oil company agreed to compromise and do the drilling in the most environmentally responsible way possible. In many of these cases, the basic issue for the environmentalists is one of development versus nondevelopment, and so an agreement that allows the development project to go ahead is not a real compromise at all—but a victory for their opponents.

Interestingly, some promoters of mediation are willing to admit that in as much as the process does promote responsible development it is not really politically neutral. Mernitz, for example, has acknowledged that "future mediated settlements will tend to favor developmental interests in the sense that some development will occur."[28] But this developmental bias poses little problem for Mernitz. This is because he assumes that development is a natural and desirable part of social and economic progress. And for him, the purpose of mediation is to promote progress—to ensure that development proceeds smoothly. In his words, "environmental mediation helps opposing parties to see the need for compromise as a means of furthering society's progress. Extensive delays, although sometimes valuable for selected interests, usually cause social, economic, emotional, and ecological traumas that are undesirable."[29]

Many environmentalists, of course, would question Mernitz's automatic equation of continuous development with the good life. Some maintain that the pursuit of the good life now requires limits to development. They argue that continuous economic growth, even in its so-called responsible forms, will only continue to drain valuable nonrenewable resources, create increasing levels of pollutants, and eventually stress our ecosystem to the breaking point. This is the argument made by Williams Ophuls in his much read book, *Ecology and the Politics of Scarcity*.[30] He argues that our increasing ecological and energy problems are merely symptoms of more basic flaws in our societal values and economic structures. And he concludes that the fundamental issue at stake in environmental politics is a choice between two incompatible sets of values and institutions. On the one side is our current advanced industrial society with its emphasis on domination of nature and increasing exploitation of its resources; and on the other, a more modest steady-state society with an economy designed to stay within our ecological limits. Thus, in Ophuls, one finds the notion of conflicting principles in its most extreme form: one not only finds disagreement over a single principle, but disagreement over world views.[31]

This view of environmental issues is also shared by some activists on the left of the environmental movement—such as the grassroots antinuclear movement in the United States and the Greens in West Germany. They believe it is a mistake merely to try to modify or regulate continuous economic development and resource exploitation, that what is needed is an a radical turn away from this destructive path.[32] Naturally, these activists tend to perceive Mernitz's notion of responsible development not as a compromise, but as a capitulation. And they may even prefer to lose a political battle outright, than to agree to a compromise that would violate their basic principles and goals. This uncompromising approach to issues is not only a characteristic of radical environmentalists—but of radical political activists in general. Activists involved in the antislavery movement, the women's suffrage movement, and the civil rights movement also refused to compromise over what they saw as matters of basic principle and morality. As a rule, then, the more radical one's analysis—the more one traces a specific dispute to some basic value and structural issues in a society—the less desirable compromise is likely to be.

Naturally, not all environmental issues involve choices between basic sets of values or ways of life. And one does not have to see environmental issues in these radical terms in order to be suspicious of compromise over environmental issues. One simply has to acknowledge that in many environmental conflicts, there are important principles at stake. In some cases, the principle involved may be a legal one, such as protecting the right of due process in environmental decisions. In other cases, one may resist compromise because it is important to take a stand in favor of an ecological principle—such as wilderness preservation. As one environmental lawyer has explained, there are simply some issues where if one agrees to negotiate and compromise over them at the very beginning, one has already lost much of the battle. "My point is based on my involvement in certain environmental issues, that there are some cases where the chance to negotiate equals giving up what you're fighting for. There are some absolutes in the world and I think lawyers are just going to have to flat-out fight to preserve them. I disagree that there are always going to be negotiations. There *are* going to be some ultimate decisions, but it should be clearly recognized that there are times when you just can't negotiate, because some things in the world are non-negotiable."[33]

Distorting and Distracting
One of the main political biases in the Conflicting Interests Model is that it encourages participants to see all issues as negotiable and amenable to compromise—when in fact many significant environmental issues involve basic matters of principle. In this way, the assumptions of this model can distort the participants' understanding of the real nature of the issues at stake. Moreover, this perspective can also distract participants from using other, more appropriate political forums to address their problems. It can be argued that issues involving principles are best dealt with in more traditional political institutions like the courts, administrative agencies, and legislatures. After all, it is the purpose of these political institutions to establish and enforce certain societal norms and principles. But by obscuring the principled nature of environmental disputes, environmental mediation may divert participants from these institutions that may be more suited to their political struggle.

Owen Fiss, a professor law at Yale University, has made a similar point. He argues that the courts are usually the best place to resolve conflicts involving basic principles, that their purpose is to "give force to the values embodied in authoritative texts such as the Constitution and the statutes: to interpret those values and bring reality into accord with them."[34] In other words, the main purpose of court decisions is to apply societal principles to conflicts—to do justice as society defines it. But, he points out, this is exactly what advocates of alternative dispute resolution fail to understand. Seeing disputes as simply involving conflicting interests, they assume that the primary purpose of litigation and the courts is simply to create peace between feuding parties—which implies that mediation is a desirable substitute. But this is a mistake. Peace and justice are quite different things, and when one substitutes mediation for litigation one may only be promoting peace without justice.[35] Just because the feuding parties come to an agreement does not mean that justice is done, or that societal norms are upheld. In the courts there is a better chance that those societal principles will be protected and applied, and for this reason litigation is often preferable to informal dispute resolution techniques like mediation. A similar point was also made in a recent report by the National Institute for Dispute Resolution: "Courts are the appropriate forum when the purpose is to establish a societal norm or legal precedent. Thus, for example, if the underlying cause of a dispute is not a disagreement over how to apply an accepted norm but rather a need to create such a principle, then courts—or the legislature—are the appropriate forum."[36]

One could take this argument even further and maintain that even when the disagreement is over how to apply an accepted norm, traditional political institutions—especially administrative and regulatory agencies—may offer more appropriate approaches than mediation. Agencies such as the EPA are required to apply and enforce certain norms that are established by Congress— norms that mediators and negotiators are under no obligation to heed. For example, as we have seen, acting in the public interest is not a norm that must be applied to mediated agreements. In contrast, the EPA and many other regulatory agencies are mandated by Congress to produce decisions that explicitly promote and maximize the public interest.[37] They are required not simply to take into account the interests of the groups involved in a specific case, but to arrive at an independent judgment about what decision would further the public interest. Thus, regulatory processes are required to transcend the pluralist political perspective present in processes like mediation. More to the point, this approach implies that principles such as the public interest are much more likely to be taken seriously in these regulatory processes than in mediation, which has no such built-in requirements. Of course, in practice, regulators inevitably make decisions that violate this norm. Congressional mandates are not a guarantee that the public interest will always be promoted by regulatory decisions. Nevertheless, the point is that this norm *is* present and there is at least the assurance that some notion of the public interest will be taken into consideration as the basis for decisions, which is not the case in environmental mediation. Furthermore, groups that believe that specific regulatory decisions violate this mandate often have the right to take agencies to court to challenge their decisions on public interest grounds—another protection not necessarily available to those who feel injured by mediation agreements. In this sense, then, in environmental disputes where the public interest is of central importance—which would seem to include most of them—one could make the case that regulatory agencies may be a more appropriate forum than mediation.

Naturally, which political forum is appropriate for which dispute will vary depending on the specifics of each case and the aims of the disputants. But the argument here is that in promoting the Conflicting Interests Model of disputes, advocates of mediation may prevent parties from making an independent judgment about political forums and divert them from political alternatives, like the courts, that may be more appropriate for their situation. In this way, the main political problems of this model are very similar to those described in the discussion of the Misunderstanding Model. The Conflicting Interests Model, like the prior model, promotes a certain perspective on environmental disputes, and it is a perspective that is not always politically neutral. It can distort and distract—distort the disputants' understanding of the real nature of those conflicts, and distract them from other, more efficacious, political strategies.

THE MEDIATOR'S REBUTTAL

Many proponents of mediation scoff at allegations that the process distorts the nature of environmental conflict, or distracts participants from more appropriate approaches. They readily admit that some environmental conflicts involve nonnegotiable matters of principle, and that mediation would bring an inappropriate perspective to these issues—but they do not see that as a problem. They argue that no reputable mediator would try to mediate such basic disputes in the first place. Most mediators, it is suggested, would quickly identify which disputes are principled and which are not, and would simply avoid attempting to mediate the former. It would be a waste of time to try to mediate those disputes, they argue, because the disputants would be unlikely to compromise. Thus, Gerald Cormick has specifically advised mediators not to attempt to mediate controversies such as those involving nuclear power plants. Recognizing that many environmentalists are philosophically opposed to nuclear power per se, he points out that "there is no possible area of accommodation and no scope for good-faith negotiation and mediation."[38]

But this suggestion that the problem of distortion can be eliminated by mediators simply avoiding principled disputes may not be as simple and workable as proponents seem to think it is. It assumes, for instance, that one can easily differentiate principled disputes from less basic ones—but this is not always the case. The boundary lines separating different kinds of disputes are obscure, and there is often a large grey area between them. Disputes do not come prepackaged with labels identifying them as "Value Conflicts" or "Misunderstandings." Even the disputants may be unclear as to the exact nature of the controversy. In such uncertain cases, the mediator plays a key role in defining the nature of the conflict; and there is an understandable inclination to define conflicts in ways which make mediation appropriate. Mediators have an obvious self-interest in expanding the market for their services, and so, as one scholar has concluded, they "face incentives to apply their techniques inappropriately."[39] Thus, there is always the temptation for mediators to take on cases that involve matters of principle, and then attempt to convince participants to compromise.

An example of a mediator who has yielded to this temptation is Dr. Irving Goldaber of the Center for the Practice of Conflict Management. He sees no problem at all with trying to mediate disputes over nuclear power plants.[40] He holds seminars for utility company executives to teach them his "win-win" approach to nuclear plant controversies. In one such seminar, a simulated negotiation resulted in "utility executives" and "environmentalists" arriving at a mutually satisfactory agreement. The agreement stipulated that the two sides would (a) cosponsor a public hearing on general nuclear issues, (b) form a joint consumer advisory committee, and (c) allow a peaceful demonstration outside the secured area of the plant.[41] One participant reported that Goldaber, quite happy with the agreement, declared, "You see? There *is* a win-win solution, ladies and gentlemen, even in your situation, which at times seems so hopeless."[42] When asked if he really believed that people in the antinuclear movement would believe they had won if the plant remained under construction, Goldaber responded that "they made some concessions, of course; but look what they're getting away with."[43]

SELLING YOUR HEALTH

One might argue that this is a unique and extreme example of the misleading use of mediation. And most reputable mediators undoubtedly would not endorse this kind of effort. However, most mediators would probably endorse the use of mediation that is sanctioned by the Massachusetts Hazardous Waste Facility Siting Act. This law is an innovative attempt to require the developers of hazardous waste treatment facilities to negotiate with local residents and officials. However, in practice, it is another example of how mediation can be used inappropriately to try to portray as

190 DISTORTING ENVIRONMENTAL CONFLICT

negotiable, issues that are best understood as matters of principle. The central issue for most residents around a hazardous waste facility is the serious health risks involved. And most consider their health and that of their family as so valuable as to be essentially nonnegotiable. But the assumption of the state-mandated mediation process in Massachusetts is that health risks should be negotiable—that the developers can economically compensate the local citizens for any increase in health risks. Thus the mediation process attempts to portray health as simply another interest, one to which a price can be attached, and one that can be bargained over like any other commodity.[44] As one of the architects of the law has pointed out, the assumption is that "people implicitly make trade-offs between health and environmental values and other values all the time."[45] Importantly, however, he also admits that most residents do not normally see the issue in that way, and that "many people blanch at the suggestion that they explicitly surrender part of their safety and tranquility in return for compensation."[46] Clearly, then, what we have in this process is an explicit attempt to change the way citizens look at health and environmental issues, and to do so in a way that will facilitate the building of the facility. This is hardly an example of mediators responsibly refusing to encourage negotiation over nonnegotiable issues.

SELECTIVE PERCEPTION
OF MULTIFACETED DISPUTES

There is yet another difficulty in the suggestion that the problem of distortion can be solved by mediators simply refusing to become involved in nonnegotiable disputes. This one is related to the fact that environmental disputes are often multifaceted, involving a mixture of different issues, some negotiable and some not. In these cases, the problem of distortion arises not because the dispute is entirely redefined by the mediator, but because they tend to view it selectively, filtering out those aspects of the conflicts they find problematic. They have a natural inclination to downplay the more basic nonnegotiable issues, and to focus participants' attention on the less important but negotiable ones. This was a complaint voiced by some respondents to the League of Women Voters' survey in Wisconsin. Several environmentalists and citizen activists said that the negotiations over environmental issues that took place in the consensus process often downplayed the most important aspects of the issues, and thus worked in the favor of industry. One local environmentalist explained how this worked concerning a dispute of mineral mining in northern Wisconsin: "None of the fundamental public policy issues concerning mining were ever discussed in the 'consensus process.' Attention was diverted from such basic questions as 'Do we need this mine— here and now—and if so, why?' to focus on details of after the fact mitigation: 'How do we make this mine nice.' "[47]

Thus, in these negotiations, the main political questions of concern to local environmentalists were largely ignored. And of course, the fact that the process assumed that the mining was going to take place, and that the only issue was environmental safeguards, worked implicitly in favor of the mining industry.

Also concerned about this tendency in environmental mediation to artificially narrow the issues being considered is David Phillips, Wildlife Projects Director for Friends of the Earth. He describes a case in Colorado involving a dispute over water use. It concerned whether and how this diminishing resource should be diverted to developing areas—an increasingly important issue in western states. In Phillips' eyes, those involved in the dispute, including some environmentalists, too quickly narrowed down the topics of discussion, and thus left out some of the most important issues. As he explained:

They all got together and one of the first things they decided was that we all have to realize that we're not going to get into the subject of growth, that we're not going to get into the idea of trying to limit diversion because we don't think that more people should be here. They all agreed on that and said, "Yeah, that will be one of our operating principles." But what good environmentalist would sit there and say that we should have as many people as could possibly be stacked in the middle of the desert in Colorado and supply them with all the water they need. Growth is part of the environmental problem there—the myth that we can make the desert bloom and put as many people there and just divert as much water from the streams to get it there. So, already from their initial operating principle, they narrowed the scope of the issue to the advantage of the development interests and the water exporters and to the disadvantage of the environmentalists. In the rush to achieve compromise and achieve consensus, there oftentimes is an unstable narrowing of the issue that later leads to problems.[48]

Again, it is easy to see both sides of this problem. On the one hand, mediators try to ensure fruitful discussions by focusing on issues that stand the best chance of resolution. And if the main goal is to arrive at some agreement, then narrowing the discussion in this way makes sense. However, if as Fiss pointed out earlier, the main goal is not just to establish peace, but to ensure that the right decision is made and that justice is done, then this process of artificially narrowing the topics may often not be environmentally desirable. Furthermore, this narrowing can work to the advantage of developers and industry, and to the disadvantage of environmentalists.[49]

OBSCURING THE FUNDAMENTAL ISSUES

It is important to emphasize that this process of narrowing the issues is not a random one—but one that tends to selectively filter out the more basic and systemic issues involved in a dispute. The tendency to divert attention from larger political issues is not unique to environmental mediation, but one that has been found in other uses of mediation as well. Researchers like Richard Abel, Jerold Auerbach, and Richard Hofrichter who have studied the political impacts of several neighborhood mediation projects set up in inner cities also have noted this problem.[50] Abel and Hofrichter have argued that informal neighborhood mediation efforts tend to portray disputes as individual grievances and thus obscure the more systematic nature of some conflicts.[51] For example, instead of understanding some urban disputes as manifestations of the problems of racial and class conflict in our society, mediators portray them as isolated problems involving individual landlords and tenants, or individual merchants and customers. Consequently, larger societal issues drop out of sight as mediators focus on the details of specific incidents and particular personalities. The problem with this, suggest the researchers, is that it discourages people from coming to a better understanding of the nature of the problems from which they are suffering. In addition, this narrow approach to social problems means that even if the specific incident is solved, the more fundamental problem may remain unsolved. For instance, you may have a case where a person settles an individual discrimination complaint with a landlord, while he continues the practice elsewhere; or an individual settlement of a product liability case, while the company continues to manufacture similar defective products. In this way, the tendency in mediation to depoliticize disputes—to ignore the underlying systemic issues involved—can discourage the processes of identifying and coming to grips with widescale social problems.

It is easy to see how this propensity to personalize and depoliticize disputes could be at work in environmental mediation as well. Mediation tends to deny that environmental problems are rooted in basic value conflicts or in the structural requirements of our economy. Often, mediation encourages us to see environmental problems as unique, isolated, local phenomena, because these kinds of problems are the easiest to mediate. But local environmental problems such as toxic waste are often only symptoms of larger and more systemic environmental problems. And even though a local problem may be resolved in an ad-hoc fashion, this may do nothing to address the more basic national problem. Moreover, if one addresses environmental problems one by one, on the local level, industry gains considerable political advantage. Industry would much rather confront environmentalists on a local level, where industry's power advantage is maximized. On the national level, such as in Congress, environmentalists are able to band together and coordinate their activities and resources to put up a much more effective fight. The odds are much more in industry's favor if they are able to define the issues as purely local ones and thus only have to confront a small and poorly funded local environmental organization.[52] Thus in environmental matters, industry can benefit greatly from a strategy of divide and conquer; and mediation, with its tendency to narrow the issues and define the problem in local terms contributes to that strategy.

So again we are back to a political theme that has already been noted several times in this chapter—the tendency of mediation to distract from other more effective forms of political action. Not surprisingly, Abel and others also found this tendency at work in the process of neighborhood mediation. As Auerbach has pointed out, the widespread use of mediation in this context, is "likely to deflect energy from political organization of groups of people with grievances in common (e.g., tenants in slums or neighborhoods slated for development) or even discourage them from developing a litigation strategy that might offer more effective leverage for social and economic change."[53]

MEDIATION AS A FORM
OF POLITICAL CONTROL

Given these political effects of mediation—to obscure the larger issues and to distract from more organized political action—one could conclude that informal dispute resolution procedures like mediation may function in our society as a subtle but powerful form of political control. Indeed, this interpretation helps to explain one of the political puzzles of mediation—why established economic and political interests have become so interested in alternative dispute resolution techniques. At first, these techniques would seem of little use to those who already have superiority in economic and political resources. But once mediation is seen as a new form of political control, the interest of these parties in the process becomes much more understandable. It becomes less surprising, for instance, that important parts of the industrial community have been strongly promoting environmental mediation. It may be that they are embracing it precisely because its obscuring and distracting tendencies can help to further bolster their political position.

The argument being made here is similar to the point made earlier in chapter 5, where we saw that governments can use environmental mediation as a way to manage public opposition to government policies. It is now being suggested that other interests as well may be able to take advantage of the political control potential present in environmental mediation. The notion that mediation may function as subtle form of political control has received some support from the research of other scholars. Richard Abel, for instance, argues that throughout the history of the alternative dispute resolution movement in the United States, mediation has been used as a way of undermining the political power of newly emerging political groups. He maintains that in the past, the search for alternatives to the courts has increased primarily "when some fairly powerful interest [has been] threatened by an increase in the number or magnitude of legal rights."[54] For example, it was not until the 1960s and 70s, when traditionally disadvantaged groups, including minorities, prisoners, tenants, the elderly, and the poor began their long overdue effort to exercise their legal rights that established authorities began to complain about clogged courts, and started their effort to funnel these "less important" cases into informal adjudication processes.[55] Jerold Auerbach has made similar observations in his historical studies and has concluded that: "Nothing, it seemed, propelled enthusiasm for alternative dispute settlement like a few legal victories that unsettled an equilibrium of privilege."[56]

Clearly, one can interpret the development of environmental mediation in this light as well. It was only in the mid-1970s when environmentalists began to exercise their expanded political powers and legal rights that industry and developers became interested in getting these issues out of the courts. In this view, then, industry's current interest in environmental mediation stems not

from a new desire to negotiate in good faith with environmentalists, but rather it is an effort to disempower environmentalists by
distracting them from more effective political strategies like litigation. And this possibility—that one of the primary functions of
environmental mediation is to depoliticize environmental issues
and to disempower environmentalists—is certainly one of the
most disturbing political implications surrounding this new
technique.

CONCLUSION

In the last several chapters we have explored a number of political
problems associated with environmental mediation, involving
such things as cooptation, imbalances in power, distortion of
issues, and so on. It is now time to draw some conclusions about
the nature of these problems. First, it should be noted that the
existence of these problems is for the most part not in dispute.
Even advocates of mediation are willing to acknowledge their
existence. But what is crucial to see is that there are two very
different ways of interpreting the significance of these problems.
When confronted with these problems in mediation, advocates
usually tend to down-play them by viewing them as exceptions—
as abuses of mediation rather than as problems inherent to the
process. Thus they argue that mediation has limitations and should
not be used when there are large imbalances of power or basic
value issues at stake. In this view, the process itself is a neutral
one, but it can be misused and abused by mediators and participants. There is, however, another way to interpret these problems—an interpretation that is supported by the analysis in the
last several chapters—and that is to see them not as abuses, but
as political biases that are built into the process itself. In this view,
the problems we have discussed are not random abuses, but systematic biases that tend to work in favor of some interests over
others. And since these biases are seen as inherent in the proce-

dures and assumptions that are imbedded in this approach, they are not as easily avoided as abuses would be.

The notion that biases can enter into mediation efforts is not an alien one to promoters of this process, but they tend to be sensitive to only certain kinds of bias. Mediators, for example, are aware of the possibility of *personal* political biases entering into their work. And the best ones make an effort to develop a professional neutrality, and try to consciously avoid letting their own political views bias the way they conduct mediation efforts.[57] But the point is that even when the mediator is politically neutral, the process itself may not be. What proponents fail to appreciate is that the main political biases in mediation eminate from the process, not the mediators. As we saw in the last chapter, mediation can be considered biased because it automatically reproduces the political imbalances present in the larger political system. In this chapter, we have seen yet another source of built-in bias, this time in the political assumptions inherent in the process of mediation itself—assumptions that are not neutral. As the cases cited here have illustrated, the assumptions about the nature of environmental conflict that are present in this approach can distort participants' understanding of environmental issues and mislead them as to the best solutions to their problems. In its essence, this is a bias rooted in the methodology of mediation. Once one assumes that mediation is the preferred method for resolving these disputes, then a certain perspective on conflict naturally follows. Or to use an analogy, if the only tool you have is a hammer, everything you encounter looks like a nail. And thus this is not a problem that can be easily avoided by mediators. Indeed, the more one practices in this profession, the more likely one is to adopt and promote these misleading assumptions about the nature of environmental disputes. Given this situation, it may do little good for critics to urge mediators to be more sensitive to the various political biases in mediation. If these biases are rooted in the requirements of the process and in the professional self-interest of the mediators, then they are probably much too entrenched to be overcome by simple exhortations.

This second interpretation, then, is one that is much more

pessimistic about the political biases in environmental mediation and about the possibility of reform—and thus one with which proponents are likely to strongly disagree. But irrespective of which interpretation of the political problems of environmental mediation one supports, the bottom line for potential participants is the same—that this process should be approached carefully and skeptically. Environmental mediation should not be accepted at face value and should not be entered into quickly. Potential participants must be careful to see through the myths of mediation— the illusion that it is a simple and easy process, that all participants around the table are equal, that the process is inherently fair, that compromise is always reasonable, and so on. In addition, they should be careful to analyze all of their political options, to accurately assess the extent of their political resources, and to come to a clear understanding of the nature of the issues at stake. Given the many pitfalls of this process and the absence of significant procedural safeguards, only the intelligence and vigilence of the participants can ensure that it is a mutually beneficial process.

CHAPTER SEVEN

The Future
of Environmental Mediation

If the current trend continues, many of the important resource allocation decisions made each year could depend on the successes of the independent mediators.

Lawrence Susskind[1]

U p to this point, the analysis of environmental mediation has focused on the political benefits and the political pitfalls. We have seen that mediation is a complex and contradictory political phenomenon. It not only opens up a new form of participation in environmental politics, but also introduces new forms of cooptation and political control. But this analysis of the potential advantages and disadvantages of environmental mediation leaves unanswered two of the most important political questions: What role is mediation likely to play in environmental politics? And what role should it play?

Needless to say, most proponents of environmental mediation forecast a rosy future. Many believe that it will become increasingly common over the next few years. Proselytizers like Lawrence Susskind and Jay D. Hair have argued that environmental mediation will come to rival litigation as one of the preferred methods of resolving environmental controversies—a state of affairs that they clearly view as desirable. As Hair put it in a 1983 speech: "My prediction is that in ten years more environmental disputes will be mediated than litigated. The forces which are pushing environmental issues out of the courtroom and into negotiated settlements are building fast and show no signs of abating. In short, mediation is a growth industry."[2]

But if the analysis in the forgoing chapters is correct, there are several good reasons to question whether mediation will expand this rapidly. Despite heavy promotion, the current demand for environmental mediation remains rather low. This is primarily because mediation is only appropriate in certain political conditions—such as where a balance of power exists between the disputants. This chapter will consider again some of these preconditions for mediation and assess to what degree they exist in environmental politics today. I will argue that many of these important preconditions will continue to be largely absent and that the prospects for the rapid growth of environmental mediation are therefore limited.

But besides the empirical question of whether the use of mediation will expand, there is also the normative question of whether it should expand. It should be clear by now that mediation is not a cure-all. It has a significant number of political problems, and these can easily lead to inequitable and cooptive agreements. Moreover, many of these political problems may be built into the process, and therefore not easily avoided. Thus it is certainly questionable whether the wholesale application of mediation to a wide variety of environmental disputes is desirable. Exploring this normative question will be the second task of this chapter. I will argue that given its drawbacks and limitations, the most appropriate role for environmental mediation is a relatively minor one. Unless it is used judiciously, it will lead to an increasing number of undesirable agreements that could contribute to the deterioration of environmental protection in the United States.

MEDIATION IN A LARGER POLITICAL CONTEXT

Predicting the future of anything in politics is a risky endeavor, and predicting the future use of environmental mediation is no exception. Indeed, it is tempting to avoid the question altogether and simply conclude that the future of mediation is in the hands of those who become involved in environmental disputes. Exactly how and when it will be used will be determined by the individual choices made by each of the participants in each of these disputes. And since these choices will vary according to the particular circumstances of the dispute, they are very hard to predict. But while this is true, it is also true that some generalizations can be made about the future uses of environmental mediation. For, as we have seen, the choices made by environmental disputants do not take place in a political vacuum, but rather take place within a larger political context. And the particular characteristics of that context have a strong impact on whether and how mediation is used. We now know, for example, that the presence or absence of certain political conditions, such as common interests, or a balance of power, strongly affects whether the parties are likely to negotiate. We also know that this power dimension also affects whether mediation is likely to be used for cooperative or cooptive purposes. Thus the role that mediation plays in environmental politics is determined in a significant way by the larger political forces at work today. Therefore, by examining these larger political forces, one should be able to make some informed speculations about how and how often environmental mediation will be used in the future.

For example, one of the political conditions that will affect how common environmental mediation efforts are likely to become is the nature and depth of the environmental disputes taking place in the United States. Successful negotiation and mediation is more likely to take place when there is widespread agreement over common interests and common values. It tends to work best in environmental controversies when there is a basic consensus over environmental values and goals and the dispute centers around differing approaches to achieving them.

Mediation is appropriate, for example, in disputes where a company and an environmental group both acknowledge that an effluent problem must be addressed, but disagree over the most efficient and expeditious way to solve the problem. Certainly some environmental conflicts fall into this category, and these will provide a number of opportunities for the effective use of mediation. But it is doubtful that implementation disputes are the most common or most significant form of environmental controversy.[3] And more importantly, it is questionable whether there exists in the United States the fundamental consensus over environmental goals and values that these kinds of disputes imply.

The notion that there is a national consensus on environmental issues has been severely undermined by the advent of the Reagan administration and its strong anti-environmental stance. The Reagan administration began by attacking what most environmentalists assumed were the basic principles of environmental regulation—such as the right and desirability of government to regulate private business and the right of the government to own and preserve public lands. Such disagreements reveal a basic lack of consensus over the principles and values animating our environmental policy in the United States. When disputes over environmental policy run this deep, mediation and negotiation are not likely to prosper. Indeed, the Reagan administration's environmental officials have often simply refused to meet with representatives of environmental organizations. In turn, those organizations have repeatedly taken the administration to court to stop the dismantling of important environmental regulations. Adversarial politics seem to be the rule these days in environmental affairs, and given the basic nature of the disputes between pro- and anti-environmental forces, this is probably appropriate.

Of course, one could argue that the disagreement over basic principles and values that characterizes current environmental politics is simply a temporary phenomenon—one that is purely a function of Reagan's unique form of dogmatic anti-environmentalism. And in fact, some environmentalists make exactly this point. They suggest that President Reagan's anti-environmental positions are an aberration that stands in stark contrast to the dominant pro-environmental sentiments in society at large. They take comfort in the public opinion polls that continue to show widespread and strong public support for strict environmental controls.[4] In this view, President Reagan is simply an anomoly and once he is out of office in 1988, the basic consensus on environmental issues will return to Washington. This interpretation of the Reagan years, if true, bodes well for environmental mediation. As the anti-environmental extremism of the Reagan administration fades, the use of negotiation and mediation could easily become more acceptable and more common.

But this interpretation of Reagan anti-environmentalism may be overly optimistic. It seems more likely that the Reagan approach to the environment is not simply the product of one politician's out-of-step beliefs, but rather the result of a significant anti-environmental backlash in this country. It is a backlash that has substantial political support, especially in the business community. In other words, the emergence of Reagan-style anti-environmentalism could indicate that there continues to exist a basic contradiction between environmental and economic goals in our society. There is no denying that environmental regulations make it more difficult and expensive to do business in the United States at a time when there is great concern over the health of our economy and the threat of foreign economic competition. And it should be remembered that President Reagan's attack on the environment has been supported by large segments of the business community. As economic times got tough, many corporations jumped onto the anti-environmental bandwagon and argued that environmental goals must take a back seat to economic expansion.[5]

If there is a basic conflict between environmental and economic goals in the United States, then Reagan's anti-environmentalism is hardly an aberration. Indeed, the aberration may have been the initial consensus on environmental issues that existed in the early 1970s. Many environmentalists prefer to think this was the norm and eagerly anticipate its return, but in fact this may have only been a honeymoon period—a period that has inevitably come to an end as the basic contradictions between economic and environmental priorities have resurfaced in the 1980s.

In this sense, then, the apparent consensus over environmental policy that one finds in the public opinion polls may be very misleading. For one thing, it is a mistake to confuse public consensus with consensus on the part of policymakers. Despite what the public espouses, there are significant numbers of both private and public policymakers who clearly do not share a strong commitment to environmental values and policy goals. In addition, it is important to remember that these polls only investigate public opinion, they do not investigate the deeper structural forces at work in society. If there is a basic conflict between environmental and economic goals in the United States, it matters little if the public chooses to recognize it or not. The effects of such an objective conflict will ultimately reveal themselves in continuing environmental problems and environmental controversies. In this way, public consensus on environmental issues may only mask a deeper reality where substantial forces are at work undermining environmental priorities.

In any case, regardless of whether our environmental problems are structural or not, it is clear that the 1980s have witnessed a renewed battle over environmental priorities in the United States. These battles have involved much more than misunderstandings, or even conflicts of interests; they have often revolved around fundamental disagreements over the basic values and principles underlying our environmental policies. There is a good chance that these conflicts will continue. This situation will, of course, tend to work against the expanded use of environmental mediation. Naturally, some mediation efforts will survive even in these hostile conditions. But when such basic conflicts exist over environmental goals, mediation is unlikely to flourish—nor should it. Mediation and compromise are usually inappropriate when fundamental principles and values are at stake.

IMBALANCES OF POWER

Another reason why environmental mediation should occupy a relatively minor role in environmental politics has to do with power. Negotiation is unlikely to take place unless there is a relative balance of power between the disputants. These balances of power are necessary to create the political stalemates that make negotiation an attractive option. Thus if environmental mediation is to become a common approach, a wide-ranging balance of power between industry and environmental groups would have to exist. Undoubtedly there will continue to be specific disputes where stand-offs will be created between these two opposing forces, and where mediation will be an appropriate alternative. But what are the general characteristics of the distribution of power between the opposing sides in environmental politics? Answering this larger question is difficult, but even a partial answer should give us a good clue about the prospects for the growth of environmental mediation.

In general, when one looks at the current conditions and trends in environmental politics, one sees evidence for a systematic imbalance of power between industry and environmentalists—one that is likely to continue and perhaps even worsen. Environmental groups have all of the disadvantages in political and economic power that afflict most public interest groups. Typically, they have limited staff, little money, and face an uphill battle to organize citizens around issues whose impacts are so diffuse. In contrast, industry organizations are well staffed, amply funded, and have a direct financial interest in these issues. For example, John Chubb, in his study of interest groups lobbying the Nuclear Regulatory Commission, found that the median budget for the five top environmental organizations was $318,000 a year, while the median budget for the electric industry lobbies was $3,500,000 a year. Similarly, the median staff of the environmental groups was twelve, while the industry groups employed an average of sixty-four.[6] For a time, in the early 1970s, environmental groups were able to overcome these inequities and become a powerful force on the national scene. Environmental issues were very much on the mind of the public. In addition, environmental groups were well organized, with growing memberships, and industry's opposition was generally weak and scattered. But this situation was temporary. Interest in environmental issues and membership in environmental organizations began to wane.[7] More importantly, by the mid-1970s, the business community was getting more politically organized. Concerned about the rise of liberal politicians and the new threats posed by public interest groups, business leaders and lobbyists met and discussed their mutual political problems. They eventually organized a coordinated political campaign whose purpose was to greatly increase the business community's influence over national policy. As Thomas Edsall has observed, the success of this campaign was one of the most important political developments of the later 1970s. In his words, "during the 1970s, the political wing of the nation's corporate sector staged one of the most remarkable campaigns in the pursuit of power in recent history. By the late 1970s and early 1980s, business, and Washington's corporate lobbying community in particular, had gained a level of influence and leverage approaching that of the boom days of the 1920s."[8]

This political campaign had several facets. One of the most important was to increase the number of corporate and trade political action committees—a development that will be discussed later. However, there were other less obvious, but equally important, parts of this campaign. One of the most inventive was the entrance of corporations into grass-roots lobbying—once the domain of environmentalists and other public interest groups. Business had always dominated in the traditional forms of one-on-one lobbying in Washington, but now they began to exploit their ability to mobilize public support for their positions. Corporate leaders realized that their institutions were in fact much better suited to grass-roots lobbying than were public interest groups. The interest and membership in public interest groups is very fluid, rising when issues have high visibility and declining when the issues become ambiguous. In contrast, corporations have a steady and ongoing interest in policies that affect them, with a stable number of employees and stockholders to mobilize. Moreover, many large corporations can mobilize a nationwide network that not only consists of employees and stockholders, but also suppliers, retailer outlets, subcontractors, salesmen, and distributors. In the later 1970s, corporations began to utilize these networks for lobbying purposes, sometimes spending millions of dollars to organize letter-writing campaigns.[9]

A second aspect of the corporate political mobilization in the 1970s was the increasing effort to use advertising to shape public opinion on political issues. Those who win political battles are often those who succeed in getting policymakers and the public to see the issue from their perspective. Political advertising can be quite useful for this purpose. One of the best known examples of corporate political propagandizing is the ongoing effort of the Mobil Corporation which regularly runs editorials on various issues in the *New York Times* and other national publications. Mobil spends almost $3.5 million a year on these kinds of advertisements. In 1978, a congressional committee estimated that corporate political advertising had then grown to $1 billion a year.[10] Needless to say, this kind of spending gives corporations a great advantage over environmental groups in the effort to sway public opinion and to shape the legislative debate over energy and environmental issues.

A third part of the corporate political offensive is the increased funding of conservative pro-business think-tanks. In another effort to alter the terms of policy debates, business funneled millions of dollars into private institutions engaged in research and scholarship on policy issues. Among the institutions that now are funded totally or partially by business are the Heritage Foundation, the American Enterprise Institute, the Hoover Institute on War, Revolution and Peace, the National Bureau of Economic Research, the Center for the Study of American Business, and the American Council for Capital Foundation. In the early seventies, many of these organizations were small and relatively insignificant, but they have grown tremendously under corporate sponsorship and many of them now exert considerable influence in shaping discussions about major policy issues. For example, the Heritage Foundation's budget in the mid-1970s was $1 million. But because of generous contributions from such benefactors as Joseph Coors, Mobil Oil, Dow Chemical, Gulf Oil, Readers Digest, and others, the budget began to grow at the rate of 40 percent a year. By 1982 its budget had reached over $7 million and the foundation had become known as one of the major influences on the Reagan administration's approach to budget cutting and deregulation.[11]

CHANGES IN POLITICAL INSTITUTIONS

In short, in recent years, the business community has engaged in a coordinated campaign to use its enormous financial resources in a variety of new ways to increase its already potent political influence. And, needless to say, environmental groups have been unable to keep up. To make matters worse for environmentalists, these increasing disadvantages in terms of resources and political influence are only part of the story. These inequities have been made even worse by recent changes in the political institutions charged with making and implementing environmental policy. Shifts in the political winds in all three branches of our federal government are further weakening the political position of environmental interests. These changes are most obvious in the administrative branch. Previously, in the Carter years, environmentalists were taken into the administration and had a large impact on regulatory decision making. But in the 1980s, environmental groups learned that this power had only been temporary; power that is given by a President can also be taken away. Many administrators sympathetic with environmental concerns were forced to leave or they simply quit in frustration, and the new appointees paid little attention to environmentalists' attempts to influence regulatory decisions. Thus, almost overnight, environmental groups lost virtually all the power they had in the administrative branch.

In contrast, Congress has been much more hospitable to environmental interests than the current administration—but even here conservationists no longer enjoy the power they had in the 1970s. After the 1980 election, Congress followed the President's lead and supported a number of large budget cuts for environmental programs, especially in the Republican dominated Senate. This changed somewhat after the 1982 election, when Congress became more reluctant to support increasing budget cutbacks in this area. But nevertheless, few new environmental initiatives have been supported by Congress in the 1980s, and environmental lobbyists have had to spend most of their time trying to preserve legislation passed in the 1970s.

In addition, it is important to note that several new trends in congressional elections will work against environmental interests in the long run. First, and most importantly, there are the changes in the financing of congressional campaigns. The late 1970s and early 1980s have witnessed the rapidly expanding role of political action committees (PACs) in congressional elections. PAC money increasingly influences who gets elected to Congress because PAC contributions are now more important than funds from political parties. Corporations have been quick to exploit the potential for PACs to translate economic power into political power, and a sharp increase in PAC spending has been one of most important aspects of the corporate campaign to increase their political power. The number of corporate PACs has skyrocketed from 89 in 1974 to 1,467 in 1982, and the number is still growing. Needless to say, most environmental groups simply cannot hope to compete with the thousands of corporate PACs who are together spending millions of dollars to support their candidates.[12] This can be a devastating political disadvantage, for it makes little difference how knowledgable and skilled environmental lobbyists are if the people elected to Congress are already deeply indebted to business interests.

There are other developments in congressional elections that also bode ill for environmental interests. The 1980s have seen a shift toward the election of more conservative members of Congress, both more conservative Democrats and more conservative Republicans. The cause of this shift is debatable; it may signify the emergence of a more conservative electorate, or it may simply represent the increased influence of PACs. But in any case, there is a trend toward a more conservative Congress. This is important because studies of congressional voting patterns on environmental issues have shown that conservatism is one of the best predictors of anti-environmental voting.[13] One of the other good predictors is the region of the country that members come from. Members from the West and South are more likely to vote against environmental legislation than members from the East. And, of course, demographic trends now require that increasingly more members of Congress will come from those regions gaining in population: the West and South.[14] Together, these trends indicate that environmentalists are likely to face an increasingly uphill battle in Congress.

Environmental groups have also suffered significant political setbacks in one of their preferred political forums—the courts. This is particularly problematic because much of the political influence of environmentalists has always depended on their ability to litigate effectively. In the 1980s this power has been undermined. For example, there have been several instances, including the Trans Alaska Pipeline, where Congress has passed legislation explicitly forbidding the courts from reviewing the environmental impacts of development projects—effectively taking away much of the litigatory power of environmentalists in these cases.[15] In addition, the current Supreme Court has made a number of rulings that have significantly undermined the litigation strategy of environmentalists—so much so that many environmental lawyers consider the Burger Court as generally inhospitable to environmental interests. Some of the most damaging rulings have involved limiting the rights of environmentalists to challenge administrative decisions on substantive environmental grounds. In *Vermont Yankee Nuclear Power Corporation v. NRDC*, the Court found that environmentalists could only challenge administrative decisions to develop nuclear power on procedural grounds, not on substantive ones.[16] Thus substantive arguments about whether nuclear power was safe or economical became essentially irrelevant. And in *Chevron v. NRDC*, the Court's ruling further restricted the role of the judiciary in independently reviewing agency interpretation of environmental regulations. In essence, it was argued that in complex environmental decisions, the courts should defer to agency expertise and not interfere.[17]

In practice, of course, this means that it is much more difficult for environmental groups to legally challenge attempts by Reagan administration officials to weaken the standards and enforcement of environmental statutes. In addition, other Burger Court decisions on such things as the scope of class-action suits also have served to weaken the standing of environmental interests in the courts. And chances are that any appointments made to the Court in the near future will only make it more politically conservative, and thus even less hospitable to environmental interests. This is not merely speculation, for already the ideological balance in many of the lower federal courts has been shifted to the right by Reagan appointees.

To make matters worse for environmentalists, the legal power and expertise of industry and developers has increased significantly since the early 1970s. In the early days of environmental litigation, it was the environmental groups that tended to have the lawyers best trained in environmental law. That situation has now changed. Industry now has the benefit of a new generation of corporate lawyers trained in the intricacies of environmental litigation. Not only has the in-house legal expertise of corporations increased, but industry has also been active in funding a set of new pro-development legal foundations (such as the Mountain States Legal Foundation that was headed by James Watt) that have been instrumental in leading the legal fight against federal environmental regulations. Not surprisingly, as industry has increased its competency in environmental law, it has also increased its use of litigation. As Professor Lettie Wenner has shown, while the number of federal court cases initiated by environmentalists have steadily declined since the mid-1970s, the number of cases initiated by industry has steadily increased. Indeed, industry initiated cases in federal appellate courts surpassed those started by environmentalists in 1975 and the gap has been widening ever since.[18] In essence, then, the political scenario one sees in the courts is similar to that in the other branches of government: environmentalists started out with a bang in the early seventies; but since then, their power has been waning, while the power of corporations has been on the rise.

To sum up, a good case can be made for a fundamental and perhaps increasing imbalance of power between environmentalists and pro-development forces, both in terms of political resources and institutional influence. And it seems likely that this imbalance will discourage the expansion of environmental mediation. Organizations with superior political and legal resources are unlikely to negotiate when they feel they can win outright. Indeed, the increasing use of litigation over environmental issues by industry could be interpreted as evidence for this trend. The behavior of officials in the Reagan administration also illustrates how those with superior power are often reluctant to consider negotiation and compromise. As a rule, appointees in environmental agencies have chosen to make unilateral regulatory decisions, with little effort to consult or negotiate with environmental groups. This all clearly suggests that the more the power of environmentalists wanes, and the more that industry and pro-development forces are able to achieve their goals through traditional political channels, the less chance there is that the use of environmental mediation will increase.

ON THE OTHER HAND . . .

Importantly, the effect of the waning power of environmentalists on the prospects for environmental mediation may not be as simple as it first appears. It is conceivable, for instance, that the weakening political position of environmentalists could actually *increase* the use of mediation. The logic here is simple: environmental groups, faced with declining influence, limited resources, and few other political options, might have to opt for mediation for lack of a better alternative. If a group lacks power and seems unable to win in conventional political forums, they may turn to mediation out of desperation. This could be the effect, for example, of the diminishing ability of environmentalists to use the courts effectively or to wield influence over administrative decisions. When these alternatives are limited, environmental groups may feel that they have little choice but to negotiate the best deal they can.

It is possible, then, that the declining power of environmentalists could force them more often into negotiations—a prospect that many proponents of mediation would undoubtedly celebrate. However, the normative implications of such a development could be questionable. For there is a good chance that while environmental mediation might prosper in these circumstances, the negotiations that take place will not be the most fair and legitimate ones. We know now that the distribution of power between disputants strongly affects the fairness of the negotiations and the equity of the outcomes. And as we have repeatedly seen, participants in mediation efforts who have little power and few options are easily taken advantage of by more powerful parties. In this sense, environmentalists without the ability to litigate would be like unions without the ability to strike. Denied their most basic weapon, they still might be able to get corporations to negotiate, but it is unlikely that the companies would do so in good faith. In short, the increasing weakness of environmental groups may encourage negotiations, but serious questions arise about the integrity and fairness of those negotiations.

This problem is not an implausible one. One of the strongest environmental proponents of mediation, Jay D. Hair of the National Wildlife Fund, has predicted that the political weakness of the environmental movement inevitably will work to increase the use of mediation.[19] He observes that the rate of technological innovation in advanced industrial societies like the United States is accelerating—the new processes and products continually developed by the petrochemical industry alone are impressive. Such advances are presenting an increasing number of threats to the environment—threats which environmentalists are finding difficult to keep up with. He argues that this burden on environmental groups to act as watchdogs over industry has now been made even worse by the recent changes in environmental agencies. Staff reductions, budget cuts, and changes in attitude have weakened these agencies' enforcement efforts, and environmental groups have had to try to take up the slack to ensure that regulations are enforced. Hair suggests that environmental groups simply lack the resources to fight all of these battles, and for this reason they will turn to mediation. "The sad fact of the matter is that environmental organizations have insufficient legal resources to fight massive noncompliance with environmental statutes. Given the wholesale disregard for both the substance and spirit of our environmental laws, we must focus on those cases that have the largest programmatic impact. . . . If environmental organizations don't find new ways to broker the local and regional environmental disputes the national groups can no longer address, too many important issues will simply slip through the cracks."[20]

Curiously, Hair draws a positive conclusion from all of this—that mediation will help beleaguered and poorly funded national environmental organizations to deal with a worsening environmental situation. He seems to suggest that local environmental groups should mediate some disputes and thus relieve national groups of some of their litigatory burden. At first glance, it might appear that such a development would be desirable, but a closer examination reveals that Hair's optimistic conclusions are questionable on a number of grounds. Mediation in these circumstances is likely to become a form of second-class justice. Smaller local groups that cannot afford to seek justice through the courts will have to settle for mediation. And needless to say, without being able to use the threat of litigation, these groups will be bargaining from a position of weakness. In addition, it is not clear that a sustained and effective mediation effort requires fewer resources than litigation. So, if a local organization cannot afford litigation, they may not be able to afford an effective mediation effort either. Thus, again, serious questions arise about the fairness and legitimacy of the mediation efforts that take place as a result of the political weakness of environmental groups.

In considering the future of environmental mediation, it is important to remember that more is not necessarily better. One must assess the quality of these negotiation efforts as well as their quantity. Whether or not the expansion of mediation is in itself a good thing depends largely on the fairness of the negotiation efforts and the legitimacy of the resulting agreements. And if the use of mediation expands because of the waning power and limited options of environmentalists, this may only encourage the kind of mediation that is biased and cooptive in nature. And this would hardly be a desirable development.

THE 10 PERCENT SOLUTION

To sum up, given the dominant characteristics of environmental politics today, the *legitimate* uses of environmental mediation seem relatively limited. The lingering conflict over basic environmental goals and values in this country, and the continuing imbalance of power between pro and anti-environmental forces would seem to constrict the opportunities for the growth of environmental mediation. We have yet to consider some of the other factors at work to limit the uses of mediation. We know, for example, that even if there is a relative balance of power between the disputants, this is unlikely to necessitate negotiation unless there is a stalemate that is *mutually* frustrating. That is often not the case. For instance, litigation can cause delays and stalemates, but often to one party's benefit. Industry may benefit from delaying the implementation of environmental regulations, and environmentalists may benefit from delaying developmental projects. Unless both parties incur large costs from such delays and stalemates, mediation is unlikely to be seen as an attractive option. These kinds of mutually frustrating impasses tend to occur in the area of labor relations, where the fate of the disputants are closely intertwined. Strikes inevitably hurt both owners and workers, an thus frequently fuel serious negotiation efforts. But similar situations do not usually exist in environmental controversies, where the disputants do not have obvious ongoing common interests, and where stalemates tend to hurt one side more than the other. This lack of mutually frustrating situations is therefore likely to dampen the demand for mediation in environmental controversies.

There are other constraints on the use of mediation as well. Some observers of mediation have argued that mediation only tends to work in particular circumstances, that is, in disputes that (a) are confined to a small geographic area, (b) are characterized by a small and well-defined group of disputants, (c) do not involve broad policy issues, (d) do not involve either-or choices, (e) where disputants are willing to place trust in the mediator, and (f) where disputants genuinely want to come to an agreement and are willing to compromise to do so.[21] All of these various limitations on the effective use of environmental mediation have led even some proponents to conclude that it can be used in only a small percentage of environmental disputes. One of the most prominent environmental mediators, Gerald Cormick of the Mediation Institute in Seattle, has concluded that mediation is really only appropriate in about 10 percent of environmental disputes.[22] The analysis here would support this modest assessment of mediation's potential role.

GOVERNMENT-MANDATED MEDIATION

Finally, it should be pointed out that there is one other political development that could change dramatically the role that environmental mediation is likely to play in the future—the growing movement to create government-mandated mediation processes. Until recently, most mediation efforts were ad-hoc and voluntary. Disputants would somehow hear about this option and arrange for a mediator, usually from one of a number of independent mediation institutes, to coordinate their negotiations. It was very much a hit-or-miss arrangement. Lately, however, there has been a concerted effort by some mediation entrepreneurs to encourage state and federal governments to sponsor or require mediation as part of the normal policymaking process. For example, Allan Talbot has urged that government begin to pressure environmental disputants to take part in mediation efforts.[23] On a more organized level, Lawrence Susskind and others at the Harvard Negotiation Project have been particularly active in promoting the institutionalization of mediation. Efforts to incorporate negotiation and mediation into governmental decision making have been made at several levels. On the federal level, there have been several informal efforts in "reg-neg" (regulatory negotiation) in which industry and environmentalists were encouraged to negotiate with government officials over proposed environmental regulations.[24]

One must look to the state level, however, to find instances where laws have been passed mandating mediation and negotiation as part of formal decision-making procedures. Several states, including Massachusetts, Wisconsin, and Rhode Island provide the option of state-sponsored negotiations in controversies over landfills, hazardous waste facilities, etc.[25] Clearly, if the idea of government-mandated mediation catches on, we could witness a substantial increase in the use of mediation in environmental controversies. But again, it should not necessarily be assumed that growth in mediation would automatically be good. It is important to assess the potential political impacts of this new approach, and to evaluate how desirable mediation would be.

Whether or not the growth of government-sponsored environmental mediation programs is desirable depends very much on how voluntary the process remains. Voluntariness is a crucial element in mediation efforts. It is one of the few safeguards built into this process and it plays a large part in ensuring that the agreements arrived at are mutually acceptable and fair. As long as participation remains voluntary there is less chance that participants will be forced into disadvantageous agreements. Some of these new government-sponsored programs, like the one in Wisconsin, are essentially voluntary in nature, and as such, should prove to be more politically acceptable. But as we saw in chapter 5, voluntariness in mediation is a complex issue. There are situations where the participation of disputants seems voluntary but in fact may be due to pressure exerted by policymakers. A judge, for example, can suggest that disputants engage in mediation, and they could easily feel that they could risk the wrath of the judge if they declined to do so. As Bacow and Wheeler point out, such judicial suggestions can easily pass over the line into coercion.[26]

Far more worrisome than this problem of informal pressure, however, is the possibility that voluntariness may be done away with altogether in some of the government-sponsored programs—that participants will be forced by law to participate in mediation efforts. This is exactly what is required in the hazardous waste facility siting laws in Massachusetts and Rhode Island. Under these laws, local citizens and officials are forced to negotiate with facility developers, and if they fail to come to an agreement, the issues are submitted to binding arbitration. But when mediation becomes required in this way, and the voluntary dimension disappears, several significant political problems can result. First, making mediation compulsory significantly increases the likelihood of its being abused. Mediation is often undesirable in situations of imbalanced power or situations where the issues involve basic nonnegotiable principles. But compulsory mediation ignores these important limitations and forces citizens to mediate irrespective of how little power they have, or irrespective of the nature of the issues involved. For example, as we saw in the last chapter, the Massachusetts hazardous waste facility siting law requires negotiation even over issues such as health risks that most residents view as inappropriate for negotiation. In this way, all of the problematic tendencies toward cooptation and issue distortion that are already present in this process could easily be made worse when disputants are given no choice but to negotiate.[27]

Moreover, such required participation usually serves to disempower some of the participants by cutting off their use of other political options. The Massachusetts law, for example, explicitly forbids local municipalities from using several of their normal regulatory powers to prevent the building of a hazardous waste facility. For instance, the act explicitly prevents localities from requiring special permits for these facilities, stipulating that "no license or permit granted a city or town shall be required for a hazardous waste facility which was not required on or before the effective date of chapter by said city or town."[28] Traditionally, municipalities have also been able to pass zoning regulations to exclude dangerous or undesirable facilities from their boundaries, but this ability is also expressly forbidden by the new hazardous waste legislation: "following the submission of notice of intent by a developer proposing to construct a hazardous waste facility, a city or town may not adopt any zoning change which would exclude the facility from the locus specified in said notice of intent."[29] The ability of local towns to block such facilities on health grounds is restricted as well. Finally, the statute severely limits the extent of judicial review over the decisions of the arbitrators. The courts are only allowed to set aside such a decision if fraud or partiality on the part of the arbitrator can be proven. Even if the communities were able to demonstrate that the arbitrator's decision was based on gross errors of law or fact, this would not be sufficient cause for the courts to overturn them.[30] Clearly, when one looks beyond the rhetoric of participation and negotiation that has accompanied this act, one finds a systematic effort to undermine the power of local governments and force them into agreements that they normally would not have endorsed.[31]

LIMITING ACCESS TO THE COURTS

The case of Massachusetts is not the only example of efforts to force negotiations by limiting the traditional political options of environmental disputants. Some proponents of mediation have suggested that access to the courts may have to be restricted in order to encourage negotiations. William Ruckelshaus, former head of the EPA under Nixon and Reagan, has argued that "if mediation is a fair way to resolve disputes, . . . then there's no reason why we can't build into statutory law the responsibility of disputants to subject these [disputes] to mediation, and to restrict access to the courts until mediation efforts have clearly failed."[32] Naturally, this possibility greatly disturbs environmentalists who have traditionally relied on access to the courts to press their case and to prevent irreversable ecological damage. As one environmentalist has complained, if such court restrictions are applied, "environmental groups, already unable to compete financially with corporations, may find it difficult to apply what has been their most potent weapon—immediate access to the courts."[33]

Such restrictions on access to the courts may not be that far off—at least if advocates of alternative dispute resolution have their way. A strong advocate of restricted access has been the National Institute for Dispute Resolution, (NIDR)—one of the leading institutions in the area of alternative dispute resolution. A recent NIDR report made it clear that they believe that alternative dispute resolution techniques like mediation are unlikely to become common unless they are mandated by the government as an alternative to litigation. They conclude in their report that "if nonlitigative methods of dispute resolution are to gain broad use, participation may have to be compulsory."[34] And the report goes on to detail two ways that participation can be mandated. First, it suggests the need for judges to have increased statutory authority to "require parties to use non-binding arbitration or mediation before submitting certain types of disputes to litigation"[35]—an approach similar to the one suggested by Ruckelshaus. In this way, environmental groups would be required to attempt to reach a settlement with the polluter through mediation before a court would hear the case. The second approach would be to create economic disincentives to discourage use of the courts and make alternatives appear more attractive. Among the suggestions: assessing a group additional costs if they refuse the settlement offered by an arbitrator and the court settlement does not turn out to be substantially higher; or increasing the costs of appeal if the appellant's position is not approved through appeal.[36] The report does mention that there may be drawbacks to instituting these compulsory forms of dispute resolution—they point out, for example, that this "might have a substantial effect on discouraging some cases that society views as important"[37]—but they seem to believe that the advantages would outweigh any such disadvantages.

WHY COMPULSORY MEDIATION?

When environmental mediation is made compulsory, it becomes a very different political animal. The loss of voluntariness would exacerbate many of mediation's most serious political drawbacks. And so we must ask why there is now such a large push for this questionable approach to mediation. It might be argued that mediation should be required because it has so many advantages over traditional approaches like litigation. This is the logic offered by

Bacow and Wheeler: "If negotiation of complex environmental issues can be beneficial not only to the parties immediately involved but to society at large, then should it not merely be encouraged but compelled?"[38] But the reasoning here is questionable. For if mediation has so many advantages over litigation, why would not disputants choose it voluntarily? Why must something so advantageous be forced on the participants? It seems odd that such an allegedly beneficial form of public participation would have to be imposed on the public from the top down.

There is a better explanation for the advocacy of compulsory mediation and it can be found if we begin to consider who would benefit most from the growth of this approach. One group that immediately comes to mind is the mediators themselves. They stand to reap potentially enormous benefits from mandated mediation. Specifically, government-sponsored mediation would solve two of the major problems undermining the stability and growth of environmental mediation: lack of money and lack of clients.

Funding always has been the Achilles heel of environmental mediation. Someone has to pay for mediation and the disputants are not always willing or able to do so. During the first years of mediation, mediation institutes and mediation efforts were primarily funded by grants from corporations and foundations. But both of these sources have significant drawbacks. Corporate funding only adds to the impression that mediation is biased toward development, and brings into question the neutrality of the mediators. Foundation money is cleaner, but ultimately unreliable. And in fact, foundation funding for environmental mediation has started to dry up in recent years, partly because they are turning their attention to other projects, and partly because of their disappointment with the poor track record of some environmental mediation institutes. As a result, many environmental mediators and mediation organizations have become somewhat desperate for funds.[39] Obviously, if state and federal governments took over the funding of mediation services, this financial problem would largely disappear.

Mandated mediation also overcomes another obstacle preventing the expansion of this approach—lack of clients. So far, relatively few disputants have voluntarily chosen to use the services of private mediators. Consequently, there have been serious questions about whether there will be enough demand to keep all mediators and institutes in business, let alone able to expand. At first it was assumed that as environmentalists and developers became aware of mediation and its advantages, there would be a natural and increasing demand for it. Millions of dollars in promotion later, the attempt to popularize environmental mediation has proven largely ineffective. As a result, several leading environmental mediation projects have concluded that there are not enough environmental clients to support their operations, and they have begun to branch out and offer to mediate a wider range of public policy disputes. It is revealing that one of the pioneering organizations in environmental mediation, The Institute for Environmental Mediation in Seattle, recently changed its name to The Mediation Institute in order to reflect their new marketing strategy. In any case, the lack of clients for mediation has led some to conclude, as the NIDR report did, that the future of mediation lies in making it compulsory. With this single step, the whole problem of demand completely disappears. And indeed, this has been used as one of the central selling points in the effort to convince mediators that government-mandated programs are desirable. No longer will they have to hustle for clients—they will get all the clients they can handle handed to them by the government. Almost overnight, mediation would change from an intriguing backwater in environmental politics into a growth industry. If this approach were pursued on a broad scale, mediation could achieve what it almost assuredly could not do on its own—it could come to rival litigation as a dispute resolution method.

BENEFITING GOVERNMENT OFFICIALS

It is important to see that many in government could also benefit from the institution of compulsory mediation. For instance, judges who feel they are overworked obviously would welcome the ability to force potential litigants to mediate first. In addition, as some commentators have pointed out, mediators employed by the courts would constitute a new stratum of subordinates for judges, and thus would enhance their status and power.[40] Compulsory mediation could also prove to be a great advantage to other government officials, like administrators. To date, many public administrators have been suspicious of techniques like mediation, often because they feel they have enough power to accomplish their goals without negotiating.[41] But administrators may find mediation useful particularly when they have to "manage" intense public opposition to government policies. Consider once again the case of the Massachusetts Hazardous Waste Facility Siting Act. Many environmentalists have speculated that the purpose of this legislation is not so much to give citizens a voice, but rather to restrict their ability to oppose waste facilities and to speed up the siting process. And in this regard, it is revealing that two of the architects of this bill wrote an article for the *Harvard Environmental Law Review* entitled "Overcoming Local Opposition to Hazardous Waste Facilities: The Massachusetts Approach."[42] As the title implies, the authors are interested in mediation primarily because it is the fastest and most effective way of *overcoming* local opposition. They warn that traditional attempts by states to force facilities on local residents often have only fueled opposition. A much more effective mode of undermining opposition, they suggest, is to combine the disempowerment of local municipalities with compulsory negotiations and the possibility of compensation.

There is already a strong inclination for government to use environmental mediation as a cooptive technique to smooth the implementation of controversial policies. But this undesirable use of mediation would increase if governments were able to limit the access of interest groups to traditional political forums and force them to participate in mediation and arbitration efforts. Unfortunately, however, what makes compulsory mediation undesirable for the public participants is exactly what makes it appealing to government officials—and this could easily fuel the movement toward institutionalizing environmental mediation.

At this point, it is too early to say just how extensive the movement toward government-sponsored mediation will be or exactly how it will be used. But it is clearly a development that needs to be watched closely. As long as mediation programs remain entirely voluntary and are offered simply as an option to disputants, they could be a healthy development. Groups have to watch out for all of the political pitfalls in the process, but at least they are free to decline mediation and to pursue other political avenues. However, government-mandated programs could easily move in the direction of compulsory mediation. When it is compulsory, mediation is no longer an additional option but is instead a *substitute* for other political processes like litigation. Such a development would thoroughly undermine any positive contributions that mediation might make, and increase the chances that it will be used primarily to disempower and coopt participating groups. It is important, then, that potential disputants in environmental controversies closely monitor any government attempts to institutionalize environmental mediation, and that they oppose efforts to make participation in these programs compulsory.

CONCLUSION

What conclusions can be drawn about the role that mediation can and should play in environmental politics in the 1980s and beyond? Environmental mediation does deserve a place in environmental politics, but its role should be a relatively small one. The number of cases in which it is appropriate are limited and it has built-in characteristics that allow it to be easily used for cooptation or political control. Environmental mediation can play a useful role in the resolution of some environmental controversies if it remains voluntary, if potential participants approach it without any illusions, and if they only join in after a thorough analysis of its advantages and disadvantages.

There are numerous forces at work, however, to push environmental mediation beyond this modest and legitimate role. First, some overzealous mediators and other proponents are promoting it as a cure-all, and have a professional self-interest in the expansion of this process. Second, a weakening environmental movement may be forced into mediation efforts for lack of other political alternatives. Third, there are those in positions of power, both in the public and private spheres, who may wish to promote mediation in order to exploit its cooptive potential. The business community can use environmental mediation to distract environmentalists from other political strategies, to distort the nature of the issues at stake, and to give the illusion of legitimacy to development projects. Those in government can use mediation to give the appearance of public participation and to undermine public opposition to controversial policies, and thus it may be in their interest to encourage the expansion of compulsory mediation. For all of these reasons, it is entirely conceivable that in the near future mediation could become a much more common approach to environmental disputes. But if the use of environmental mediation grows for these reasons, it will function primarily as a form of cooptation and political control—not as an egalitarian form of public participation in environmental decisions. Therefore, this kind of expansion of mediation should be strongly resisted, both by those who are committed to genuine democratic participation in political decisions, and by those who care about the quality of the environment in the United States.

On balance, environmental mediation is a process that should be approached with much caution and skepticism. In spite of the extravagant claims, mediation's potential is modest and its problems are many. And while it is something new in environmental politics, it is not something separate from environmental politics. It is an intensely political phenomenon—it contains its own political biases and it is inseparably linked to all the powerplays and struggles over principles and values that characterize environmental politics as a whole. It is a mistake to view mediation as the solution to the political problems that afflict the courts and other traditional policymaking institutions. Indeed, it is prone to the very same problems of expense, exclusion, inequality, and distortion that are present in all other approaches to environmental decision making. Environmental mediation is best understood not as an alternative to environmental politics as usual, but as a strange new form of it. When potential participants keep that crucial point in mind—that mediation is basically political—they will be in a better position to perceive its potential pitfalls and will be more likely to avoid them.

Epilogue

Environmental mediation is not an isolated political phenomenon. It is one part of a larger alternative dispute resolution movement in the United States, and some political analysts have expressed hope that techniques like mediation can eventually be used to resolve some of our most pressing political, economic, social, and racial problems. Thus, the use of mediation in environmental disputes is a forerunner of additional attempts to use alternative dispute resolution techniques in other public policy areas. But are such efforts wise or practical? Naturally, these are difficult questions to answer without a careful examination of specific issues and techniques. However, the conclusions about environmental mediation reached in this book can shed some initial light on these questions, and they would seem to suggest that we approach such political efforts with a healthy amount of skepticism.

Again, at first glance, there seems little wrong with efforts to increase communication and cooperation over controversial political issues. Indeed, efforts to increase dialogue and understanding between competing political groups should be encouraged. However, as the last several chapters have shown, it would be naive to assume that these kinds of negotiations could routinely resolve the festering political problems that we face as a nation. Moreover, widescale efforts to apply dispute resolution techniques to public policy problems could easily multiply the serious political problems, like the distortion of issues and the exploitation of weaker political groups, that we have already seen accompany environmental mediation.

The fundamental flaw underlying any attempt to rely on dispute resolution to resolve public policy conflicts is that such well-meaning efforts ultimately rest on a false understanding of what politics is all about. Politics is not simply about communication, it is also about power struggles. It is not only about common interests, but about conflicting interests as well. And it not only involves horse-trading, but competition between conflicting values and different moral visions. These are the elemental characteristics of politics in American society today. Any political process that ignores these basic political facts is ultimately built upon false hopes. Processes built upon false understandings and false hopes will, at best, only enjoy limited political success. At worst, the illusions built into such processes will not only make them politically irrelevant, but also will make them politically hazardous. We have seen, for example, how the illusion of egalitarianism in mediation can mask crucial inequalities in power and serve to legitimate unfair agreements.

Thus, if there is a larger political lesson to be learned from our experiences with environmental mediation, it is one concerning the need for political realism. We need to realize that we are not yet at the dawn of a cooperative society, and that inescapable struggles over power and visions of the good society still lie at the center of the important political battles taking place in America.

Notes

Introduction

1. The description of this case adapted from Robert Golten, "Mediation," pp. 63–64.

2. William D. Ruckelshaus, "Environmental Dispute Resolution," p. 1.

3. William Clark, "Excerpts of Remarks," p. 3.

4. See for example, the articles by Hair and by Reilly.

5. Louis Fernandez, "Let's Try Cooperation Instead of Confrontation," pp. 519, 514.

6. This brief history adapted from Scott Mernitz, *Mediation of Environmental Disputes,* Chapter 5.

7. For a longer description of this dispute, see Gerald Cormick, "Mediating Environmental Controversies," pp. 219–223.

8. For a list of mediation institutes and current mediation projects, see current issues of *Resolve,* available free from the Conservation Foundation in Washington, D. C.

9. A few words should be said about terminology. Throughout the book I will usually refer to this new approach as "environmental mediation." Although this is a common label, some proponents prefer the phrase "environmental dispute resolution." They find "environmental mediation" to be too narrow a term and feel that "environmental dispute resolution" is the best general term to describe the wide variety of approaches in this field. (There are times, for instance, when negotiations will take place between disputing parties without the use of a third-party mediator.) However, I find "environmental dispute resolution" to be an overly vague and somewhat awkward term. I believe that "environmental mediation" is a more convenient and less technical term that gives the reader a better feeling for the essence of this approach. It should be kept in mind, however, that I often will be using this term loosely, as an umbrella term to describe the entire field.

10. For a description of this project, see Tom Alexander, "A Promising Try at Environmental Detente for Coal." Also, for a more lengthy description of the various forms of third-party intervention into environmental disputes, see John McCory, "Environmental Mediation," pp. 52–56; or Howard Bellman, et al., "Environmental Conflict Resolution," pp. 1–7.

11. See Gail Bingham, "Does Negotiations Hold a Promise for Regulatory Reform?" pp. 1–8.

12. For a description of some of these state-sponsored negotiation projects, see the Winter/Spring 1983 issue of *Resolve*.

13. For a description of some successful (and some not so successful) cases of environmental mediation, see Allan Talbot, *Settling Things*.

14. Jay D. Hair, "Winning Through Mediation," p. 528.

15. Susskind, Lawrence, "Environmental Mediation and the Accountability Problem," pp. 2–5.

16. See, for example, Scott Mernitz, *Mediation of Environmental Disputes;* Kent Gilbreath, ed., *Business and the Environment;* and Tom Alexander, "A Promising Try at Environmental Detente for Coal."

17. Quoted in Peter Steinhart, "Talking It Over," p.10.

18. A good sample of these materials would include: Lawrence Bacow and Michael Wheeler, *Environmental Dispute Resolution;* Lawrence Susskind, Lawrence Bacow, and Michael Wheeler, *Resolving Environmental Regulatory Disputes;* Scott Mernitz, *Mediation of Environmental Disputes;* Roger Fisher and William Ury, *Getting to Yes;* Lawrence Susskind and Alan Weinstein, "Towards a Theory of Environmental Dispute Resolution," Susan L. Carpenter and W. J. D. Kennedy, "Environmental Conflict Management;" James L. Creighton, "A Tutorial: Acting as a Conflict Conciliator;" Gerald Cormick, "Mediating Environmental Controversies." Among the professional newsletters are *Resolve: A Quarterly Newsletter on Environmental Dispute Resolution,* available from the Conservation Foundation in Washington, D. C., and *The Mediator,* published by the Institute for Environmental Negotiation at the University of Virginia in Charlottesville.

19. Bacow and Wheeler, *Environmental Dispute Resolution,* p. 362.

20. Allan Talbot, *Settling Things;* Laura Lake, ed., *Environmental Mediation;* the books by Mernitz, Susskind et al., and Bacow and Wheeler also contain a number of interesting case studies.

21. See, for example, Lon Fuller, "The Forms and Limits of Adjudication;" and Frank Sander, "Varieties of Dispute Resolution."

22. Some good examples of this critical approach are Jerold Auerbach, *Justice Without Law;* Richard Abel's two volume collection *The Politics of Informal Justice;* and Christine Harrington, *Shadow Justice.*

22. Dorothy Lagerroos and Caryl Terrell, *Report on the League of Women Voters' Survey on the Consensus Process.*

23. For example, see Lawrence Susskind "Resolving Environmental Disputes Through Ad-Hocracy," pp. 3–5.

24. For a good summary of the cooptation problems inherent in many citizen participation techniques, see Sherry Arnstein, "A Ladder of Citizen Participation," pp. 216–224.

25. Michael Crozier, Samuel Huntington, and Joji Watanuki, *The Crisis of Democracy,* pp. 59–115.

26. Mancur Olson, *The Rise and Decline of Nations.*

27. Felix Rohatyn, "How About Domestic Cooperation?"

28. Ford Foundation, *New Approaches to Conflict Resolution,* p.v.

1. MEDIATION VERSUS TRADITIONAL POLITICAL INSTITUTIONS

1. Lawrence Susskind and Connie Ozawa, "Mediated Negotiation in the Public Sector," pp. 2–3.

2. Susskind and Ozawa, p. 16.

3. Environmental Law Center, "Environmental Mediation in Vermont," p. 5.

4. National Institute for Dispute Resolution (NIDR), "Paths to Justice," p. 9.

5. Scott Mernitz, *Mediation of Environmental Disputes*, p. 48.

6. NIDR, "Paths to Justice," p. 8.

7. For a good description of this case and the mediation effort that finally resolved it, see Allan R. Talbot, *Settling Things*, ch. 1.

8. A more detailed and critical discussion of these time and expense questions will take place in chapter 3.

9. Environmental Law Center, "Environmental Mediation in Vermont," p. 5.

10. Robert Bartlett, *The Reserve Mining Controversy*.

11. Louis Fernandez, "Lets Try Cooperation Instead of Confrontation," pp. 519, 513.

12. Fernandez, p. 514.

13. See William K. Reilly, "Conservation in the 1980's."

14. Laura Lake, *Environmental Mediation*, ch. 2.

15. Susskind and Ozawa, p. 17. Lettie Wenner disagrees with this point and has suggested that environmental controversies end up in the courts, not because of the procedural inadequacies of legislative and administrative approaches, but because whoever loses in these decisions inevitably seeks to win in another political forum—in this case, the courts. I touch on this point a bit later in my discussion of the disadvantages of win–lose decision making.

16. Susskind and Ozawa, p. 16.

17. Lake, p. 17.

18. Lake, p. 17.

19. Alan Stone, *Regulation and Its Alternatives*, p. 189.

20. Stone, pp. 186–189. Also, for a discussion of how vague legislation is passed for primarily symbolic purposes, see Murray Edelman, *The Symbolic Uses of Politics*.

21. John S. Dryzek, *Conflict and Choice in Resource Management*, p. 21.

22. Lawrence Susskind, "Resolving Environmental Disputes Through Ad-Hocracy," p. 3–4.

23. For an excellent study of the problems that environmentalists have in lobbying in the administrative branch, see John Chubb, *Interest Groups in the Bureaucracy*.

24. Lake, p. 15.

25. Joseph Sax, *Defending the Environment*.

26. Jay D. Hair, "Winning Through Mediation," p. 529.

27. Susskind and Ozawa, pp. 2–3.

28. The main source for the description of this case was Talbot's *Settling Things*. I supplemented his account with information from local newspapers and interviews with some of the participants.

29. Susskind and Ozawa, p. 16.

30. Richard Neely, *Why Courts Don't Work*, p. 166.

31. Susskind, "Resolving Environmental Disputes Through Ad Hocracy," p. 4.

32. Susskind, "Resolving Environmental Disputes Through Ad Hocracy," p. 3.

33. Lawrence Susskind, *The Importance of Citizen Participation and Consensus Building in the Land Use Planning Process*.

34. Susskind and Ozawa, p. 27.

35. Susskind and Ozawa, p. 18; Vermont Law Center, p. 6. This lack of judicial expertise is also one of the main complaints of Donald Horowitz in his book, *The Courts*

and Social Policy. On the other hand, Joseph Sax believes that the lack of judicial expertise on environmental matters is not really much of a problem: "Courts are never asked to resolve technical questions—they are only asked to determine whether a party appearing before them has effectively borne the burden of proving that which he asserts. Thus the questions is not one of substituting judicial knowledge for that of experts, but whether a judge is sufficiently capable of understanding the evidence put forward by expert witnesses to decide whether the party who has the burden of proof has adduced evidence adequate to support his conclusion. Why this question has seemed particularly troublesome in this context of environmental litigation is rather perplexing—courts are called upon frequently to decide cases in which the evidence of technical experts is crucial. Medical malpractice, product safety, and industrial accidents, to take only a few examples, are routine grist for the judicial mill" (Sax, p. 150).

36. Roger Fisher and William Ury, *Getting to Yes*, p. 28.

37. Edward Krinsky, a speech given at the Conference on Environmental Mediation.

38. Carole Pateman, *Participation and Democratic Theory*, p. 27.

2. THE ADVANTAGES OF INFORMALITY

1. Another version of this common mediator's fable can be found in Roger Fisher and William Ury, *Getting to Yes*, p. 59.

2. National Institute for Dispute Resolution, "Paths to Justice,", p. 10.

3. Susan Cook, speech to the Conference of Environmental Mediation.

4. W. J. D. Kennedy, "Applying Dispute Resolution to the Environmental Area," pp. 1–2.

5. For an illuminating discussion of how mediators manipulate negotiating discussions into order to reframe the issues, see Susan S. Silbey and Sally E. Merry, "Mediator Settlement Strategies."

6. James L. Creighton, "A Tutorial," p. 120.

7. Creighton, p. 121.

8. Ford Foundation, "Mediating Social Conflict," p. 5.

9. Creighton, p. 120.

10. Creighton, p. 121.

11. Silbey and Merry, "Mediator Settlement Strategies,"

12. Silbey and Merry, pp. 25–26.

13. Ford Foundation, p. 5.

14. Creighton, pp. 120–121.

15. Susan L. Carpenter and W. J. D. Kennedy, "Environmental Conflict Management," pp. 67–74.

16. Mark Dowie, "Atomic Psyche-Out," p. 23.

17. Silbey and Merry, p. 26. For a brief discussion of how miscommunication can undermine negotiations, see Timothy Sullivan, *Resolving Development Disputes Through Negotiations*, pp. 36–38.

18. William J. Dittrich, County Park Board member, phone interview by author, November 24, 1981.

19. Gail Bingham, Conservation Foundation, phone interview by author, September 21, 1981.

20. This point has also been made by researchers in other fields. In her study of participatory democracy in town meetings, Jane Mansbridge found that face-to-face contact between people encouraged emphathy and mutual understanding. She argues that

some studies by psychologists confirm this tendency. Jane Mansbridge, *Beyond Adversarial Democracy*, pp. 270–273.

21. Allan Talbot, *Environmental Mediation*, p. 10.

22. Talbot, p. 10.

23. Bob Partlow, "Portage Island,", p. 3E.

24. Tom Alexander, "A Promising Try at Environmental Detente," p. 102.

25. Talbot, p. 4.

26. Donald B. Strauss, "Managing Complexity," p. 662.

27. Lawrence Bacow and Michael Wheeler, *Environmental Dispute Resolution*, p. 76.

28. Howard Bellman, interview by author, September 25, 1981.

29. Kai N. Lee, "Neutral' Interveners in Environmental Disputes," pp. 30–32. For a more extended discussion of joint problemsolving, see Bacow and Wheeler, ch. 4.

30. Lee, p. 31.

31. Fisher and Ury, p. 64.

32. Straus, p. 662.

33. Straus, p. 662.

34. Lee, p. 32.

35. Fisher and Ury, pp. 58–83.

36. Fisher and Ury, p. 41.

37. Fisher and Ury, pp. 43–44.

38. For a description of this case, see Gerald Cormick, "Mediating Environmental Controversies," pp. 219–224.

39. Talbot, p. 11.

40. Peter Bachrach, "Interest, Participation, and Democratic Theory," p. 43.

41. Lawrence S. Bacow and James R. Milkey, "Responding to local opposition to hazardous waste facilities," pp. 1, 4–8.

42. Fisher and Ury, p. 43.

43. William Clark, "Excerpts of Remarks by Secretary Clark to the National Wildlife Federation Conservation Conference," p. 3.

3. SEPARATING MYTH FROM REALITY

1. Howard Bellman, interview by author, Oberlin, Ohio, September 25, 1981.

2. Kent Gilbreath, ed., *Business and the Environment*, p. 529.

3. See for example, L. Forer, *The Death of the Law;* and Jerold Auerbach, "A Plague of Lawyers."

4. Dean Manning, "Hyperlexis: Our National Disease," p. 767.

5. "Debunking Litigation Magic," *Newsweek,* November 21, 1983, p. 98.

6. For a good analysis of the work done by the Civil Litigation Research Project, see Marc Galanter, "Reading the Landscapes of Disputes," pp. 4–72.

7. National Institute for Dispute Resolution, "Paths to Justice", p. 7.

8. Lettie M. Wenner, *The Environmental Decade in Court,* p. 21.

9. Charles Warren, "The Hopeful Future of Mediation," p. 9.

10. Wenner, pp. 17–18; William D. Ruckelshaus, "Environmental Dispute Resolution."

11. Gail Bingham, *Resolving Environmental Disputes.*

12. Bingham, pp. 11–12.

13. Bingham, p. 12.

14. Bingham, p. 12.

15. Joseph L. Sax, *Defending the Environment*, pp. 115–120.
16. Sax, p. 118.
17. David Schoenbrod, "Limits and Dangers of Environmental Meditation,".
18. Bingham, p. 11.
19. Bingham, p. 11.
20. Bingham, p. 11.
21. Jonathan Lash, attorney for the National Resource Defense Council, telephone interview by author, September 1984.
22. Bingham, p. 3.
23. This lack of grass-roots demand for mediation has also been confirmed by other studies of informal dispute resolution processes. See, for example, Christine Harrington, "The Politics of Participation and Nonparticipation in Dispute Processes."
24. These and other figures from the Buckles' study come from notes taken at their presentation at the Law and Society Conference in June of 1984 in Boston. Requests for a written copy of their final study report have not been responded to.
25. Quoted in Phillip Shabecoff, "Mediating, Not Suing, Over the Environment," p. 16.
26. As we will see in the next chapter, there may also be another reason for this lack of demand—the fact that many environmentalists are suspicious of this process and suspect that it may be used to their disadvantage.
27. Gerald Cormick, summarized in *Environmental Mediation*, p. 17.
28. Gerald Cormick and Leah Patton, "Environmental Mediation in the U.S.," p. 10.
29. For a more lengthy description of this case see Allan R. Talbot, *Settling Things*, chapter 1.
30. The question of power and how it is distributed in environmental disputes will be discussed in greater detail in later chapters, especially chapters 5 and 7.
31. Cormick, "An Effective Alternative," p. 17.
32. Jerold S. Auerbach, *Justice Without Law*, chs. 1 and 2.
33. Auerbach, p. 52.
34. Ford Foundation, "The National Institute for Dispute Resolution," p. 1.
35. Bob Partlow, "Portage Island," p. 3E.
36. Ted Becker, "Review of Jerold Auerbach, *Justice without Law?*," p. 797.
37. Bellman, interview.
38. Gerald Cormick, "Environmental Mediation in the U.S.," p. 10.
39. Bellman, interview.
40. Bellman, interview.
41. Bellman, interview.
42. Bellman, interview.
43. Carole Pateman, *Participation and Democratic Theory*, p. 25.
44. J. J. Rousseau, *The Social Contract*, p. 96.

4. MEDIATION AS SEDUCTION

1. Adapted from a story by Joey Adams, *Reader's Digest,* March 1983, p. 130.
2. Quoted in James Crowfoot, "Negotiations," p. 25.
3. Peter Steinhart, "Talking It Over," p. 10.
4. Tom Alexander, "A Promising Try at Environmental Detente for Coal," pp. 94–102.

5. Geoffrey O'Gara, "Should This Marriage Be Saved?" pp. 11–13.

6. Bill Barich, "Playing Environmental Let's Make a Deal," p. 20.

7. Conservation Foundation, *A Report on the Year 1984*, pp. 94–95.

8. Nancy Shute, "A Guide to Environmental Groups," pp. 56–58.

9. The concern about cooptation arose early in scholarly writings about citizen participation efforts; see Philip Selznick, *TVA and the Grass Roots*. For more recent discussions of this problem see Sherry R. Arnstein, "A Ladder of Citizen Participation." pp. 216–224; and Harold Savitch, "Powerlessness in an Urban Ghetto," pp. 19–56.

10. Jane J. Mansbridge, *Beyond Adversary Democracy*

11. Mansbridge, pp. 276–277.

12. All of these examples of tricks of the trade were adapted from examples given in Chester L. Karrass, *Give and Take*.

13. Information on Inyo County groundwater negotiations was obtained from a telephone interview, October 15, 1984, with Ellen Hardebeck from the League of Women Voters in Inyo County who has been a close observer of these talks.

14. National Institute for Dispute Resolution, "Paths to Justice," p. 15.

15. NIDR, p. 17.

16. Kai N. Lee, " 'Neutral' Intervenors in Environmental Disputes," p. 24.

17. Gail Bingham, Conservation Foundation, telephone interview by author, September 22, 1981.

18. James Benson, Director of the Institute for Ecological Studies, telephone interview by author, November 17, 1981.

19. Herb Cohen, *You Can Negotiate Anything*, p. 241.

20. Cohen, p. 242.

21. For a lengthy (and laudatory) description of this negotiation effort see Alexander, "A Promising Try."

22. O'Gara, p. 11.

23. Alexander, p. 94.

24. Alexander, p. 101.

25. Alexander, p. 95.

26. O'Gara, p. 11.

27. Alexander, p. 96.

28. "DoE Grants $85,000 to Halt 'Nuclear Phobia,' " *Not Man Apart*, (December 1984), 14 (10):15

29. Arnstein, p. 218–219.

30. For a description of this mediation effort, see Katherine Fitzpatrick-Lins, John A. S. McGlennon, and Glenn F. Tiedt, "Conflict Resolution in Railroad Right-of-Way Disputes."

31. Fitzpatrick-Lins et al, p. 6.

32. Mary Douglas and Aaron Wildavsky, *Risk and Culture*.

33. For a discussion of this point, see David Cohen, "The Public Interest Movement and Citizen Participation."

34. Joan Nice, "Stalemates spawn new breed," p. 4.

35. Patrick Parenteau.

36. Gerald Cormick, "Intervention and Self-Determination in Environmental Disputes," p. 5; and Gerald Cormick, "Environmental Mediation in the U.S.," p. 11.

37. Allan R. Talbot, *Settling Things*, p. 63.

38. Howard Bellman, interview by author.

39. Deborah M. Kolb, *The Mediators*.

40. Kolb, ch. 5.

41. Kolb, p. 210, n.7.

42. Kolb, p. 117.

43. Kolb, p. 125.

44. Kolb, p. 126.

45. Kolb, p. 120.

46. Kolb, p. 162.

47. Kolb, pp. 118–120 and pp. 128–133.

48. Kolb, p. 130.

49. Kolb, p. 166.

50. Kolb, p. 166.

5. MEDIATION AND INEQUALITIES OF POWER

1. Adapted from a story told by Thomas R. Colosi, "On Ethics: Of Lions, Lambs, and Underdogs," address given to Society of Professionals in Dispute Resolution Conference on Ethics, Philadelphia, 1983.

2. James Crowfoot, "Negotiations," p. 35. This is by far the best discussion of the inherent connections between mediation and theories of political power. His basic point is that mediation is a desirable approach if one assumes a pluralist perspective, but that if one holds to elite theory assumptions, mediation becomes seen as primarily a form of manipulation and cooptation.

3. Owen Fiss, "Against Settlement," pp. 1073–1092.

4. Malcolm D. Rivken, "Negotiated Development," p. 4.

5. This statement from Robert Golten, and many of the other statements from mediators in this chapter come from interviews conducted by Andrew Sachs in the preparation for his Masters thesis "An Analysis of Practitioners Theories."

6. Howard Bellman, interviewed by Andrew Sachs, March 22–23, 1984.

7. These figures come from a study done by the Wisconsin League of Women Voters. Some of this information came from Dorothy Lagerroos and Caryl Terrell, "Report on the League of Women Voters' Survey on the Consensus Process." Other figures came from survey data that was not included in this final report, but which the League kindly allowed me to review.

8. E. E. Schattschneider, "The Scope and Bias of the Pressure System," Grant McConnell, *Private Power and American Democracy;* Charles Lindblom, *Politics and Markets,* see especially part 5.

9. Mancur Olson, *The Logic of Collective Action*.

10. Timothy Sullivan, *Resolving Development Disputes Through Negotiations*, pp. 188–190.

11. Sullivan, pp. 188–190.

12. Reports of this kind of bias in the selection of participants can be found in responses to the Lagerroos and Terrell's Wisconsin League of Women Voters study cited above. They are contained in written responses not included in the final report, but that are available from the League.

13. Another "objective" selection criterion sometimes used by mediators is who is involved in the litigation taking place over this dispute. But again this gets back to the issue of power—for it is those groups that are less powerful that usually are unable to take part in the court battles over a particular dispute, and thus tend to be left out of the subsequent negotiations.

14. Howard Bellman, interview by author.

15. Olson, pp. 165–167.

16. Lagerroos and Terrell, p. 5.

17. Lagerros and Terrell.

18. These quotes are found in responses to the League's survey that are not included in the final report, but that are available upon request.

19. Quote from Lagerroos and Terrell study.

20. Lagerroos and Terrell.

21. For a discussion of the Reagan administration's campaign of deregulation in the area of the environment, from a conservationist's point of view, see Jonathan Lash, *A Season of Spoils.*

22. Lettie Wenner, "Judicial Oversight of Environmental Deregulation," p. 186.

23. Alan S. Miller, "Steel Industry Effluent Limitations," p. 10095.

24. The following account of the Thriftway case is based in large part on an article by Frank O'Donnell that was reproduced in the *Congressional Record,* March 7, 1983, 129 (26): E848–E 849.

25. For a discussion of this issue, see *Lead In Gasoline: Public Health Dangers: Hearing before a Subcommittee on the House Committee on Government Operations,* 97th Cong., 2d sess., April 14, 1982.

26. Not all mediators are insensitive to the importance of the public interest. See Gerald Cormick, "Intervention and Self-Determination in Environmental Disputes," pp. 1, 3–6.

27. Cormick, p. 4

28. Lawrence Susskind, "Environmental Mediation and the Accountability Problem," p. 38.

29. Timothy Sullivan, "Resolving Development Disputes Through Negotiation," p. 7.

30. Lawrence Bacow and James Milkey, "Responding to Local Opposition to Hazardous Waste Facilities."

31. For a discussion of efforts in this direction, see Lawrence Bacow and Michael Wheeler, *Environmental Dispute Resolution,* ch. 12.

32. Jerold Auerbach, *Justice Without Law,* p. 136.

33. Sam Gusman, interviewed by Andrew Sachs, March 17, 1984.

34. James Benson, environmental activist, telephone interview by author, November 17, 1981.

35. David Doniger, attorney for Natural Resource Defense Fund, interview by author, Washington, D. C., August 30, 1984.

36. Patrick Parenteau.

37. Dana Duxbury, "Another View," p. 9. It should be pointed out that the Massachusetts law does make provision for grants to local towns to help them with technical issues, but apparently Ms. Duxbury and the local residents find those inadequate to deal with this problem, especially at the early stages of the dispute.

38. Lagerroos and Terrell.

39. Roger Fisher and William Ury, *Getting to Yes,* pp. 106–111.

40. For a further discussion of coercion in other forms of alternative dispute resolution besides environmental mediation, see L. R. Singer, *The Growth of Non-Judicial Dispute Resolution;* and H. McIssac, "Mandatory Conciliation Custody/Visitation Matters," pp 73–81.

41. Christine Harrington, "Voluntariness, Consent, and Coercion in Adjudicating

Minor Disputes," p. 145. Owen Fiss has also argued that mediated agreements can sometimes be compared to plea bargains where the defendant's agreement often could hardly be considered voluntary. See Fiss, "Against Settlement," p. 1075.

42. Susskind, *Environmental Mediation*, p. 15.

43. Benson interview.

44. "Ground Water Bill Opposed," p. 6.

45. Lagerroos and Terrell.

46. Gail Bingham, *Resolving Environmental Disputes*, p. 5

47. For a discussion of how this approach limits the bargaining power of participants, see Sullivan, p. 193.

48. Jeffrey Miller, interviewed by Andrew Sachs, March 20, 1984.

49. Peter Clark and Wendy Emrich, "New Tools for Resolving Environmental Disputes," pp. i, 2.

50. Clark and Emrich, p. 12.

51. Peter Bachrach and Morton Baratz, "Two Faces of Power."

52. Peter Bachrach and Morton Baratz, "Decisions and Non-decisions," p. 632.

53. Cynthia Sampson, "Wisconsin Ensures Local-Level Negotiations in Siting Waste Management Facilities," p. 3.

54. Miller interview by Sachs.

55. The description of this dispute was adapted from Katherine Fitzpatrick-Lins, John A. S. McGlennon, and Glenn F. Tiedt, "Conflict Resolution in Railroad Right-of-Way Disputes."

56. Fitzpatrick-Lins et al., p. 6.

57. Saul Alinsky, *Rules for Radicals*, p. 13.

58. Private developmental groups have also used similar preemptive strategies to try to manage conflict over development projects. See Douglas J. Amy, "The Politics of Environmental Mediation," p. 12.

59. James Wall, "Mediation," p. 164.

60. Susskind, "Environmental Mediation," p. 15.

61. Susan Carpenter and John Kennedy, *ACCORD* Associates, interviewed by Andrew Sachs, March 14, 1984.

62. Howard Bellman interview by Sachs.

63. Bellman interview by Sachs.

64. Thomas Colosi, interviewed by Andrew Sachs, April 2, 1984.

65. Colosi interview by Sachs.

6. DISTORTING THE NATURE OF ENVIRONMENTAL CONFLICT

1. Amory Lovins, *Soft Energy Paths*, p. 12.

2. Thomas Colosi, interviewed by Andrew Sachs, April 2, 1984. This same point was made by Lon Fuller: "The central quality of mediation [is] its capacity to reorient the parties towards each other, not by imposing rules on them, but by helping them achieve a new and shared perception of their relationship, a perception that will redirect their attitude and dispositions to one another." Quoted in Joseph Stulberg, "The Theory and Practice of Mediation," p. 91.

3. Susan Carpenter quoted in Kai Lee, "'Neutral' Interveners in Environmental Disputes," p. 32.

4. Lee, pp. 3 and 31.

5. See Jay D. Hair, "Winning through Mediation," p. 528.

6. Gilbreath, p. 445.

7. Gilbreath, p. 528.

8. William K. Reilly, "Conservation in the 1980's."

9. Christopher Palmer, "Business and Environmentalists,"

10. Brock Evans, "Environmentalists and Utilities," p. 496.

11. Jonathan Lash, staff lawyer with Natural Resource Defense Council, telephone interview by author, August 5, 1984.

12. Jane J. Mansbridge, *Beyond Adversarial Democracy*, p. 5

13. Roger Fisher and William Ury, *Getting to Yes*, p. 84.

14. Cormick, "Environmental Mediation in the U.S.," p. 9.

15. For an example of this kind of perspective on environmental issues, see William Ophuls, *Ecology and the Politics of Scarcity*.

16. Laurence Tribe, Corinne Schelling, and John Voss, eds., *When Values Conflict*, p. 4.

17. Gerald Cormick, "Mediating Environmental Controversies," p. 215.

18. Lawrence Bacow and Michael Wheeler, *Environmental Dispute Resolution*, p. 364.

19. Emily Joffee, "Peace of Mindlessness," *The New Republic*, March 12, 1984.

20. Joffee, p. 18.

21. In making a similar point, Silbey and Merry have noted that mediators will often "rephrase demands and accounts in order to eliminate loaded language which might connote moral blame or liability." Susan Silbey and Sally Merry, "Mediator Settlement Strategies," p. 22.

22. Quote comes from a survey conducted by Dorothy Lagerroos and Caryl Terrell, *Report on the League of Women Voters' Survey on the Consensus Process*.

23. Lagerroos and Terrell.

24. David Brower quoted in Bill Barich, "Playing Environmental Let's Make a Deal," p. 20.

25. Scott Mernitz, *Mediation of Environmental Disputes*, p. 163.

26. Malcolm Rivkin, "Negotiated Development."

27. Mernitz, p. 163.

28. Mernitz, p. 163.

29. Mernitz, p. 158.

30. William Ophuls, *Ecology and the Politics of Scarcity*. See especially Chapter 8.

31. Others have also portrayed the choices that face us in environmental and energy policy in these kinds of stark and dichotomous terms. See Amory Lovins, *Soft Energy Paths*; and Herman Daly, *Steady-State Economics*.

32. For example, one radical critic, Timothy Lukes, has criticized the mainstream environmental movement for only attempting to check the worst excesses of corporate capitalism and for not trying to reconstitute capitalism itself into a more environmentally benign economic system. Timothy Lukes, "Notes on a Deconstructionist Ecology," p. 23.

33. Quoted in Northern Rockies Action Group, "Selected Transcripts from the NRAG Conference on Negotiations," p. 21.

34. Owen Fiss, "Against Settlement," p. 1085.

35. Fiss, p. 1085.

36. National Institute for Dispute Resolution, "Paths to Justice," p. 10.

37. For a more detailed discussion of the advantages of regulatory process over mediation in promoting the public interest see David Schoenbrod, "Limits and Dangers of Environmental Mediation," pp. 1466–1471.

38. Gerald Cormick, "Mediating Environmental Controversies," p. 218.

39. Lee, p. 3.

40. For a description of Goldaber's work, see Mark Dowie, "Atomic Psyche-Out,"

41. Dowie, p. 50.

42. Dowie, p. 50.

43. Dowie, p. 50.

44. The common assumption that some things have no price and are not negotiable has a number of important political and policy implications, but unfortunately there is not space to discuss them here. For a fascinating and useful discussion of this topic and its implications for environmental policy, see Steven Kelman, *What Price Incentives*, pp. 54–83.

45. Lawrence Bacow and James R. Milkey, "Overcoming Local Opposition to Hazardous Waste Facilities," p. 276.

46. Bacow and Milkey, p. 276.

47. Lagerroos and Terrell.

48. David Phillips, Wildlife Projects Director of Friends of the Earth, telephone interview by author, September 13, 1984.

49. Observers of labor-management negotiations have also noticed this narrowing processes at work there. In particular, there is a tendency for negotiations to focus on economic issues, rather than on larger and more political issues such as worker participation in management. There are undoubtedly a number of reasons for this, but Deborah Kolb found that labor mediators play a role in this narrowing process, in large part because they find economic issues easier to work with and generate compromises over. As she observed, "the mediator's skills are well suited to the consideration of monetary issues and are not as applicable to [other] demands." See Deborah Kolb, *The Mediators*, p. 169.

50. These scholars are among the best who are attempting to understand the larger political implications of the increasing use of informal dispute resolution in American society. See, Richard Abel, "The Contradiction of Informal Justice," pp. 267–320; Richard Hofrichter, "Neighborhood Justice and The Social Control Problems of American Capitalism"; and Jerold Auerbach, *Justice Without Law?*

51. Abel, pp. 289–291.

52. This preference by industry for a case-by-case approach and the resulting political advantages has been confirmed by Professor John Chubb in his study of political participation in the regulation of the nuclear power industry. He found that the utility industry prefers to address the licensing of each new nuclear power plant on a case-by-case basis because this "increases the participatory burden upon public interest groups and other financially deficient interests." See John E. Chubb, *Interest Groups in the Bureaucracy*, p. 95.

53. Quoted in Hofrichter, p. 400.

54. Auerbach, p. 144.

55. Auerbach, p. 124.

56. Auerbach, p. 128.

57. Naturally, not all mediators succeed in keeping their personal political opinions from affecting their work—and this may indeed be a significant source of political bias in the process. But in this book I am not so much concerned with the biases introduced by individual mediators; rather, I am interested in the political biases that are inherent to the process itself. The former problem can be solved by replacing the mediator, the latter is not so easily remedied.

7. THE FUTURE OF ENVIRONMENTAL MEDIATION

1. Lawrence Susskind, "Environmental Mediation and the Accountability Problem," pp. 2–5.

2. Jay D. Hair, "Winning Through Mediation," p. 527.

3. This point was stressed by David Doniger of the Natural Resources Defense Council, an attorney who participated in an early effort at regulatory negotiation.

4. For an illuminating discussion of these surveys, see Robert Cameron Mitchel, "Public Opinion and Environmental Politics in the 1970s and 1980s," pp. 51–74.

5. For an account of the corporate attack on environmental regulations in the 1980s, see Susan Tolchin and Martin Tolchin, *Dismantling America*.

6. John E. Chubb, *Interest Groups and the Bureaucracy*, p. 102. For another discussion of the disadvantages that environmentalist typically suffer from in their effort to lobbying Congress and the administrative branch, see Laura Lake, *Environmental Mediation*, pp. 17–20.

7. There was a surge in membership in many environmental organizations as a reaction to election of Ronald Reagan and the appointment of James Watt, but those numbers now seem to be shrinking again. This is a further indication of the volatility and unreliability of participation in these groups.

8. Thomas Byrne Edsall, *The New Politics of Inequality*, p. 107. Much of the argument in this section follows along the points made by Edsall in chapter 3 of his insightful book. Another book useful in analyzing the increase of corporate power in the United States is Charles Lindblom's *Politics and Markets*.

9. Edsall, pp. 111–112, 115–116.

10. Edsall, p. 116.

11. Edsall, pp. 117–120.

12. For a general discussion of the political problems stemming from the increases in PAC spending in congressional races, see Mark Green, *Who Runs Congress?* pp. 29–45, 51–57.

13. Henry C. Kenski and Margaret Corgan Kenski, "Congress Against the President," pp. 112.

14. Kenski and Kenski, pp. 114.

15. George Coggins, "Some Suggestions for Future Plaintiffs," p. 312.

16. *Vermont Yankee Nuclear Power Corporation v. NRDC et al.*, 38 CCH. S. Ct. Bull. p. B 1471 (April 1978).

17. For a mention of this case and some of its implications for mediation, see Patricia M. Wald, "Negotiation of Environmental Disputes," p. 3.

18. Lettie M. Wenner, *The Environmental Decade in Court*, p. 43.

19. Hair, p. 530.

20. Hair, p. 531.

21. "Environmental Mediation," pp. 17–19.

22. "Environmental Mediation," p. 17.

23. Allan Talbot, *Settling Things*, p. 93.

24. For a discussion of the theory of reg-neg, especially on the federal level, see Gail Bingham, "Does Negotiation Hold a Promise for Regulatory Reform?", pp. 1–8; and Richard Stewart, "Regulation, Innovation, and Administrative Law."

25. For a description and discussion of these state programs from a mediators point of view, see *Resolve: A Quarterly Newsletter on Environmental Dispute Resolution*, Winter, Spring 1983.

26. Lawrence Bacow and Michael Wheeler, *Environmental Dispute Resolution*, pp. 324–325.

27. For a discussion of some of the other problems, including lack of goodfaith bargaining, that characterize mandatory negotiations, see Timothy Sullivan, "The Difficulties of Mandatory Negotiations."

28. Denise Provost, "The Massachusetts Hazardous Waste Facility Siting Act," p. 737.

29. Provost, p. 737.

30. Lawrence Bacow and James Milkey, "Overcoming Local Opposition to Hazardous Waste Facilities," pp. 297–298.

31. For a good discussion of the legal dimensions of this kind of preemption of local power, including questions of due process, see Provost's "The Massachusetts Hazardous Waste."

32. Quoted in Ron Arnold, "Loggers vs. Environmentalists," p. 19.

33. Bill Barich, "Playing Environmental Let's Make a Deal," p. 20.

34. National Institute for Dispute Resolution (NIDR), "Paths to Justice," p. 22.

35. NIDR, p. 22.

36. NIDR, p. 21.

37. NIDR, p. 21.

38. Bacow and Wheeler, p. 328.

39. The Harvard Negotiation Project seems to be the one exception to this funding drought. As one mediator commented somewhat jealously, "Companies and foundations seem to be competing to see who can give the most money to Harvard."

40. Richard Abel, ed., *The Politics of Informal Justice*, p. 302.

41. For a discussion of why administrators are reluctant to get involved in negotiation efforts, see Lawrence Susskind and Alan Weinstein, "Toward A Theory of Environmental Dispute Resolution," pp.352–353.

42. Bacow and Milkey.

Bibliography

Abel, Richard, ed. *The Politics of Informal Justice.* 2 vols. New York: Academic Press, 1982.

Abel, Richard. "The Contradiction of Informal Justice." In Abel, ed. *The Politics of Informal Justice,* pp. 267–310.

Alexander, Tom. "A Promising Try at Environmental Detente for Coal." *Fortune,* February 13, 1978, pp. 94–102.

Alinsky, Saul. *Rule for Radicals.* New York: Vintage Books, 1971.

Amy, Douglas J. "The Politics of Environmental Mediation." *Ecology Law Quarterly* (1983); 2(1): 1–19.

Arnold, Ron. "Loggers vs. Environmentalist: Friends Or Foes." *Logging Management* (February 1978), 1:16–19.

Arnstein, Sherry. "A Ladder of Citizen Participation."*AIP Journal* (July 1969), pp. 216–24.

Auerbach, Jerold. *Justice Without Law: Resolving Disputes Without Lawyers.* New York: Oxford University Press, 1983.

——"A Plague of Lawyers." *Harpers,* October 1976.

Bachrach, Peter. "Interest, Participation, and Democratic Theory." In J. Ronald Pennock and John W. Chapman, eds., *Participation In Politics.* pp. 39–55.

Bachrach, Peter and Morton Baratz. "Two Faces of Power." *American Political Science Review*(1962), 56:947–952.

——"Decisions and Nondecisions: An Analytic Framework." *American Political Science Review* (1963), 57:635–642.

Bacow, Lawrence S. and James R. Milkey. "Responding to Local Opposition to Hazardous Waste Facilities: the Massachusetts Approach." *Resolve* (Winter/Spring 1983), 1:4–8.

——"Overcoming Local Opposition to Hazardous Waste Facilities: The Massachusetts Approach." *Harvard Environmental Law Review,* 6:263–303.

Bacow, Lawrence and Michael Wheeler. *Environmental Dispute Resolution.* New York: Plenum Press, 1984.

Barich, Bill. "Playing Environmental Let's Make a Deal." *Outside* (February 1978), p. 20.

Bartlett, Robert. *The Reserve Mining Controversy: Science, Technology, and Environmental Quality.* Bloomington: Indiana University Press, 1980.

Becker, Ted. Review of *Justice Without Law?* by Jerold Auerbach. *American Political Science Review* (Fall 1984), p. 797.

Bellman, Howard. Interview by author in Oberlin, Ohio. September 25, 1981.

——Interview by Andrew Sachs. March 22–23, 1984.

Bellman, Howard et al., "Environmental Conflict Resolution: Practitioners' Perspective of An Emerging Field." *Environmental Consensus* (Winter 1981), pp. 1–7.

Benson, James. Telephone interview by author. November 17, 1981.

Bingham, Gail. Telephone interview by author. September 22, 1981.

——"Does Negotiation Hold a Promise for Regulatory Reform?" *Resolve: A Quarterly Newsletter on Environmental Dispute Resolution* (Fall 1981), pp. 1–8.

——*Resolving Environmental Disputes: A Decade of Experience* (Executive Summary), Washington, D. C.: Conservation Foundation, 1985.

Carpenter, Susan and W. J. D. Kennedy. "Environmental Conflict Management." *Environmental Professional* (1980), 67–74.

Carpenter, Susan and John Kennedy. Interview by Andrew Sachs. March 14, 1984.

Chubb, John. *Interest Groups In the Bureaucracy.* Stanford: Stanford University Press, 1983.

Clark, Peter and Wendy Emrich. "New Tools For Resolving Environmental Disputes." Washington D. C.: Council on Environmental Quality and Resource and Land Investigations Program, Geological Survey, U. S. Department of the Interior, 1980.

Clark, William. "Excerpts of Remarks by Secretary William Clark to the National Wildlife Federation Conservation Conference, December 7, 1983." Washington, D. C.: Department of Interior.

Coggins, George. "Some Suggestions for Future Plaintiffs." *Kansas Law Review* (1976), 24:312.

Cohen, David. "The Public Interest Movement and Citizen Participation." In Stuart Langton, ed., *Citizen Participation in America.* pp. 55–64.

Cohen, Herb. *You Can Negotiate Anything.* New York: Bantam Books, 1980.

Colosi, Thomas. Interview by Andrew Sachs. April 2, 1984.

Conservation Foundation. "Environmental Mediation: An Effective Alternative?" Washington, D. C.: Conservation Foundation, 1978.

——"Report of the Year 1984." Washington, D. C.: Conservation Foundation, 1985.

——*Resolve: A Quarterly Newsletter on Environmental Dispute Resolution.* Washington, D.C.: Conservation Foundation.

Cook, Susan. "Excerpts from a speech to The Conference of Environmental Mediation in Columbus, Ohio. November 15–16, 1984."

Cormick, Gerald. "Mediating Environmental Controversies: Perspectives and First Experience." *Earth Law Journal* (1976), 2:215–224.

——"Environmental Mediation in the U.S.: Experience and Future Directions." Seattle: Mediation Institute, 1981. Mimeo.

——"Intervention and Self-determination In Environmental Disputes: A Mediator's Perspective." *Resolve* (Winter 1982), 1: 3–6.

Creighton, James L. "A Tutorial: Acting As a Conflict Conciliator." *Environmental Professional* (1980), 2:119–127.

Crowfoot, James. "Negotiations: An Effective Tool For Citizen Organizations?" *Northern Rockies Action Group Paper* (Fall 1980) Helena, Mont.: Northern Rockies Action Group.

Crozier, Michel, Samuel Huntington, and Joji Watanuki. *The Crisis of Democracy.* New York: New York University Press, 1975.

Daly, Herman. *Steady–State Economics.* San Francisco: Freeman, 1977.

Dittrich, William J. Telephone interview by author. November 24, 1981.

Doniger, David. Interview by author in Washington, D.C. August 30, 1984.

Douglas, Mary and Aaron Wildavsky. *Risk and Culture.* Berkeley: University of California Press, 1982.

Dowie, Mark. "Atomic Psyche-Out: The Nuclear Industry's Strategy to Divide and Destroy the Opposition." *Mother Jones* (May 1981), pp. 21–23, 47–85.

Dryzek, John S. *Conflict and Choice In Resource Management: The Case of Alaska.* Boulder, Colo.: Westview Press, 1983.

Duxbury, Dana. "Another View." *Resolve* (Winter/Spring 1983), p. 9.

Edelman, Murray. *The Symbolic Uses of Politics.* Urbana: University of Illinois Press, 1967.

Edsall, Thomas Byrne. *The New Politics of Inequality.* New York: Norton, 1984.

Environmental Law Center. "Environmental Mediation In Vermont." South Royalton: Vermont Law School Publication Series, 1982.

Evans, Brock. "Environmentalists and Utilities: Let's Get Together." In Gilbreath, *Business and the Environment,* pp. 493–504.

Fernandez, Louis. "Let's Try Cooperation Instead of Confrontation." In Gilbreath, ed., *Business and the Environment,* pp. 563–819.

Fisher, Roger and William Ury. *Getting to Yes: Negotiating Without Giving In.* Boston: Houghton Mifflin, 1981.

Fiss, Owen. "Against Settlement." *The Yale Law Journal.* (May 1984), 93:1073–1092.

Fitzpatrick-Lins, Katherine, John A. S. McGlennon, and Glenn F. Tiedt. "Conflict Resolution in Railroad Right-of-Way Disputes: Columbia, Missouri, and Douglas County, Nebraska," U. S. Geological Survey and the Council on Environmental Quality (May 1981), Report No. 80–874.

Ford Foundation. "New Approaches to Conflict Resolution." New York: Ford Foundation, 1978.

——"Mediating Social Conflict." New York: Ford Foundation, 1978.

——"The National Institute for Dispute Resolution." New York: Ford Foundation, 1981.

Forer, Lois. *The Death of the Law.* New York: McKay, 1975.

Fuller, Lon. "The Forms and Limits of Adjudication." *Harvard Law Review* (1978), 92:294–404

Galanter, Marc. "Reading the Landscapes of Disputes: What We Know and Don't Know (and Think We Know) About Our Allegedly Contentious and Litigious Society." *UCLA Law Review* (October 1983), 31:4–72.

Gilbreath, Kent, ed. *Business and the Environment: Toward Common Ground.* 2d ed. Washington, D.C.: Conservation Foundation, 1984.

Golten, Robert. "Mediation: A Sellout For Conservation Advocates, Or a Bargain." *The Environmental Professional* (1980), 2:62–66.

——Interview by Andrew Sachs, March 16, 1984.

Green, Mark. *Who Runs Congress?* New York: Dell, 1984.

Gusman, Sam. Interview by Andrew Sachs. March 17, 1984.

Hair, John D. "Winning Through Mediation." In Gilbreath, ed., *Business and the Environment,* pp. 527–533.

Hardebeck, Ellen. Telephone interview by author. October 15, 1984.

Harrington, Christine, "Voluntariness, Consent, and Coercion in Adjudicating Minor Disputes: The Neighborhood Justice Center." In John Brigham, ed., *Policy Implementation,* pp. 131–158. Beverly Hills: Sage, 1980.

——"The Politics of Participation and Nonparticipation in Dispute Processes." *Law and Policy* (April 1984), 6:203–230.

——*Shadow Justice: The Ideology and Institutionalization of Alternatives to Court.* Boston: Greenwood Press, 1985.

Harter, Philip S. "Regulatory Negotiation: The Experience So Far." *Resolve* (Winter 1984), 1:5–10.

Hofrichter, Richard. "Neighborhood Justice and the Social Control Problems of American Capitalism." In Abel, ed., *The Politics of Informal Justice,* pp. 207–248.

Horowitz, Donald. "The Courts and Social Policy." Washington, D. C.: Brookings Institution, 1977.

Institute for Environmental Negotiation. *The Mediator.* Charlottesville: University of Virginia.

Karrass, Chester L. *Give and Take: The Complete Guide to Negotiating Strategies and Tactics.* New York: Crowell, 1970.

Kelman, Steven. *What Price Incentives.* Boston: Auburn House, 1981.

Kennedy, W. J. D. "Applying Dispute Resolution to the Environmental Area." Speech before the Second National Conference on Environmental Dispute Resolution, Washington, D. C., October 1–2, 1984.

Kenski, Henry C. and Margaret Corgan Kenski. "Congress Against the President." In Vig and Kraft, eds., *Environmental Policy In the 1980s,* pp 97–120.

Kolb, Deborah M. *The Mediators.* Cambridge: MIT Press, 1983.

Krinsky, Edward. Speech given at the Conference on Environmental Mediation, Columbus, Ohio, November 15–16, 1983.

Lagerroos, Dorothy and Caryl Terrell. *Report on the League of Women Voters' Survey on the Consensus Process*. Madison: League of Women Voters of Wisconsin, 1984.

Lake, Laura, ed. *Environmental Mediation: The Search for Consensus*. Boulder, Colo: Westview Press, 1980.

Lash, Jonathan. Interview by author. September 1984.

——Interview by author. August 5, 1984.

——*A Season of Spoils*. New York: Pantheon Books, 1984.

Lee, Kai N. "'Neutral' Interveners in Environmental Disputes: An Analytic Framework." University of Washington Institute for Environmental Studies, Seattle, June 1982. Mimeo.

Lindblom, Charles. *Politics and Markets*. New York: Basic Books, 1977.

Lovins, Amory. *Soft Energy Paths*. Cambridge: Ballinger, 1977.

Lowi, Theodore. *The End of Liberalism*. New York: Morton, 1970.

Lukes, Timothy. "Notes on A Deconstructionist Ecology." *New Political Science* (Spring 1983), 11:20–32.

Manning, Dean. "Hyperlexis: Our National Disease." *New York University Law Review*, 71:18

Mansbridge, Jane. *Beyond Adversarial Democracy*. Chicago: University of Chicago Press, 1983.

McConnell, Grant. *Private Power and American Democracy*. New York: Knopf, 1967.

McCory, John. "Environmental Mediation: Another Piece of the Puzzle." *Vermont Law Review* (1981), 6(1):50–83.

McIssac, H. "Mandatory Conciliation Custody/Visitation Matters: California''s Bold Stroke." *Conciliation Courts Review*, (1981, 19(2):73–81.

Mernitz, Scott. *Mediation of Environmental Disputes: A Sourcebook*. New York: Praeger, 1980.

Miller, Alan S. "Steel Industry Effluent Limitations: Success at the Negotiating Table." *Environmental Law Reporter* (1984), 8(4):10094–95.

Miller, Jeffrey. Interview by Andrew Sachs. March 20, 1984.

Mitchell, Robert Cameron. "Public Opinion and Environmental Politics in the 1970s and 1980s." In Vig and Kraft, eds., *Environmental Policy in the 1980s*, pp. 51–74.

National Institute for Dispute Resolution. "Paths to Justice: Major Public Policy Issues of Dispute Resolution." Prepared for the Department of Justice, Office of Legal Policy, January 1984.

Neely, Richard. *Why Courts Don't Work*. New York: McGraw-Hill, 1982.

Nice, Joan. "Stalemates Spawn New Breed: The Eco-Mediators." *High Country News*, March 23, 1979, pp. 4–6.

Northern Rockies Action Group. "Selected Transcripts from the NRAG Conference on Negotiations." *NRAG Papers* (Fall, 1980).

O'Gara, Geoffrey. "Should This Marriage Be Saved?" *Environmental Action*, March 11, 1978, pp. 10–13.

Olson, Mancur. *The Logic of Collective Action.* Cambridge: Harvard University Press, 1965.

——*The Rise and Decline of Nations.* New Haven: Yale University Press, 1983.

Ophuls, William. *Ecology and the Politics of Scarcity.* San Francisco: Freeman, 1977.

Palmer, Christopher. "Business and Environmentalists: A Peace ̇ ̇oposal." In Gilbreath, ed., *Business and the Environment.* pp. 483–486.

Parenteau, Patrick. Speech given at the Ohio Alliance for Enviroumental Edu cation Seventh Annual Environmental Education Conference, Columbuᵥ, Ohio, November 16, 1983.

Partlow, Bob. "Portage Island: Agreement Is Most Valuable In Terms of Indians and Non-Indians Being Able to Work Together.' *Bellingham Herald*, April 22, 1979, p.3E.

Pateman, Carole. *Participation and Democratic Theory.* Cambridge, Eng.: Cambridge University Press, 1970.

Phillips, David. Telephone interview by author. September 13, 1984.

Provost, Denise. "The Massachusetts Hazardous Waste Facility Siting Act: What Impact on Municipal Power to Exclude and Regulate?" *Environmental Affairs* (1982–1983), 10:715–793.

Reilly, William K. "Conservation in the 1980's: Building on a Firm Foundation." In Gilbreath, ed., *Business in the Environment*, pp. 463–472.

Rivken, Malcolm D. "Negotiated Development: A Breakthrough in Environmental Development Controversies." Washington, D.C.: Conservation Foundation, 1977.

Rohatyn, Felix. "How About Domestic Cooperation?" *New York Times*, June 7, 1983, p. A19.

Rousseau, J. J. *The Social Contract.* New York: Penguin Books, 1968.

Ruckelshaus, William D. "The Environmental Dispute Resolution, October 1, 1984." Transcript of remarks William D. Ruckelshaus at the Conservation Foundation's Second National Conference. Washington, D. C.: Conservation Foundation, 1984.

Sachs, Andrew. "An Analysis of Practitioners' Theories: The Dependence of Negotiating Power Upon Political Power in Environmental Disputes." Masters thesis, MIT, 1985.

Sampson, Cynthia. "Wisconsin Ensures Local-Level Negotiations in Siting Waste Management Facilities." *Resolve* (Winter/Spring 1983), p. 3.

Sander, Frank. "Varieties of Dispute Resolution." *Federal Decisions Rules* (1976), 70:111–134.

Savitch, Harold. "Powerlessness In an Urban Ghetto." *Polity* (1972), 5:19–56.

Sax, Joseph. *Defending the Environment: A Strategy for Citizen Action.* New York: Knopf, 1971.

Schattschneider, E. E. "The Scope and Bias of the Pressure System." In Michael P. Smith. ed., *American Politics and Public Policy*. New York: Random House, 1973.

Schoenbrod, David. "Limits and Dangers of Environmental Mediation: A Review Essay." *New York University Law Review* (1983), 38 153–76.

Selznick, Philip. *TVA and the Grass Roots*. Berkeley: University of California Press, 1949.

Shabecoff, Phillip. "Mediating, Not Suing, Over the Environment." *New York Times*, May 29, 1983, p. 16.

Shute, Nancy. "A Guide to Environmental Groups." *Country Journal* (January 1984), pp. 56–58.

Silbey, Susan S. and Sally E. Merry, "Mediator Settlement Strategies." Paper presented at the American Sociological Association Annual Meetings. Wellesley, Mass., 1984. (Available from the authors at Wellesley College, Wellesley, Mass.)

Singer, L. R. *The Growth of Non-Judicial Dispute Resolution: Speculations on the Effects of Justice for the Poor and on the Role of Legal Services*. Washington, D. C., Legal Services Corporation, 1979.

Steinhart, Peter. "Talking It Over." *Audubon* (1984), 86:(1)8–15.

Stewart, Richard. "Regulation, Innovation and Administrative Law: A Conceptual Framework." *California Law Review* (1981), Vol. 69.

Stone, Alan. *Regulation and Its Alternatives*. Washington, D.C.: Congressional Quarterly Press, 1982.

Strauss, Donald B. "Managing Complexity: A New Look At Environmental Mediation." *Environmental Science and Technology* (1979), 13(6):661–665

Stulberg, Joseph. "The Theory and Practice of Mediation: A Reply to Professor Susskind." *Vermont Law Review* (1981), 6:85–117.

Sullivan, Timothy. "Resolving Development Disputes Through Negotiation." Berkeley: Graduate School of Public Policy. 1984. Mimeo.

——*Resolving Development Disputes Through Negotiations*. New York: Plenum Press, 1985.

Susskind, Lawrence. "The Importance of Citizen Participation and Consensus Building In the Land Use Planning Process." Cambridge: MIT Environmental Impact Assessment Project, 1977.

——"Resolving Environmental Disputes Through Ad-Hocracy." *Environmental Consensus*, Summer 1980, pp. 3–5.

——"Environmental Mediation and the Accountability Problem" *Vermont Law Review* (1981) 6(1):1–47.

Susskind, Lawrence and Alan Weinstein. "Toward a Theory of Environmental Dispute Resolution." *Boston College Environmental Affairs Law Review* (1980), 9:311–357.

Susskind, Lawrence, Lawrence Bacow, and Michael Wheeler. *Resolving Environmental Regulatory Disputes*. Cambridge: Schenkman, 1983.

Susskind, Lawrence and Connie Ozawa. "Mediated Negotiation in the Public Sector: Objectives, Procedures and the Difficulties of Measuring Success." Cambridge: Harvard Law School Negotiation Project. 1984. Mimeo.

Talbot, Allan. *Environmental Mediation: Three Case Studies.* Seattle: Mediation Institute, 1981.

——*Settling Things: Six Case Studies in Environmental Mediation.* Washington, D.C.: Conservation Foundation, 1983.

Tolchin, Susan and Martin Tolchin. *Dismantling America.* Boston: Hougton Mifflin, 1983.

Tribe, Laurence, Corinne Schelling, and John Voss, eds. *When Values Conflict: Essays on Environmental Analysis, Discourse, and Decision.* Cambridge: Ballinger, 1976.

Vig, Norman and Michael Kraft, eds. *Environmental Policy in the 1980s: Reagan's New Agenda.* Washington, D. C.: Congressional Quarterly Press, 1984.

Wald, Patricia M. "Negotiation of Environmental Disputes: A New Role for Courts?" *Columbia Journal of Environmental Law* (December 1984), pp. 1–33.

Wall, James. "Mediation: Analysis, Review and Proposed Research." *Journal of Conflict Resolution* (March 1981), 25(1):157–180.

Warren, Charles. "The Hopeful Future of Mediation." In *Environmental Mediation: An Effective Alternative?* Washington, D.C.: Conservation Foundation, 1978.

Wenner, Lettie M. *The Environmental Decade in Court.* Bloomington: Indiana University Press, 1982.

——"Judicial Oversight of Environmental Deregulation." In Vig and Kraft, eds., *Environmental Policy in the 1980s.*

——Interview by author in Washington, D.C. September 1, 1984.

Wisconsin State Journal. "Ground Water Bill Opposed." October 1, 1983, Section 1, p. 6.

Index